Play-Making

William Archer

Contents

PREFATORY NOTE 7
BOOK I PROLOGUE 8
CHAPTER I INTRODUCTORY 8
CHAPTER II THE CHOICE OF A THEME 16
CHAPTER III DRAMATIC AND UNDRAMATIC 24
CHAPTER IV THE ROUTINE OF COMPOSITION 40
CHAPTER V DRAMATIS PERSONAE 53
BOOK II THE BEGINNING 58
CHAPTER VI THE POINT OF ATTACK: SHAKESPEARE AND IBSEN 58
CHAPTER VII EXPOSITION: ITS END AND ITS MEANS 74
CHAPTER VIII THE FIRST ACT 86
CHAPTER IX "CURIOSITY" AND "INTEREST" 101
CHAPTER X FORESHADOWING, NOT FORESTALLING 113
BOOK III THE MIDDLE 121
CHAPTER XI TENSION AND ITS SUSPENSION 121
CHAPTER XII PREPARATION: THE FINGER-POST 129
CHAPTER XIII THE OBLIGATORY SCENE 143
CHAPTER XIV THE PERIPETY 164
CHAPTER XV PROBABILITY, CHANCE, AND COINCIDENCE 173
CHAPTER XVI LOGIC 186
CHAPTER XVII KEEPING A SECRET 192
BOOK IV THE END 200
CHAPTER XVIII CLIMAX AND ANTICLIMAX 200
CHAPTER XIX CONVERSION 207
CHAPTER XX BLIND-ALLEY THEMES--AND OTHERS 213
CHAPTER XXI THE FULL CLOSE 220
BOOK V EPILOE 231
CHAPTER XXII CHARACTER AND PSYCHOLOGY 231
CHAPTER XXIII DIALOGUE AND DETAILS 237

PLAY-MAKING

BY
William Archer

To
Brander Matthews
Guide Philosopher and Friend

PREFATORY NOTE

This book is, to all intents and purposes, entirely new. No considerable portion of it has already appeared, although here and there short passages and phrases from articles of bygone years are embedded --indistinguishably, I hope--in the text. I have tried, wherever it was possible, to select my examples from published plays, which the student may read for himself, and so check my observations. One reason, among others, which led me to go to Shakespeare and Ibsen for so many of my illustrations, was that they are the most generally accessible of playwrights.

If the reader should feel that I have been over lavish in the use of footnotes, I have two excuses to allege. The first is that more than half of the following chapters were written on shipboard and in places where I had scarcely any books to refer to; so that a great deal had to be left to subsequent enquiry and revision. The second is that several of my friends, dramatists and others, have been kind enough to read my manuscript, and to suggest valuable afterthoughts.

LONDON
January, 1912

BOOK I PROLOGUE

CHAPTER I
INTRODUCTORY

There are no rules for writing a play. It is easy, indeed, to lay down negative recommendations--to instruct the beginner how *not* to do it. But most of these "don'ts" are rather obvious; and those which are not obvious are apt to be questionable. It is certain, for instance, that if you want your play to be acted, anywhere else than in China, you must not plan it in sixteen acts of an hour apiece; but where is the tyro who needs a text-book to tell him that? On the other hand, most theorists of to-day would make it an axiom that you must not let your characters narrate their circumstances, or expound their motives, in speeches addressed, either directly to the audience, or ostensibly to their solitary selves. But when we remember that, of all dramatic openings, there is none finer than that which shows Richard Plantagenet limping down the empty stage to say--

"Now is the winter of our discontent   Made glorious summer by this sun of York;   And all the clouds that lour'd upon our house   In the deep bosom of the ocean buried"--

we feel that the axiom requires large qualifications. There are no absolute rules, in fact, except such as are dictated by the plainest common sense. Aristotle himself did not so much dogmatize as analyse, classify, and generalize from, the practices of the Attic dramatists. He said, "you had better" rather than "you must." It was Horace, in an age of deep dramatic decadence, who re-stated the pseudo-Aristotelian formulas of the Alexandrians as though they were unassailable dogmas of art.

How comes it, then, that there is a constant demand for text-books of the art and craft of drama? How comes it that so many people--and I among the number--who could not write a play to save their lives, are eager to tell others how to do so? And, stranger still, how comes it that so many people are willing to sit at the feet of these instructors? It is not so with the novel. Popular as is that form of literature, guides to novel-writing, if they exist at all, are comparatively rare. Why are people possessed with the idea that the art of dramatic fiction differs from that of narrative fiction, in that it can and must be taught?

The reason is clear, and is so far valid as to excuse, if not to justify, such works as the present. The novel, as soon as it is legibly written, exists, for what it is worth. The page of black and white is the sole intermediary between the creative and the perceptive brain. Even the act of printing merely widens the possible appeal: it does not alter its nature. But the drama, before it can make its proper appeal at all, must be run through a highly complex piece of mechanism--the theatre--the precise conditions of which are, to most beginners, a fascinating mystery. While they feel a strong inward conviction of their ability to master it, they are possessed with an idea, often exaggerated and superstitious, of its technical complexities. Having, as a rule, little or no opportunity of closely examining or experimenting with it, they are eager to "read it up," as they might any other machine. That is the case of the average aspirant, who has neither the instinct of the theatre fully developed in his blood, nor such a congenital lack of that instinct as to be wholly inapprehensive of any technical difficulties or problems. The intelligent novice, standing between these extremes, tends, as a rule, to overrate the efficacy of theoretical instruction, and to expect of analytic criticism more than it has to give.

There is thus a fine opening for pedantry on the one side, and quackery on the other, to rush in. The pedant, in this context, is he who constructs a set of rules from metaphysical or psychological first principles, and professes to bring down a dramatic decalogue from the Sinai of some lecture-room in the University of Weissnichtwo. The quack, on the other hand, is he who generalizes from the worst practices of the most vulgar theatrical journeymen, and has no higher ambition than to interpret the oracles of the box-office. If he succeeded in so doing, his function would not be wholly despicable; but as he is generally devoid of insight, and as, moreover, the oracles of the box-office vary from season to season, if not from month to month, his lucubrations are about as valuable as those of Zadkiel or Old Moore.[1]

What, then, is the excuse for such a discussion as is here attempted? Having admitted that there are no rules for dramatic composition, and that the quest of such rules is apt to result either in pedantry or quackery, why should I myself set forth upon so fruitless and foolhardy an enterprise? It is precisely because I am alive to its dangers that I have some hope of avoiding them. Rules there are none; but it does not follow that some of the thousands who are fascinated by the art of the playwright may not profit by having their attention called, in a plain and practical way, to some of its problems and possibilities. I have myself felt the need of some such handbook, when would-be dramatists have come to me for advice and guidance. It is easy to name excellent treatises on the drama; but the aim of such books is to guide the judgment of the critic rather than the creative impulse of the playwright. There are also valuable collections of dramatic criticisms; but any practical hints that they may contain are scattered and unsystematic. On the other hand, the advice one is apt to give to beginners--"Go to the theatre; study its conditions and mechanism for yourself"--is, in fact, of very doubtful value. It might, in many cases, be wiser to warn the aspirant to keep himself unspotted from the playhouse. To send him there is to imperil, on the one hand, his originality of vision, on the other, his individuality of method. He may fall under the influence of some great master, and see life only through his eyes; or he may become so habituated to the current tricks of the theatrical trade as to lose all sense of their conventionality and falsity, and find himself, in the end, better fitted to write what I have called a quack handbook than a living play. It would be ridiculous, of course, to urge an aspirant positively to avoid the theatre; but the common advice to steep himself in it is beset with dangers.

It may be asked why, if I have any guidance and help to give, I do not take it myself, and write plays instead of instructing others in the art. This is a variant of an ancient and fallacious jibe against criticism in general. It is quite true that almost all critics who are worth their salt are "stickit" artists. Assuredly, if I had the power, I should write plays instead of writing about them; but one may have a great love for an art, and some insight into its principles and methods, without the innate faculty required for actual production. On the other hand, there is nothing to show that, if I were a creative artist, I should be a good mentor for beginners. An accomplished painter may be the best teacher of painters; but an accomplished dramatist is scarcely the best guide for dramatists. He cannot analyse his own practice, and discriminate between that in it which is of universal validity, and that which may be good for him, but would be bad for any one else. If he happened to be a great man, he would inevitably, even if unconsciously, seek to impose upon his disciples his individual attitude towards life; if he were a lesser man, he would teach them only his tricks. But dramatists do not, as a matter of fact, take pupils or write handbooks.[2] When they expound their principles of art, it is generally in answer to, or in anticipation of, criticism--with a view, in short, not to helping others, but to defending themselves. If beginners, then, are to find any systematic guidance, they must turn to the critics, not to the dramatists; and no person of common sense holds it a reproach to a critic to tell him that he is a "stickit" playwright.

If questions are worth discussing at all, they are worth discussing gravely. When, in the following pages, I am found treating with all solemnity matters of apparently trivial detail, I beg the reader to believe that very possibly I do not in my heart overrate their importance. One thing is certain, and must be emphasized from the outset: namely, that if any part of the dramatist's art can be taught, it is only a comparatively mechanical and formal part--the art of structure. One may learn how to tell a story in good dramatic form: how to develop and marshal it in such a way as best to seize and retain the interest of a theatrical audience. But no teaching or study can enable a man to choose or invent a good story, and much less to do that which alone lends dignity to dramatic story-telling--to observe and portray human character. This is the aim and end of all serious drama; and it will be apt to appear as though, in the following pages, this aim and end were ignored. In reality it is not so. If I hold comparatively mechanical questions of pure craftsmanship to be worth discussing, it is because I believe that only by aid of competent craftsmanship can the greatest genius enable his creations to live and breathe upon the stage. The profoundest insight into human nature and destiny cannot find valid expression through the medium of the theatre without some understanding of the peculiar art of dramatic construction. Some people are born with such an instinct for this art, that a very little practice renders them masters of it. Some people are born with a hollow in their cranium where the bump of drama ought to be. But between these extremes, as I said before, there are many people with moderately developed and cultivable faculty; and it is these who, I trust, may find some profit in the following discussions.[3] Let them not forget, however, that the topics treated of are merely the indispensable rudiments of the art, and are not for a moment to be mistaken for its ultimate and incommunicable secrets. Beethoven could not have composed the Ninth Symphony without a mastery of harmony and counterpoint; but there are thousands of masters of harmony and counterpoint who could not compose the Ninth Symphony.

The art of theatrical story-telling is necessarily relative to the audience to whom the story is to be told. One must assume an audience of a certain status and characteristics before one can rationally discuss the best methods of appealing to its intelligence and its sympathies. The audience I have throughout assumed is drawn from what may be called the ordinary educated public of London and New York. It is not an ideal or a specially selected audience; but it is somewhat above the average of the theatre-going public, that average being sadly pulled down by the myriad frequenters of musical farce and absolutely worthless melodrama. It is such an audience as assembles every night at, say, the half-dozen best theatres of each city. A peculiarly intellectual audience it certainly is not. I gladly admit that theatrical art owes much, in both countries, to voluntary organizations of intelligent or would-be intelligent[4] playgoers, who have combined to provide themselves with forms of drama which specially interest them, and do not attract the great public. But I am entirely convinced that the drama renounces its chief privilege and glory when it waives its claim to be a popular art, and is content to address itself to coteries, however "high-browed." Shakespeare did not write for a coterie: yet he produced some works of considerable subtlety and profundity. Moliere was popular with the ordinary parterre of his day: yet his plays have endured for over two centuries, and the end of their vitality does not seem to be in sight. Ibsen did not write for a coterie, though special and regrettable circumstances have made him, in England, something of a coterie-poet. In Scandinavia, in Germany, even in America, he casts his spell over great audiences, if not through long runs (which are a vice of the merely commercial theatre), at any rate through frequently-repeated representations. So far as I know, history records no instance of a playwright failing to gain the ear of his contemporaries, and then being recognized and appreciated by posterity. Alfred de Musset might, perhaps, be cited as a case in point; but he did not write with a view to the stage, and made no bid for contemporary popularity. As soon as it occurred to people to produce his plays, they were found to be delightful. Let no playwright, then, make it his boast that he cannot disburden his soul within the three hours' limit, and cannot produce plays intelligible or endurable to any audience but a band of adepts. A popular audience, however, does not necessarily mean the mere riff-raff of the theatrical public. There is a large class of playgoers, both in England and America, which is capable of appreciating work of a high intellectual order, if only it does not ignore the fundamental conditions of theatrical presentation. It is an audience of this class that I have in mind throughout the following pages; and I believe that a playwright who despises such an audience will do so to the detriment, not only of his popularity and profits, but of the artistic quality of his work.

Some people may exclaim: "Why should the dramatist concern himself about his audience? That may be all very well for the mere journeymen of the theatre, the hacks who write to an actor-manager's order--not for the true artist! He has a soul above all such petty considerations. Art, to him, is simply self-expression. He writes to please himself, and has no thought of currying favour with an audience, whether intellectual or idiotic." To this I reply simply that to an artist of this way of thinking I have nothing to say. He has a perfect right to express himself in a whole literature of so-called plays, which may possibly be studied, and even acted, by societies organized to that laudable end. But the dramatist who declares his end to be mere self-expression stultifies himself in that very phrase. The painter may paint, the sculptor model, the lyric poet sing, simply to please himself,[5] but the drama has no meaning except in relation to an audience. It is a portrayal of life by means of a mechanism so devised as to bring it home to a considerable number of people assembled in a given place. "The public," it has been well said, "constitutes the theatre." The moment a playwright confines his work within the two or three hours' limit prescribed by Western custom for a theatrical performance, he is currying favour with an audience. That limit is imposed simply by the physical endurance and power of sustained attention that can be demanded of Western human beings assembled in a theatre. Doubtless an author could express himself more fully and more subtly if he ignored these limitations; the moment he submits to them, he renounces the pretence that mere self-expression is his aim. I know that there are haughty-souls who make no such submission, and express themselves in dramas which, so far as their proportions are concerned, might as well be epic poems or historical romances.[6] To them, I repeat, I have nothing to say. The one and only subject of the following discussions is the best method of fitting a dramatic theme for representation before an audience assembled in a theatre. But this, be it noted, does not necessarily mean "writing down" to the audience in question. It is by obeying, not by ignoring, the fundamental conditions of his craft that the dramatist may hope to lead his audience upward to the highest intellectual level which he himself can attain.

These pages, in short, are addressed to students of play-writing who sincerely desire to do sound, artistic work under the conditions and limitations of the actual, living playhouse. This does not mean, of course, that they ought always to be studying "what the public wants." The dramatist should give the public what he himself wants--but in such form as to make it comprehensible and interesting in a theatre.

* * * * *

Notes:
[1: It is against "technic" in this sense of the term that the hero of Mr. Howells's admirable novel, *The Story of a Play*, protests in vigorous and memorable terms. "They talk," says Maxwell, "about a knowledge of the stage as if it were a difficult science, instead of a very simple piece of mechanism whose limitations and possibilities anyone may see at a glance. All that their knowledge of it comes to is claptrap, pure and simple.... They think that their exits and entrances are great matters and that they must come on with such a speech, and go off with another; but it is not of the least importance how they come or go, if they have something interesting to say or do." Maxwell, it must be remembered, is speaking of technic as expounded by the star actor, who is shilly-shallying--as star actors will--over the production of his play. He would not, in his calmer moments, deny that it is of little use to have something interesting to say, unless you know how to say it interestingly. Such a denial would simply be the negation of the very idea of art.]

[2: A dramatist of my acquaintance adds this footnote: "But, by the Lord! They have to give advice. I believe I write more plays of other people's than I do of my own."]

[3: It may be hoped, too, that even the accomplished dramatist may take some interest in considering the reasons for things which he does, or does not do, by instinct.]

[4: This is not a phrase of contempt. The would-be intelligent playgoer is vastly to be preferred to the playgoer who makes a boast of his unintelligence.]

[5: In all the arts, however, the very idea of craftsmanship implies some sort of external percipient, or, in other words, some sort of an audience. In point of sheer self-expression, a child's scrabblings with a box of crayons may deserve to rank with the most masterly canvas of Velasquez or Vermeer. The real difference between the dramatist and other artists, is that they can be ***their own audience***, in a sense in which he cannot.]

[6: Let me guard against the possibility that this might be interpreted as a sneer at *The Dynasts*--a great work by a great poet.]

CHAPTER II
THE CHOICE OF A THEME

The first step towards writing a play is manifestly to choose a theme. Even this simple statement, however, requires careful examination before we can grasp its full import. What, in the first place, do we mean by a "theme"? And, secondly, in what sense can we, or ought we to, "choose" one?

"Theme" may mean either of two things: either the subject of a play, or its story. The former is, perhaps, its proper or more convenient sense. The theme of **Romeo and Juliet** is youthful love crossed by ancestral hate; the theme of **Othello** is jealousy; the theme of **Le Tartufe** is hypocrisy; the theme of **Caste** is fond hearts and coronets; the theme of **Getting Married** is getting married; the theme of **Maternite** is maternity. To every play it is possible, at a pinch, to assign a theme; but in many plays it is evident that no theme expressible in abstract terms was present to the author's mind. Nor are these always plays of a low class. It is only by a somewhat artificial process of abstraction that we can formulate a theme for *As You Like It*, for *The Way of the World*, or for *Hedda Gabler*.

The question now arises: ought a theme, in its abstract form, to be the first germ of a play? Ought the dramatist to say, "Go to, I will write a play on temperance, or on woman's suffrage, or on capital and labour," and then cast about for a story to illustrate his theme? This is a possible, but not a promising, method of procedure. A story made to the order of a moral concept is always apt to advertise its origin, to the detriment of its illusive quality. If a play is to be a moral apologue at all, it is well to say so frankly--probably in the title--and aim, not at verisimilitude, but at neatness and appositeness in the working out of the fable. The French ***proverbe*** proceeds on this principle, and is often very witty and charming.[1] A good example in English is ***A Pair of Spectacles***, by Mr. Sydney Grundy, founded on a play by Labiche. In this bright little comedy every incident and situation bears upon the general theme, and pleases us, not by its probability, but by its ingenious appropriateness. The dramatic fable, in fact, holds very much the same rank in drama as the narrative fable holds in literature at large. We take pleasure in them on condition that they be witty, and that they do not pretend to be what they are not.

A play manifestly suggested by a theme of temporary interest will often have a great but no less temporary success. For instance, though there was a good deal of clever character-drawing in ***An Englishman's Home***, by Major du Maurier, the theme was so evidently the source and inspiration of the play that it will scarcely bear revival. In America, where the theme was of no interest, the play failed.

It is possible, no doubt, to name excellent plays in which the theme, in all probability, preceded both the story and the characters in the author's mind. Such plays are most of M. Brieux's; such plays are Mr. Galsworthy's ***Strife*** and ***Justice***. The French plays, in my judgment, suffer artistically from the obtrusive predominance of the theme--that is to say, the abstract element--over the human and concrete factors in the composition. Mr. Galsworthy's more delicate and unemphatic art eludes this danger, at any rate in ***Strife***. We do not remember until all is over that his characters represent classes, and his action is, one might almost say, a sociological symbol. If, then, the theme does, as a matter of fact, come first in the author's conception, he will do well either to make it patently and confessedly dominant, as in the ***proverbe***, or to take care that, as in ***Strife***, it be not suffered to make its domination felt, except as an afterthought.[2] No outside force should appear to control the free rhythm of the action.

The theme may sometimes be, not an idea, an abstraction or a principle, but rather an environment, a social phenomenon of one sort or another. The author's primary object in such a case is, not to portray any individual character or tell any definite story, but to transfer to the stage an animated picture of some broad aspect or phase of life, without concentrating the interest on any one figure or group. There are theorists who would, by definition, exclude from the domain of drama any such cinematograph-play, as they would probably call it; but we shall see cause, as we go on, to distrust definitions, especially when they seek to clothe themselves with the authority of laws. Tableau-plays of the type here in question may even claim classical precedent. What else is Ben Jonson's **Bartholomew Fair**? What else is Schiller's **Wallensteins Lager**? Amongst more recent plays, Hauptmann's **Die Weber** and Gorky's **Nachtasyl** are perhaps the best examples of the type. The drawback of such themes is, not that they do not conform to this or that canon of art, but that it needs an exceptional amount of knowledge and dramaturgic skill to handle them successfully. It is far easier to tell a story on the stage than to paint a picture, and few playwrights can resist the temptation to foist a story upon their picture, thus marring it by an inharmonious intrusion of melodrama or farce. This has often been done upon deliberate theory, in the belief that no play can exist, or can attract playgoers, without a definite and more or less exciting plot. Thus the late James A. Herne inserted into a charming idyllic picture of rural life, entitled **Shore Acres**, a melodramatic scene in a lighthouse, which was hopelessly out of key with the rest of the play. The dramatist who knows any particular phase of life so thoroughly as to be able to transfer its characteristic incidents to the stage, may be advised to defy both critical and managerial prejudice, and give his tableau-play just so much of story as may naturally and inevitably fall within its limits.

One of the most admirable and enthralling scenes I ever saw on any stage was that of the Trafalgar Square suffrage meeting in Miss Elizabeth Robins's **Votes for Women**. Throughout a whole act it held us spellbound, while the story of the play stood still, and we forgot its existence. It was only within a few minutes of the end, when the story was dragged in neck and crop, that the reality of the thing vanished, and the interest with it.

* * * * *

If an abstract theme be not an advisable starting-point, what is? A character? A situation? Or a story? On this point it would be absurd to lay down any rule; the more so as, in many cases, a playwright is quite unable to say in what form the germ of a play first floated into his mind. The suggestion may come from a newspaper paragraph, from an incident seen in the street, from an emotional adventure or a comic misadventure, from a chance word dropped by an acquaintance, or from some flotsam or jetsam of phrase or fable that has drifted from the other end of history. Often, too, the original germ, whatever it may be, is transformed beyond recognition before a play is done.[3] In the mind of the playwright figs grow from thistles, and a silk purse--perhaps a Fortunatus' purse--may often be made from a sow's ear. The whole delicate texture of Ibsen's **Doll's House** was woven from a commonplace story of a woman who forged a cheque in order to redecorate her drawing-room. Stevenson's romance of **Prince Otto** (to take an example from fiction) grew out of a tragedy on the subject of Semiramis!

One thing, however, we may say with tolerable confidence: whatever may be the germ of a play--whether it be an anecdote, a situation, or what not--the play will be of small account as a work of art unless character, at a very early point, enters into and conditions its development. The story which is independent of character--which can be carried through by a given number of ready-made puppets--is essentially a trivial thing. Unless, at an early stage of the organizing process, character begins to take the upper hand--unless the playwright finds himself thinking, "Oh, yes, George is just the man to do this," or, "That is quite foreign to Jane's temperament"--he may be pretty sure that it is a piece of mechanism he is putting together, not a drama with flesh and blood in it. The difference between a live play and a dead one is that in the former the characters control the plot, while in the latter the plot controls the characters. Which is not to say, of course, that there may not be clever and entertaining plays which are "dead" in this sense, and dull and unattractive plays which are "live."

A great deal of ink has been wasted in controversy over a remark of Aristotle's that the action or *muthos*, not the character or *ethos*, is the essential element in drama. The statement is absolutely true and wholly unimportant. A play can exist without anything that can be called character, but not without some sort of action. This is implied in the very word "drama," which means a doing, not a mere saying or existing. It would be possible, no doubt, to place Don Quixote, or Falstaff, or Peer Gynt, on the stage, and let him develop his character in mere conversation, or even monologue, without ever moving from his chair. But it is a truism that deeds, not words, are the demonstration and test of character; wherefore, from time immemorial, it has been the recognized business of the theatre to exhibit character in action. Historically, too, we find that drama has everywhere originated in the portrayal of an action--some exploit or some calamity in the career of some demi-god or hero. Thus story or plot is by definition, tradition, and practical reason, the fundamental element in drama; but does it therefore follow that it is the noblest element, or that by which its value should be measured? Assuredly not. The skeleton is, in a sense, the fundamental element in the human organism. It can exist, and, with a little assistance, retain its form, when stripped of muscle and blood and nerve; whereas a boneless man would be an amorphous heap, more helpless than a jelly-fish. But do we therefore account the skeleton man's noblest part? Scarcely. It is by his blood and nerve that he lives, not by his bones; and it is because his bones are, comparatively speaking, dead matter that they continue to exist when the flesh has fallen away from them. It is, therefore, if not a misreading of Aristotle,[4] at any rate a perversion of reason, to maintain that the drama lives by action, rather than by character. Action ought to exist for the sake of character: when the relation is reversed, the play may be an ingenious toy, but scarcely a vital work of art.

*   *   *   *   *

It is time now to consider just what we mean when we say that the first step towards play-writing is the "choice" of a theme.

In many cases, no doubt, it is the plain and literal fact that the impulse to write some play--any play--exists, so to speak, in the abstract, unassociated with any particular subject, and that the would-be playwright proceeds, as he thinks, to set his imagination to work, and invent a story. But this frame of mind is to be regarded with suspicion. Few plays of much value, one may guess, have resulted from such an abstract impulse. Invention, in these cases, is apt to be nothing but recollection in disguise, the shaking of a kaleidoscope formed of fragmentary reminiscences. I remember once, in some momentary access of ambition, trying to invent a play. I occupied several hours of a long country walk in, as I believed, creating out of nothing at all a dramatic story. When at last I had modelled it into some sort of coherency, I stepped back from it in my mind, as it were, and contemplated it as a whole. No sooner had I done so than it began to seem vaguely familiar. "Where have I seen this story before?" I asked myself; and it was only after cudgelling my brains for several minutes that I found I had re-invented Ibsen's **Hedda Gabler**. Thus, when we think we are choosing a plot out of the void, we are very apt to be, in fact, ransacking the store-house of memory. The plot which chooses us is much more to be depended upon--the idea which comes when we least expect it, perhaps from the most unlikely quarter, clamours at the gates of birth, and will not let us rest till it be clothed in dramatic flesh and blood.[5] It may very well happen, of course, that it has to wait--that it has to be pigeon-holed for a time, until its due turn comes.[6] Occasionally, perhaps, it may slip out of its pigeon-hole for an airing, only to be put back again in a slightly more developed form. Then at last its convenient season will arrive, and the play will be worked out, written, and launched into the struggle for life. In the sense of selecting from among a number of embryonic themes stored in his mind, the playwright has often to make a deliberate choice; but when, moved by a purely abstract impulse, he goes out of set purpose to look for a theme, it may be doubted whether he is likely to return with any very valuable treasure-trove.[7]

The same principle holds good in the case of the ready-made poetic or historical themes, which are--rightly or wrongly--considered suitable for treatment in blank verse. Whether, and how far, the blank verse drama can nowadays be regarded as a vital and viable form is a question to be considered later. In the meantime it is sufficient to say that whatever principles of conception and construction apply to the modern prose drama, apply with equal cogency to the poetic drama. The verse-poet may perhaps take one or two licenses denied to the prose-poet. For instance, we may find reason to think the soliloquy more excusable in verse than in prose. But fundamentally, the two forms are ruled by the same set of conditions, which the verse-poet, no less than the prose-poet, can ignore only at his peril. Unless, indeed, he renounces from the outset all thought of the stage and chooses to produce that cumbrous nondescript, a "closet drama." Of such we do not speak, but glance and pass on. What laws, indeed, can apply to a form which has no proper element, but, like the amphibious animal described by the sailor, "cannot live on land and dies in the water"?

To return to our immediate topic, the poet who essays dramatic composition on mere abstract impulse, because other poets have done so, or because he is told that it pays, is only too likely to produce willy-nilly a "closet drama." Let him beware of saying to himself, "I will gird up my loins and write a play. Shall it be a Phaedra, or a Semiramis, or a Sappho, or a Cleopatra? A Julian, or an Attila, or a Savanarola, or a Cromwell?" A drama conceived in this reach-me-down fashion will scarcely have the breath of life in it. If, on the other hand, in the course of his legendary, romantic, or historical reading, some character should take hold upon his imagination and demand to be interpreted, or some episode should, as it were, startle him by putting on vivid dramatic form before his mind's eye, then let him by all means yield to the inspiration, and try to mould the theme into a drama. The real labour of creation will still lie before him; but he may face it with the hope of producing a live play, not a long-drawn rhetorical anachronism, whether of the rotund or of the spasmodic type.

*   *   *   *   *

Notes:
[1: For instance, *Il ne faut jurer de rien. Il faut qu'une porte soit ouverte ou fermee. Un bienfait n'est jamais perdu.* There is also a large class of pieces of which the title, though not itself a proverb, makes direct allusion to some fable or proverbial saying: for example, *Les Brebis de Panurge, La Chasse aux Corbeaux, La Cigale chez les Fourmis*.]

[2: I learn, on the best authority, that I am wrong, in point of fact, as to the origin of *Strife*. The play arose in Mr. Galsworthy's mind from his actually having seen in conflict the two men who were the prototypes of Anthony and Roberts, and thus noted the waste and inefficacy arising from the clash of strong characters unaccompanied by balance. It was accident that led him to place the two men in an environment of capital and labour. In reality, both of them were, if not capitalists, at any rate on the side of capital. This interesting correction of fact does not invalidate the theory above stated.]

[3: Mr. Henry Arthur Jones writes to me: "Sometimes I start with a scene only, sometimes with a complete idea. Sometimes a play splits into two plays, sometimes two or three ideas combine into a concrete whole. Always the final play is altered out of all knowledge from its first idea." An interesting account of the way in which two very different plays by M. de Curel: *L'Envers d'une Sainte* and *L'Invitee*,--grew out of one and the same initial idea, may be found in ***L'Annee Psychologique***, 1894, p. 121.]

[4: In my discussion of this point, I have rather simplified Aristotle's position. He appears to make action the essential element in tragedy and not merely the necessary vehicle of character. "In a play," he says, "they do not act in order to portray the characters, they include the characters for the sake of the action. So that it is the action in it, ***i.e.*** its Fable or Plot, that is the end and purpose of the tragedy, and the end is everywhere the chief thing. Besides this, a tragedy is impossible without action, but there may be one without character." (Bywater's Translation.) The last sentence is, in my view, the gist of the matter; the preceding sentences greatly overstate the case. There was a lively controversy on the subject in the ***Times*** Literary Supplement in May, 1902. It arose from a review of Mr. Phillips's ***Paolo and Francesco***, and Mr. Andrew Lang, Mr. Churton Collins, and Mr. A.B. Walkley took part in it.]

[5: "Are the first beginnings of imaginative conception directed by the will? Are they, indeed, conscious at all? Do they not rather emerge unbidden from the vague limbo of sub-consciousness?" A.B. Walkley, ***Drama and Life***, p. 85.]

[6: Sardou kept a file of about fifty ***dossiers***, each bearing the name of an unwritten play, and containing notes and sketches for it. Dumas, on the other hand, always finished one play before he began to think of another. See ***L'Annee Psychologique***, 1894, pp. 67, 76.]

[7: "My experience is," a dramatist writes to me, "that you never deliberately choose a theme. You lie awake, or you go walking, and suddenly there flashes into your mind a contrast, a piece of spiritual irony, an old incident carrying some general significance. Round this your mind broods, and there is the germ of your play." Again be writes: "It is not advisable for a playwright to start out at all unless he has so felt or seen something, that he feels, as it matures in his mind, that he must express it, and in dramatic form."]

CHAPTER III
DRAMATIC AND UNDRAMATIC

It may be well, at this point, to consider for a little what we mean when we use the term "dramatic." We shall probably not arrive at any definition which can be applied as an infallible touchstone to distinguish the dramatic from the undramatic. Perhaps, indeed, the upshot may rather be to place the student on his guard against troubling too much about the formal definitions of critical theorists.

The orthodox opinion of the present time is that which is generally associated with the name of the late Ferdinand Brunetiere. "The theatre in general," said that critic, "is nothing but the place for the development of the human will, attacking the obstacles opposed to it by destiny, fortune, or circumstances." And again: "Drama is a representation of the will of man in conflict with the mysterious powers or natural forces which limit and belittle us; it is one of us thrown living upon the stage, there to struggle against fatality, against social law, against one of his fellow-mortals, against himself, if need be, against the ambitions, the interests, the prejudices, the folly, the malevolence of those who surround him."[1]

The difficulty about this definition is that, while it describes the matter of a good many dramas, it does not lay down any true differentia--any characteristic common to all drama, and possessed by no other form of fiction. Many of the greatest plays in the world can with difficulty be brought under the formula, while the majority of romances and other stories come under it with ease. Where, for instance, is the struggle in the *Agamemnon*? There is no more struggle between Clytemnestra and Agamemnon than there is between the spider and the fly who walks into his net. There is not even a struggle in Clytemnestra's mind. Agamemnon's doom is sealed from the outset, and she merely carries out a pre-arranged plot. There is contest indeed in the succeeding plays of the trilogy; but it will scarcely be argued that the ***Agamemnon***, taken alone, is not a great drama. Even the ***Oedipus*** of Sophocles, though it may at first sight seem a typical instance of a struggle against Destiny, does not really come under the definition. Oedipus, in fact, does not struggle at all. His struggles, in so far as that word can be applied to his misguided efforts to escape from the toils of fate, are all things of the past; in the actual course of the tragedy he simply writhes under one revelation after another of bygone error and unwitting crime. It would be a mere play upon words to recognize as a dramatic "struggle" the writhing of a worm on a hook. And does not this description apply very closely to the part played by another great protagonist--Othello to wit? There is no struggle, no conflict, between him and Iago. It is Iago alone who exerts any will; neither Othello nor Desdemona makes the smallest fight. From the moment when Iago sets his machination to work, they are like people sliding down an ice-slope to an inevitable abyss. Where is the conflict in ***As You Like It***? No one, surely, will pretend that any part of the interest or charm of the play arises from the struggle between the banished Duke and the Usurper, or between Orlando and Oliver. There is not even the conflict, if so it can be called, which nominally brings so many hundreds of plays under the Brunetiere canon--the conflict between an eager lover and a more or less reluctant maid. Or take, again, Ibsen's ***Ghosts***--in what valid sense can it be said that that tragedy shows us will struggling against obstacles? Oswald, doubtless, wishes to live, and his mother desires that he should live; but this mere will for life cannot be the differentia that makes of ***Ghosts*** a drama. If the reluctant descent of the "downward path to death" constituted drama, then Tolstoy's ***Death of Ivan Ilytch*** would be one of the greatest dramas ever written--which it certainly is not. Yet again, if we want to see will struggling against obstacles, the classic to turn to is not ***Hamlet***, not ***Lear***, but ***Robinson Crusoe***; yet no one, except a pantomime librettist, ever saw a drama in Defoe's narrative. In a Platonic dialogue, in ***Paradise Lost***, in ***John Gilpin***, there is a struggle of will against obstacles; there is none in ***Hannele***, which, nevertheless, is a deeply-moving drama. Such a struggle is characteristic of all great fiction, from ***Clarissa Harlowe*** to ***The House with the Green Shutters***; whereas in many plays the struggle, if there be any at all, is the merest matter of form (for instance, a quite conventional love-story), while the real interest resides in something quite different.

The plain truth seems to be that conflict is *one* of the most dramatic elements in life, and that many dramas--perhaps most--do, as a matter of fact, turn upon strife of one sort or another. But it is clearly an error to make conflict indispensable to drama, and especially to insist--as do some of Brunetiere's followers--that the conflict must be between will and will. A stand-up fight between will and will--such a fight as occurs in, say, the ***Hippolytus*** of Euripides, or Racine's ***Andromaque***, or Moliere's ***Tartufe***, or Ibsen's ***Pretenders***, or Dumas's ***Francillon***, or Sudermann's ***Heimat***, or Sir Arthur Pinero's ***Gay Lord Quex***, or Mr. Shaw's ***Candida***, or Mr. Galsworthy's ***Strife***--such a stand-up fight, I say, is no doubt one of the intensest forms of drama. But it is comparatively rare at any rate as the formula of a whole play. In individual scenes a conflict of will is frequent enough; but it is, after all, only one among a multitude of equally telling forms of drama. No one can say that the Balcony Scene in ***Romeo and Juliet*** is undramatic, or the "Galeoto fu il libro" scene in Mr. Stephen Phillips's ***Paolo and Francesca***; yet the point of these scenes is not a clash, but an ecstatic concordance, of wills. Is the death-scene of Cleopatra undramatic? Or the Banquet scene in ***Macbeth***? Or the pastoral act in ***The Winter's Tale***? Yet in none of these is there any conflict of wills. In the whole range of drama there is scarcely a passage which one would call more specifically dramatic than the Screen Scene in ***The School for Scandal***; yet it would be the veriest quibbling to argue that any appreciable part of its effect arises from the clash of will against will. This whole comedy, indeed, suffices to show the emptiness of the theory. With a little strain it is possible to bring it within the letter of the formula; but who can pretend that any considerable part of the attraction or interest of the play is due to that possibility?

The champions of the theory, moreover, place it on a metaphysical basis, finding in the will the essence of human personality, and therefore of the art which shows human personality raised to its highest power. It seems unnecessary, however, to apply to Schopenhauer for an explanation of whatever validity the theory may possess. For a sufficient account of the matter, we need go no further than the simple psychological observation that human nature loves a fight, whether it be with clubs or with swords, with tongues or with brains. One of the earliest forms of mediaeval drama was the "estrif" or "flyting"--the scolding-match between husband and wife, or between two rustic gossips. This motive is glorified in the quarrel between Brutus and Cassius, degraded in the patter of two "knockabout comedians." Certainly there is nothing more telling in drama than a piece of "cut-and-thrust" dialogue after the fashion of the ancient "stichomythia." When a whole theme involving conflict, or even a single scene of the nature described as a "passage-at-arms," comes naturally in the playwright's way, by all means let him seize the opportunity. But do not let him reject a theme or scene as undramatic merely because it has no room for a clash of warring wills.

There is a variant of the "conflict" theory which underlines the word "obstacles" in the above-quoted dictum of Brunetiere, and lays down the rule: "No obstacle, no drama." Though far from being universally valid, this form of the theory has a certain practical usefulness, and may well be borne in mind. Many a play would have remained unwritten if the author had asked himself, "Is there a sufficient obstacle between my two lovers?" or, in more general terms, "between my characters and the realization of their will?" There is nothing more futile than a play in which we feel that there is no real obstacle to the inevitable happy ending, and that the curtain might just as well fall in the middle of the first act as at the end of the third. Comedies abound (though they reach the stage only by accident) in which the obstacle between Corydon and Phyllis, between Lord Edwin and Lady Angelina, is not even a defect or peculiarity of character, but simply some trumpery misunderstanding[2] which can be kept afoot only so long as every one concerned holds his or her common sense in studious abeyance. "Pyramus and Thisbe without the wall" may be taken as the formula for the whole type of play. But even in plays of a much higher type, the author might often ask himself with advantage whether he could not strengthen his obstacle, and so accentuate the struggle which forms the matter of his play. Though conflict may not be essential to drama, yet, when you set forth to portray a struggle, you may as well make it as real and intense as possible.

It seems to me that in the late William Vaughn Moody's drama, **The Great Divide**, the body of the play, after the stirring first act, is weakened by our sense that the happy ending is only being postponed by a violent effort. We have been assured from the very first--even before Ruth Jordan has set eyes on Stephen Ghent--that just such a rough diamond is the ideal of her dreams. It is true that, after their marriage, the rough diamond seriously misconducts himself towards her; and we have then to consider the rather unattractive question whether a single act of brutality on the part of a drunken husband ought to be held so unpardonable as to break up a union which otherwise promises to be quite satisfactory. But the author has taken such pains to emphasize the fact that these two people are really made for each other, that the answer to the question is not for a moment in doubt, and we become rather impatient of the obstinate sulkiness of Ruth's attitude. If there had been a real disharmony of character to be overcome, instead of, or in addition to, the sordid misadventure which is in fact the sole barrier between them, the play would certainly have been stronger, and perhaps more permanently popular.

In a play by Mr. James Bernard Fagan, *The Prayer of the Sword*, we have a much clearer example of an inadequate obstacle. A youth named Andrea has been brought up in a monastery, and destined for the priesthood; but his tastes and aptitudes are all for a military career. He is, however, on the verge of taking his priestly vows, when accident calls him forth into the world, and he has the good fortune to quell a threatened revolution in a romantic Duchy, ruled over by a duchess of surpassing loveliness. With her he naturally falls in love; and the tragedy lies, or ought to lie, in the conflict between this earthly passion and his heavenly calling and election. But the author has taken pains to make the obstacle between Andrea and Ilaria absolutely unreal. The fact that Andrea has as yet taken no irrevocable vow is not the essence of the matter. Vow or no vow, there would have been a tragic conflict if Andrea had felt absolutely certain of his calling to the priesthood, and had defied Heaven, and imperilled his immortal soul, because of his overwhelming passion. That would have been a tragic situation; but the author had carefully avoided it. From the very first--before Andrea had ever seen Ilaria--it had been impressed upon us that he had no priestly vocation. There was no struggle in his soul between passion and duty; there was no struggle at all in his soul. His struggles are all with external forces and influences; wherefore the play, which a real obstacle might have converted into a tragedy, remained a sentimental romance--and is forgotten.

* * * * *

What, then, is the essence of drama, if conflict be not it? What is the common quality of themes, scenes, and incidents, which we recognize as specifically dramatic? Perhaps we shall scarcely come nearer to a helpful definition than if we say that the essence of drama is ***crisis***. A play is a more or less rapidly-developing crisis in destiny or circumstance, and a dramatic scene is a crisis within a crisis, clearly furthering the ultimate event. The drama may be called the art of crises, as fiction is the art of gradual developments. It is the slowness of its processes which differentiates the typical novel from the typical play. If the novelist does not take advantage of the facilities offered by his form for portraying gradual change, whether in the way of growth or of decay, he renounces his own birthright, in order to trespass on the domain of the dramatist. Most great novels embrace considerable segments of many lives; whereas the drama gives us only the culminating points--or shall we say the intersecting culminations?--two or three destinies. Some novelists have excelled precisely in the art with which they have made the gradations of change in character or circumstance so delicate as to be imperceptible from page to page, and measurable, as in real life, only when we look back over a considerable period. The dramatist, on the other hand, deals in rapid and startling changes, the "peripeties," as the Greeks called them, which may be the outcome of long, slow processes, but which actually occur in very brief spaces of time. Nor is this a merely mechanical consequence of the narrow limits of stage presentation. The crisis is as real, though not as inevitable, a part of human experience as the gradual development. Even if the material conditions of the theatre permitted the presentation of a whole ***Middlemarch*** or ***Anna Karenine***--as the conditions of the Chinese theatre actually do--some dramatists, we cannot doubt, would voluntarily renounce that license of prolixity, in order to cultivate an art of concentration and crisis. The Greek drama "subjected to the faithful eyes," as Horace phrases it, the culminating points of the Greek epic; the modern drama places under the lens of theatrical presentment the culminating points of modern experience.

But, manifestly, it is not every crisis that is dramatic. A serious illness, a lawsuit, a bankruptcy, even an ordinary prosaic marriage, may be a crisis in a man's life, without being necessarily, or even probably, material for drama. How, then, do we distinguish a dramatic from a non-dramatic crisis? Generally, I think, by the fact that it develops, or can be made naturally to develop, through a series of minor crises, involving more or less emotional excitement, and, if possible, the vivid manifestation of character. Take, for instance, the case of a bankruptcy. Most people, probably, who figure in the **Gazette** do not go through any one, or two, or three critical moments of special tension, special humiliation, special agony. They gradually drift to leeward in their affairs, undergoing a series of small discouragements, small vicissitudes of hope and fear, small unpleasantnesses, which they take lightly or hardly according to their temperament, or the momentary state of their liver. In this average process of financial decline, there may be--there has been--matter for many excellent novels, but scarcely for a drama. That admirable chapter in **Little Dorrit,** wherein Dickens describes the gradual degradation of the Father of the Marshalsea, shows how a master of fiction deals with such a subject; but it would be quite impossible to transfer this chapter to the stage. So, too, with the bankruptcy of Colonel Newcome--certain emotional crises arising from it have, indeed, been placed on the stage, but only after all Thackeray's knowledge of the world and fine gradations of art had been eliminated. Mr. Hardy's **Mayor of Casterbridge** has, I think, been dramatized, but not, I think, with success. A somewhat similar story of financial ruin, the grimly powerful **House with the Green Shutters**, has not even tempted the dramatiser. There are, in this novel, indeed, many potentially dramatic crises; the trouble is that they are too numerous and individually too small to be suitable for theatrical presentment. Moreover, they are crises affecting a taciturn and inarticulate race,[3] a fact which places further difficulties in the way of the playwright. In all these cases, in short, the bankruptcy portrayed is a matter of slow development, with no great outstanding moments, and is consequently suited for treatment in fiction rather than in drama.

But bankruptcy sometimes occurs in the form of one or more sudden, sharp crises, and has, therefore, been utilized again and again as a dramatic motive. In a hundred domestic dramas or melodramas, we have seen the head of a happy household open a newspaper or a telegram announcing the failure of some enterprise in which all his fortune is embarked. So obviously dramatic is this incident that it has become sadly hackneyed. Again, we have bankruptcy following upon a course of gambling, generally in stocks. Here there is evident opportunity, which has been frequently utilized, for a series of crises of somewhat violent and commonplace emotion. In American drama especially, the duels of Wall Street, the combats of bull and bear, form a very popular theme, which clearly falls under the Brunetiere formula. Few American dramatists can resist the temptation of showing some masterful financier feverishly watching the "ticker" which proclaims him a millionaire or a beggar. The "ticker" had not been invented in the days when Ibsen wrote *The League of Youth*, otherwise he would doubtless have made use of it in the fourth act of that play. The most popular of all Bjoernson's plays is specifically entitled *A Bankruptcy*. Here the poet has had the art to select a typical phase of business life, which naturally presents itself in the form of an ascending curve, so to speak, of emotional crises. We see the energetic, active business man, with a number of irons in the fire, aware in his heart that he is insolvent, but not absolutely clear as to his position, and hoping against hope to retrieve it. We see him give a great dinner-party, in order to throw dust in the eyes of the world, and to secure the support of a financial magnate, who is the guest of honour. The financial magnate is inclined to "bite," and goes off, leaving the merchant under the impression that he is saved. This is an interesting and natural, but scarcely a thrilling, crisis. It does not, therefore, discount the supreme crisis of the play, in which a cold, clear-headed business man, who has been deputed by the banks to look into the merchant's affairs, proves to him, point by point, that it would be dishonest of him to flounder any longer in the swamp of insolvency, into which he can only sink deeper and drag more people down with him. Then the bankrupt produces a pistol and threatens murder and suicide if the arbiter of his fate will not consent to give him one more chance; but his frenzy breaks innocuous against the other's calm, relentless reason. Here we have, I repeat, a typically dramatic theme: a great crisis, bringing out vivid manifestations of character, not only in the bankrupt himself, but in those around him, and naturally unfolding itself through a series of those lesser crises, which we call interesting and moving scenes. The play is scarcely a great one, partly because its ending is perfunctory, partly because Bjoernson, poet though he was, had not Ibsen's art of "throwing in a little poetry" into his modern dramas. I have summarized it up to its culminating point, because it happened to illustrate the difference between a bankruptcy, dramatic in its nature and treatment, and those undramatic bankruptcies to which reference has been made. In *La Douloureuse*, by Maurice Donnay, bankruptcy is incidentally employed to bring about a crisis of a different order. A ball is proceeding at the house of a Parisian financier, when the whisper spreads that the host is ruined, and has committed suicide in a room above; whereupon the guests, after a moment of flustered consternation, go on supping and dancing![4] We are not at all deeply interested in the host or his fortunes. The author's purpose is to illustrate, rather crudely, the heartlessness of plutocratic Bohemia; and by means of the bankruptcy and suicide he brings about what may be called a crisis of collective character.[5]

* * * * *

As regards individual incidents, it may be said in general that the dramatic way of treating them is the crisp and staccato, as opposed to the smooth or legato, method. It may be thought a point of inferiority in dramatic art that it should deal so largely in shocks to the nerves, and should appeal by preference, wherever it is reasonably possible, to the cheap emotions of curiosity and surprise. But this is a criticism, not of dramatic art, but of human nature. We may wish that mankind took more pleasure in pure apprehension than in emotion; but so long as the fact is otherwise, that way of handling an incident by which the greatest variety of poignancy of emotion can be extracted from it will remain the specifically dramatic way.

We shall have to consider later the relation between what may be called primary and secondary suspense or surprise--that is to say between suspense or surprise actually experienced by the spectator to whom the drama is new, and suspense or surprise experienced only sympathetically, on behalf of the characters, by a spectator who knows perfectly what is to follow. The two forms of emotion are so far similar that we need not distinguish between them in considering the general content of the term "dramatic." It is plain that the latter or secondary form of emotion must be by far the commoner, and the one to which the dramatist of any ambition must make his main appeal; for the longer his play endures, the larger will be the proportion of any given audience which knows it beforehand, in outline, if not in detail.

As a typical example of a dramatic way of handling an incident, so as to make a supreme effect of what might else have been an anti-climax, one may cite the death of Othello. Shakespeare was faced by no easy problem. Desdemona was dead, Emilia dead, Iago wounded and doomed to the torture; how was Othello to die without merely satiating the audience with a glut of blood? How was his death to be made, not a foregone conclusion, a mere conventional suicide, but the culminating moment of the tragedy? In no single detail, perhaps, did Shakespeare ever show his dramatic genius more unmistakably than in his solution of this problem. We all remember how, as he is being led away, Othello stays his captors with a gesture, and thus addresses them:

> "Soft you; a word or two, before you go.
> I have done the state some service, and they know 't;
> No more of that. I pray you, in your letters,
> When you shall these unlucky deeds relate,
> Speak of me as I am; nothing extenuate,
> Nor set down aught in malice, then must you speak
> Of one that loved not wisely but too well;
> Of one not easily jealous, but, being wrought,
> Perplex'd in the extreme; of one whose hand,
> Like the base Indian, threw a pearl away
> Richer than all his tribe; of one whose subdued eyes,
> Albeit unused to the melting mood,
> Drop tears as fast as the Arabian trees
> Their medicinal gum. Set you down this;
> And say besides, that in Aleppo once,
> Where a malignant and a turban'd Turk
> Beat a Venetian and traduced the state,
> I took by the throat the circumcised dog,
> And smote him--thus!"

What is the essence of Shakespeare's achievement in this marvellous passage? What is it that he has done? He has thrown his audience, just as Othello has thrown his captors, off their guard, and substituted a sudden shock of surprise for a tedious fulfilment of expectation. In other words, he has handled the incident crisply instead of flaccidly, and so given it what we may call the specific accent of drama.

Another consummate example of the dramatic handling of detail may be found in the first act of Ibsen's ***Little Eyolf***. The lame boy, Eyolf, has followed the Rat-wife down to the wharf, has fallen into the water, and been drowned. This is the bare fact: how is it to be conveyed to the child's parents and to the audience?

A Greek dramatist would probably have had recourse to a long and elaborately worked-up "messenger-speech," a pathetic recitation. That was the method best suited to the conditions, and to what may be called the prevailing tempo, of the Greek theatre. I am far from saying that it was a bad method: no method is bad which holds and moves an audience. But in this case it would have had the disadvantage of concentrating attention on the narrator instead of on the child's parents, on the mere event instead of on the emotions it engendered. In the modern theatre, with greater facilities for reproducing the actual movement of life, the dramatist naturally aims at conveying to the audience the growing anxiety, the suspense and the final horror, of the father and mother. The most commonplace playwright would have seen this opportunity and tried to make the most of it. Every one can think of a dozen commonplace ways in which the scene could be arranged and written; and some of them might be quite effective. The great invention by which Ibsen snatches the scene out of the domain of the commonplace, and raises it to the height of dramatic poetry, consists in leaving it doubtful to the father and mother what is the meaning of the excitement on the beach and the confused cries which reach their ears, until one cry comes home to them with terrible distinctness, "The crutch is floating!" It would be hard to name any single phrase in literature in which more dramatic effect is concentrated than in these four words--they are only two words in the original. However dissimilar in its nature and circumstances, this incident is comparable with the death of Othello, inasmuch as in each case the poet, by a supreme felicity of invention, has succeeded in doing a given thing in absolutely the most dramatic method conceivable. Here we recognize in a consummate degree what has been called the "fingering of the dramatist"; and I know not how better to express the common quality of the two incidents than in saying that each is touched with extraordinary crispness, so as to give to what in both cases has for some time been expected and foreseen a sudden thrill of novelty and unexpectedness. That is how to do a thing dramatically.[6]

And now, after all this discussion of the "dramatic" in theme and incident, it remains to be said that the tendency of recent theory, and of some recent practice, has been to widen the meaning of the word, until it bursts the bonds of all definition. Plays have been written, and have found some acceptance, in which the endeavour of the dramatist has been to depict life, not in moments of crisis, but in its most level and humdrum phases, and to avoid any crispness of touch in the presentation of individual incidents. "Dramatic," in the eyes of writers of this school, has become a term of reproach, synonymous with "theatrical." They take their cue from Maeterlinck's famous essay on "The Tragic in Daily Life," in which he lays it down that: "An old man, seated in his armchair, waiting patiently, with his lamp beside him--submitting with bent head to the presence of his soul and his destiny--motionless as he is, does yet live in reality a deeper, more human, and more universal life than the lover who strangles his mistress, the captain who conquers in battle, or the husband who 'avenges his honour.'" They do not observe that Maeterlinck, in his own practice, constantly deals with crises, and often with violent and startling ones.

At the same time, I am far from suggesting that the reaction against the traditional "dramatic" is a wholly mistaken movement. It is a valuable corrective of conventional theatricalism; and it has, at some points, positively enlarged the domain of dramatic art. Any movement is good which helps to free art from the tyranny of a code of rules and definitions. The only really valid definition of the dramatic is: Any representation of imaginary personages which is capable of interesting an average audience assembled in a theatre. We must say "representation of imaginary personages" in order to exclude a lecture or a prize-fight; and we must say "an average audience" (or something to that effect) in order to exclude a dialogue of Plato or of Landor, the recitation of which might interest a specially selected public. Any further attempt to limit the content of the term "dramatic" is simply the expression of an opinion that such-and-such forms of representation will not be found to interest an audience; and this opinion may always be rebutted by experiment. In all that I have said, then, as to the dramatic and the non-dramatic, I must be taken as meaning: "Such-and-such forms and methods have been found to please, and will probably please again. They are, so to speak, safer and easier than other forms and methods. But it is the part of original genius to override the dictates of experience, and nothing in these pages is designed to discourage original genius from making the attempt." We have already seen, indeed, that in a certain type of play--the broad picture of a social phenomenon or environment--it is preferable that no attempt should be made to depict a marked crisis. There should be just enough story to afford a plausible excuse for raising and for lowering the curtain.[7]

Let us not, however, seem to grant too much to the innovators and the quietists. To say that a drama should be, or tends to be, the presentation of a crisis in the life of certain characters, is by no means to insist on a mere arbitrary convention. It is to make at once an induction from the overwhelming majority of existing dramas, and a deduction from the nature and inherent conditions of theatrical presentation. The fact that theatrical conditions often encourage a violent exaggeration of the characteristically dramatic elements in life does not make these elements any the less real or any the less characteristically dramatic. It is true that crispness of handling may easily degenerate into the pursuit of mere picture-poster situation; but that is no reason why the artist should not seek to achieve crispness within the bounds prescribed by nature and common sense. There is a drama--I have myself seen it--in which the heroine, fleeing from the villain, is stopped by a yawning chasm. The pursuer is at her heels, and it seems as though she has no resource but to hurl herself into the abyss. But she is accompanied by three Indian servants, who happen, by the mercy of Providence, to be accomplished acrobats. The second climbs on the shoulders of the first, the third on the shoulders of the second; and then the whole trio falls forward across the chasm, the top one grasping some bush or creeper on the other side; so that a living bridge is formed, on which the heroine (herself, it would seem, something of an acrobat) can cross the dizzy gulf and bid defiance to the baffled villain. This is clearly a dramatic crisis within our definition; but, no less clearly, it is not a piece of rational or commendable drama. To say that such-and-such a factor is necessary, or highly desirable, in a dramatic scene, is by no means to imply that every scene which contains this factor is good drama. Let us take the case of another heroine--Nina in Sir Arthur Pinero's *His House in Order*. The second wife of Filmer Jesson, she is continually being offered up as a sacrifice on the altar dedicated to the memory of his adored first wife. Not only her husband, but the relatives of the sainted Annabel, make her life a burden to her. Then it comes to her knowledge--she obtains absolute proof--that Annabel was anything but the saint she was believed to be. By a single word she can overturn the altar of her martyrdom, and shatter the dearest illusion of her persecutors. Shall she speak that word, or shall she not? Here is a crisis which comes within our definition just as clearly as the other;[8] only it happens to be entirely natural and probable, and eminently illustrative of character. Ought we, then, to despise it because of the element it has in common with the picture-poster situation of preposterous melodrama? Surely not. Let those who have the art--the extremely delicate and difficult art--of making drama without the characteristically dramatic ingredients, do so by all means; but let them not seek to lay an embargo on the judicious use of these ingredients as they present themselves in life.

* * * * *

Notes:[1: *Etudes Critiques*, vol. vii, pp. 153 and 207.]

[2: In the most aggravated cases, the misunderstanding is maintained by a persevering use of pronouns in place of proper names: "he" and "she" being taken by the hearer to mean A. and B., when the speaker is in fact referring to X. and Y. This ancient trick becomes the more irritating the longer the *quiproquo* is dragged out.]

[3: The Lowland Scottish villager. It is noteworthy that Mr. J.M. Barrie, who himself belongs to this race, has an almost unique gift of extracting dramatic effect out of taciturnity, and even out of silence.]

[4: There is a somewhat similar incident in Clyde Fitch's play, *The Moth and the Flame*.]

[5: *Les Corbeaux*, by Henri Becque, might perhaps be classed as a bankruptcy play, though the point of it is that the Vigneron family is not really bankrupt at all, but is unblushingly fleeced by the partner and the lawyer of the deceased Vigneron, who play into each other's hands.]

[6: "Dramatic" has recently become one of the most overworked words in the vocabulary of journalism. It constantly appears, not only in the text of the picturesque reporter, but in head-lines and on bulletin-boards. When, on July 20, 1911, Mr. Asquith wrote to Mr. Balfour to inform him that the King had guaranteed the creation of peers, should it prove necessary for the passing of the Parliament Bill, one paper published the news under this head-line: "DRAMATIC ANNOUNCEMENT BY THE PRIME MINISTER," and the parliamentary correspondent of another paper wrote: "With dramatic suddenness and swiftness, the Prime Minister hurled his thunderbolt at the wavering Tory party yesterday." As a matter of fact, the letter was probably not "hurled" more suddenly or swiftly than the most ordinary invitation to dinner: nor can its contents have been particularly surprising to any one. It was probably the conclusiveness, the finality, of the announcement that struck these writers as "dramatic." The letter put an end to all dubiety with a "short, sharp shock." It was, in fact, crisp. As a rule, however, "dramatic" is employed by the modern journalist simply as a rather pretentious synonym for the still more hackneyed "startling."]

[7: As a specimen, and a successful specimen, of this new technic, I may cite Miss Elizabeth Baker's very interesting play, **Chains**. There is absolutely no "story" in it, no complication of incidents, not even any emotional tension worth speaking of. Another recent play of something the same type, **The Way the Money Goes**, by Lady Bell, was quite thrilling by comparison. There we saw a workman's wife bowed down by a terrible secret which threatened to wreck her whole life--the secret that she had actually run into debt to the amount of L30. Her situation was dramatic in the ordinary sense of the word, very much as Nora's situation is dramatic when she knows that Krogstad's letter is in Helmer's hands. But in **Chains** there is not even this simple form of excitement and suspense. A city clerk, oppressed by the deadly monotony and narrowness of his life, thinks of going to Australia--and doesn't go: that is the sum and substance of the action. Also, by way of underplot, a shopgirl, oppressed by the deadly monotony and narrowness of her life, thinks of escaping from it by marrying a middle-aged widower--and doesn't do it. If any one had told the late Francisque Sarcey, or the late Clement Scott, that a play could be made out of this slender material, which should hold an audience absorbed through four acts, and stir them to real enthusiasm, these eminent critics would have thought him a madman. Yet Miss Baker has achieved this feat, by the simple process of supplementing competent observation with a fair share of dramatic instinct.]

[8: If the essence of drama is crisis, it follows that nothing can be more dramatic than a momentous choice which may make or mar both the character and the fortune of the chooser and of others. There is an element of choice in all action which is, or seems to be, the product of free will; but there is a peculiar crispness of effect when two alternatives are clearly formulated, and the choice is made after a mental struggle, accentuated, perhaps, by impassioned advocacy of the conflicting interests. Such scenes are **Coriolanus**, v. 3, the scene between Ellida, Wangel, and the Stranger in the last act of *The Lady from the Sea*, and the concluding scene of **Candida**.]

CHAPTER IV
THE ROUTINE OF COMPOSITION

As no two people, probably, ever did, or ever will, pursue the same routine in play-making, it is manifestly impossible to lay down any general rules on the subject. There are one or two considerations, however, which it may not be wholly superfluous to suggest to beginners.

An invaluable insight into the methods of a master is provided by the scenarios and drafts of plays published in Henrik Ibsen's ***Efterladte Skrifter***. The most important of these "fore-works," as he used to call them, have now been translated under the title of ***From Ibsen's Workshop*** (Scribner), and may be studied with the greatest profit. Not that the student should mechanically imitate even Ibsen's routine of composition, which, indeed, varied considerably from play to play. The great lesson to be learnt from Ibsen's practice is that the play should be kept fluid or plastic as long as possible, and not suffered to become immutably fixed, either in the author's mind or on paper, before it has had time to grow and ripen. Many, if not most, of Ibsen's greatest individual inspirations came to him as afterthoughts, after the play had reached a point of development at which many authors would have held the process of gestation ended, and the work of art ripe for birth. Among these inspired afterthoughts may be reckoned Nora's great line, "Millions of women have done that"--the most crushing repartee in literature--Hedvig's threatened blindness, with all that ensues from it, and Little Eyolf's crutch, used to such purpose as we have already seen.

This is not to say that the drawing-up of a tentative scenario ought not to be one of the playwright's first proceedings. Indeed, if he is able to dispense with a scenario on paper, it can only be because his mind is so clear, and so retentive of its own ideas, as to enable him to carry in his head, always ready for reference, a more or less detailed scheme. Go-as-you-please composition may be possible for the novelist, perhaps even for the writer of a one-act play, a mere piece of dialogue; but in a dramatic structure of any considerable extent, proportion, balance, and the interconnection of parts are so essential that a scenario is almost as indispensable to a dramatist as a set of plans to an architect. There is one dramatist of note whom one suspects of sometimes working without any definite scenario, and inventing as he goes along. That dramatist, I need scarcely say, is Mr. Bernard Shaw. I have no absolute knowledge of his method; but if he schemed out any scenario for **Getting Married** or **Misalliance**, he has sedulously concealed the fact--to the detriment of the plays.[1]

The scenario or skeleton is so manifestly the natural ground-work of a dramatic performance that the playwrights of the Italian *commedia dell' arte* wrote nothing more than a scheme of scenes, and left the actors to do the rest. The same practice prevailed in early Elizabethan days, as one or two MS. "Plats," designed to be hung up in the wings, are extant to testify. The transition from extempore acting regulated by a scenario to the formal learning of parts falls within the historical period of the German stage. It seems probable that the romantic playwrights of the sixteenth and seventeenth centuries, both in England and in Spain, may have adopted a method not unlike that of the drama of improvisation, that is to say, they may have drawn out a scheme of entrances and exits, and then let their characters discourse (on paper) as their fancy prompted. So, at least, the copious fluency of their dialogue seems to suggest. But the typical modern play is a much more close-knit organism, in which every word has to be weighed far more carefully than it was by playwrights who stood near to the days of improvisation, and could indulge in "the large utterance of the early gods." Consequently it would seem that, until a play has been thought out very clearly and in great detail, any scheme of entrances and exits ought to be merely provisional and subject to indefinite modification. A modern play is not a framework of story loosely draped in a more or less gorgeous robe of language. There is, or ought to be, a close interdependence between action, character and dialogue, which forbids a playwright to tie his hands very far in advance.

As a rule, then, it would seem to be an unfavourable sign when a drama presents itself at an early stage with a fixed and unalterable outline. The result may be a powerful, logical, well-knit piece of work; but the breath of life will scarcely be in it. Room should be left as long as possible for unexpected developments of character. If your characters are innocent of unexpected developments, the less characters they.[2] Not that I, personally, have any faith in those writers of fiction, be they playwrights or novelists, who contend that they do not speak through the mouths of their personages, but rather let their personages speak through them. "I do not invent or create" I have heard an eminent novelist say: "I simply record; my characters speak and act, and I write down their sayings and doings." This author may be a fine psychologist for purposes of fiction, but I question his insight into his own mental processes. The apparent spontaneity of a character's proceedings is a pure illusion. It means no more than that the imagination, once set in motion along a given line, moves along that line with an ease and freedom which seems to its possessor preternatural and almost uncanny.[3]

Most authors, however, who have any real gift for character-creation probably fall more or less under this illusion, though they are sane enough and modest enough to realize that an illusion it is.[4] A character will every now and then seem to take the bit between his teeth and say and do things for which his creator feels himself hardly responsible. The playwright's scheme should not, then, until the latest possible moment, become so hard and fast as to allow his characters no elbow room for such manifestations of spontaneity. And this is only one of several forms of afterthought which may arise as the play develops. The playwright may all of a sudden see that a certain character is superfluous, or that a new character is needed, or that a new relationship between two characters would simplify matters, or that a scene that he has placed in the first act ought to be in the second, or that he can dispense with it altogether, or that it reveals too much to the audience and must be wholly recast.[5]

These are only a few of the re-adjustments which have constantly to be made if a play is shaping itself by a process of vital growth; and that is why the playwright may be advised to keep his material fluid as long as he can. Ibsen had written large portions of the play now known to us as **Rosmersholm** before he decided that Rebecca should not be married to Rosmer. He also, at a comparatively late stage, did away with two daughters whom he had at first given to Rosmer, and decided to make her childlessness the main cause of Beata's tragedy.

Perhaps I insist too strongly on the advisability of treating a dramatic theme as clay to be modelled and remodelled, rather than as wood or marble to be carved unalterably and once for all. If so, it is because of a personal reminiscence. In my early youth, I had, like everybody else, ambitions in the direction of play-writing; and it was my inability to keep a theme plastic that convinced me of my lack of talent. It pleased me greatly to draw out a detailed scenario, working up duly to a situation at the end of each act; and, once made, that scenario was like a cast-iron mould into which the dialogue had simply to be poured. The result was that the play had all the merits of a logical, well-ordered essay. My situations worked out like the Q.E.D.'s of Euclid. My characters obstinately refused to come to life, or to take the bit between their teeth. They were simply cog-wheels in a pre-arranged mechanism. In one respect, my two or three plays were models--in respect of brevity and conciseness. I was never troubled by the necessity of cutting down--so cruel a necessity to many playwrights.[6] My difficulty was rather to find enough for my characters to say-- for they never wanted to say anything that was not strictly germane to the plot. It was this that made me despair of play-writing, and realize that my mission was to teach other people how to write plays. And, similarly, the aspirant who finds that his people never want to say more than he can allow them to say--that they never rush headlong into blind alleys, or do things that upset the balance of the play and have to be resolutely undone--that aspirant will do well not to be over-confident of his dramatic calling and election. There may be authors who can write vital plays, as Shakespeare is said (on rather poor evidence)[7] to have done, without blotting a line; but I believe them to be rare. In our day, the great playwright is more likely to be he who does not shrink, on occasion, from blotting an act or two.

There is a modern French dramatist who writes, with success, such plays as I might have written had I combined a strong philosophical faculty with great rhetorical force and fluency. The dramas of M. Paul Hervieu have all the neatness and cogency of a geometrical demonstration. One imagines that, for M. Hervieu, the act of composition means merely the careful filling in of a scenario as neat and complete as a schedule.[8] But for that very reason, despite their undoubted intellectual power, M. Hervieu's dramas command our respect rather than our enthusiasm. The dramatist should aim at *being* logical without *seeming* so.[9]

It is sometimes said that a playwright ought to construct his play backwards, and even to write his last act first.[10] This doctrine belongs to the period of the well-made play, when climax was regarded as the one thing needful in dramatic art, and anticlimax as the unforgivable sin. Nowadays, we do not insist that every play should end with a tableau, or with an emphatic *mot de la fin*. We are more willing to accept a quiet, even an indecisive, ending.[11] Nevertheless it is and must ever be true that, at a very early period in the scheming of his play, the playwright ought to assure himself that his theme is capable of a satisfactory ending. Of course this phrase does not imply a "happy ending," but one which satisfies the author as being artistic, effective, inevitable (in the case of a serious play), or, in one word, "right." An obviously makeshift ending can never be desirable, either from the ideal or from the practical point of view. Many excellent plays have been wrecked on this rock. The very frequent complaint that "the last act is weak" is not always or necessarily a just reproach; but it is so when the author has clearly been at a loss for an ending, and has simply huddled his play up in a conventional and perfunctory fashion. It may even be said that some apparently promising themes are deceptive in their promise, since they are inherently incapable of a satisfactory ending. The playwright should by all means make sure that he has not run up against one of these blind-alley themes.[12] He should, at an early point, see clearly the end for which he is making, and be sure that it is an end which he actively desires, not merely one which satisfies convention, or which "will have to do."

Some dramatists, when a play is provisionally mapped out, do not attempt to begin at the beginning and write it as a coherent whole, but make a dash first at the more salient and critical scenes, or those which specially attract their imagination. On such a point every author must obviously be a law unto himself. From the theoretical point of view, one can only approve the practice, since it certainly makes for plasticity. It is evident that a detached scene, written while those that lead up to it are as yet but vaguely conceived, must be subject to indefinite modification.[13] In several of Ibsen's very roughest drafts, we find short passages of dialogue sketched out even before the names have been assigned to the characters, showing that some of his earliest ideas came to him, as it were, ready dramatized. One would be tempted to hope much of an author who habitually and unaffectedly thus "lisped in dialogue for the dialogue came."

Ought the playwright, at an early stage in the process of each act, to have the details of its scene clearly before him? Ought he to draw out a scene-plot, and know, from moment to moment, just where each character is, whether He is standing on the hearthrug and She sitting on the settee, or *vice versa*? There is no doubt that furniture, properties, accidents of environment, play a much larger part in modern drama than they did on the Elizabethan, the eighteenth century, or even the early-Victorian stage. Some of us, who are not yet centenarians, can remember to have seen rooms on the stage with no furniture at all except two or three chairs "painted on the flat." Under such conditions, it was clearly useless for the playwright to trouble his head about furniture, and even "positions" might well be left for arrangement at rehearsal. This carelessness of the environment, however, is no longer possible. Whether we like it or no (and some theorists do not like it at all), scenery has ceased to be a merely suggestive background against which the figures stand out in high relief. The stage now aims at presenting a complete picture, with the figures, not "a little out of the picture," but completely in it. This being so, the playwright must evidently, at some point in the working out of his theme, visualize the stage-picture in considerable detail; and we find that almost all modern dramatists do, as a matter of fact, pay great attention to what may be called the topography of their scenes, and the shifting "positions" of their characters. The question is: at what stage of the process of composition ought this visualization to occur? Here, again, it would be absurd to lay down a general rule; but I am inclined to think, both theoretically and from what can be gathered of the practice of the best dramatists, that it is wisest to reserve it for a comparatively late stage. A playwright of my acquaintance, and a very remarkable playwright too, used to scribble the first drafts of his play in little notebooks, which he produced from his pocket whenever he had a moment to spare--often on the top of an omnibus. Only when the first draft was complete did he proceed to set the scenes, as it were, and map out the stage-management. On the other hand, one has heard of playwrights whose first step in setting to work upon a particular act was to construct a complete model of the scene, and people it with manikins to represent the characters. As a general practice, this is scarcely to be commended. It is wiser, one fancies, to have the matter of the scene pretty fully roughed-out before details of furniture, properties, and position are arranged.[14] It may happen, indeed, that some natural phenomenon, some property or piece of furniture, is the very pivot of the scene; in which case it must, of course, be posited from the first. From the very moment of his conceiving the fourth act of *Le Tartufe*, Moliere must have had clearly in view the table under which Orgon hides; and Sheridan cannot have got very far with the Screen Scene before he had mentally placed the screen. But even where a great deal turns on some individual object, the detailed arrangements of the scene may in most cases be taken for granted until a late stage in its working out.

One proviso, however, must be made; where any important effect depends upon a given object, or a particular arrangement of the scene, the playwright cannot too soon assure himself that the object comes well within the physical possibilities of the stage, and that the arrangement is optically[15] possible and effective. Few things, indeed, are quite impossible to the modern stage; but there are many that had much better not be attempted. It need scarcely be added that the more serious a play is, or aspires to be, the more carefully should the author avoid any such effects as call for the active collaboration of the stage-carpenter, machinist, or electrician. Even when a mechanical effect can be produced to perfection, the very fact that the audience cannot but admire the ingenuity displayed, and wonder "how it is done," implies a failure of that single-minded attention to the essence of the matter in hand which the dramatist would strive to beget and maintain. A small but instructive example of a difficult effect, such as the prudent playwright will do well to avoid, occurs in the third act of Ibsen's *Little Eyolf*. During the greater part of the act, the flag in Allmers's garden is hoisted to half-mast in token of mourning; until at the end, when he and Rita attain a serener frame of mind, he runs it up to the truck. Now, from the poetic and symbolic point of view, this flag is all that can be desired; but from the practical point of view it presents grave difficulties. Nothing is so pitifully ineffective as a flag in a dead calm, drooping nervelessly against the mast; and though, no doubt, by an ingenious arrangement of electric fans, it might be possible to make this flag flutter in the breeze, the very fact of its doing so would tend to set the audience wondering by what mechanism the effect was produced, instead of attending to the soul-struggles of Rita and Allmers. It would be absurd to blame Ibsen for overriding theatrical prudence in such a case; I merely point out to beginners that it is wise, before relying on an effect of this order, to make sure that it is, not only possible, but convenient from the practical point of view. In one or two other cases Ibsen strained the resources of the stage. The illumination in the last act of ***Pillars of Society*** cannot be carried out as he describes it; or rather, if it were carried out on some exceptionally large and well-equipped stage, the feat of the mechanician would eclipse the invention of the poet. On the other hand, the abode of the Wild Duck in the play of that name is a conception entirely consonant with the optics of the theatre; for no detail at all need be, or ought to be, visible, and a vague effect of light is all that is required. Only in his last melancholy effort did Ibsen, in a play designed for representation, demand scenic effects entirely beyond the resources of any theatre not specially fitted for spectacular drama, and possible, even in such a theatre, only in some ridiculously makeshift form.

There are two points of routine on which I am compelled to speak in no uncertain voice--two practices which I hold to be almost equally condemnable. In the first place, no playwright who understands the evolution of the modern theatre can nowadays use in his stage-directions the abhorrent jargon of the early nineteenth century. When one comes across a manuscript bespattered with such cabalistic signs as "R.2.E.," "R.C.," "L.C.," "L.U.E.," and so forth, one sees at a glance that the writer has neither studied dramatic literature nor thought out for himself the conditions of the modern theatre, but has found his dramatic education between the buff covers of ***French's Acting Edition***. Some beginners imagine that a plentiful use of such abbreviations will be taken as a proof of their familiarity with the stage; whereas, in fact, it only shows their unfamiliarity with theatrical history. They might as well set forth to describe a modern battleship in the nautical terminology of Captain Marryat. "Right First Entrance," "Left Upper Entrance," and so forth, are terms belonging to the period when there were no "box" rooms or "set" exteriors on the stage, when the sides of each scene were composed of "wings" shoved on in grooves, and entrances could be made between each pair of wings. Thus, "R. 1 E." meant the entrance between the proscenium and the first "wing" on the right, "R. 2 E." meant the entrance between the first pair of "wings," and so forth. "L.U.E." meant the entrance at the left between the last "wing" and the back cloth. Now grooves and "wings" have disappeared from the stage. The "box" room is entered, like any room in real life, by doors or French windows; and the only rational course is to state the position of your doors in your opening stage-direction, and thereafter to say in plain language by which door an entrance or an exit is to be made. In exterior scenes where, for example, trees or clumps of shrubbery answer in a measure to the old "wings," the old terminology may not be quite meaningless; but it is far better eschewed. It is a good general rule to avoid, so far as possible, expressions which show that the author has a stage scene, and not an episode of real life, before his eyes. Men of the theatre are the last to be impressed by theatrical jargon; and when the play comes to be printed, the general reader is merely bewildered and annoyed by technicalities, which tend, moreover, to disturb his illusion.

A still more emphatic warning must be given against another and more recent abuse in the matter of stage-directions. The "L.U.E.'s," indeed, are bound very soon to die a natural death. The people who require to be warned against them are, as a rule, scarcely worth warning. But it is precisely the cleverest people (to use clever in a somewhat narrow sense) who are apt to be led astray by Mr. Bernard Shaw's practice of expanding his stage-directions into essays, disquisitions, monologues, pamphlets. This is a practice which goes far to justify the belief of some foreign critics that the English, or, since Mr. Shaw is in question, let us say the inhabitants of the British Islands, are congenitally incapable of producing a work of pure art. Our novelists--Fielding, Thackeray, George Eliot--have been sufficiently, though perhaps not unjustly, called over the coals for their habit of coming in front of their canvas, and either gossiping with the reader or preaching at him. But, if it be a sound maxim that the novelist should not obtrude his personality on his reader, how much more is this true of the dramatist! When the dramatist steps to the footlights and begins to lecture, all illusion is gone. It may be said that, as a matter of fact, this does not occur: that on the stage we hear no more of the disquisitions of Mr. Shaw and his imitators than we do of the curt, and often non-existent, stage-directions of Shakespeare and his contemporaries. To this the reply is twofold. First, the very fact that these disquisitions are written proves that the play is designed to be printed and read, and that we are, therefore, justified in applying to it the standard of what may be called literary illusion. Second, when a playwright gets into the habit of talking around his characters, he inevitably, even if unconsciously, slackens his endeavour to make them express themselves as completely as may be in their own proper medium of dramatic action and dialogue. You cannot with impunity mix up two distinct forms of art--the drama and the sociological essay or lecture. To Mr. Shaw, of course, much may, and must, be forgiven. His stage-directions are so brilliant that some one, some day, will assuredly have them spoken by a lecturer in the orchestra while the action stands still on the stage. Thus, he will have begotten a bastard, but highly entertaining, form of art. My protest has no practical application to him, for he is a standing exception to all rules. It is to the younger generation that I appeal not to be misled by his seductive example. They have little chance of rivalling him as sociological essayists; but if they treat their art seriously, and as a pure art, they may easily surpass him as dramatists. By adopting his practice they will tend to produce, not fine works of art, but inferior sociological documents. They will impair their originality and spoil their plays in order to do comparatively badly what Mr. Shaw has done incomparably well.

The common-sense rule as to stage directions is absolutely plain; be they short, or be they long, they ought always to be ***impersonal***. The playwright who cracks jokes in his stage-directions, or indulges in graces of style, is intruding himself between the spectator and the work of art, to the inevitable detriment of the illusion. In preparing a play for the press, the author should make his stage-directions as brief as is consistent with clearness. Few readers will burden their memory with long and detailed descriptions. When a new character of importance appears, a short description of his or her personal appearance and dress may be helpful to the reader; but even this should be kept impersonal. Moreover, as a play has always to be read before it can be rehearsed or acted, it is no bad plan to make the stage-directions, from the first, such as tend to bring the play home clearly to the reader's mental vision. And here I may mention a principle, based on more than mere convenience, which some playwrights observe with excellent results. Not merely in writing stage-directions, but in visualizing a scene, the idea of the stage should, as far as possible, be banished from the author's mind. He should see and describe the room, the garden, the sea-shore, or whatever the place of his action may be, not as a stage-scene, but as a room, garden, or sea-shore in the real world. The cultivation of this habit ought to be, and I believe is in some cases, a safeguard against theatricality.

* * * * *

Notes:

[1: Sardou wrote careful and detailed scenarios, Dumas *fils* held it a waste of time to do so. Pailleron wrote "enormous" scenarios, Meilhac very brief ones, or none at all. Mr. Galsworthy, rather to my surprise, disdains, and even condemns, the scenario, holding that a theme becomes lifeless when you put down its skeleton on paper. Sir Arthur Pinero says: "Before beginning to write a play, I always make sure, by means of a definite scheme, that there is *a* way of doing it; but whether I ultimately follow that way is a totally different matter." Mr. Alfred Sutro practically confesses to a scenario. He says: "Before I start writing the dialogue of a play, I make sure that I shall have an absolutely free hand over the entrances and exits: in other words, that there is ample and legitimate reason for each character appearing in any particular scene, and ample motive for his leaving it." Mr. Granville Barker does not put on paper a detailed scenario. He says: "I plan the general scheme, and particularly the balance of the play, in my head; but this, of course, does not depend entirely on entrances and exits." Mr. Henry Arthur Jones says: "I know the leading scenes, and the general course of action in each act, before I write a line. When I have got the whole story clear, and divided into acts, I very carefully construct the first act, as a series of scenes between such and such of the characters. When the first act is written I carefully construct the second act in the same way--and so on. I sometimes draw up twenty scenarios for an act before I can get it to go straight."]

[2: A friend of the late Clyde Fitch writes to me: "Fitch was often astonished at the way in which his characters developed. He tried to make them do certain things: they did others."]

[3: This account of the matter seems to find support in a statement, by M. François de Curel, an accomplished psychologist, to the effect that during the first few days of work at a play he is "clearly conscious of creating," but that gradually he gets "into the skin" of his characters, and appears to work by instinct. No doubt some artists are actually subject to a sort of hallucination, during which they seem rather to record than to invent the doings of their characters. But this somewhat morbid condition should scarcely be cultivated by the dramatist, whose intelligence should always keep a light rein on his more instinctive mental processes. See *L'Annee Psychologique*, 1894. p. 120.]

[4: Sir Arthur Pinero says: "The beginning of a play to me is a little world of people. I live with them, get familiar with them, and *they* tell me the story." This may sound not unlike the remark of the novelist above quoted; but the intention was quite different. Sir Arthur simply meant that the story came to him as the characters took on life in his imagination. Mr. H.A. Jones writes: "When you have a character or several characters you haven't a play. You may keep these in your mind and nurse them till they combine in a piece of action; but you haven't got your play till you have theme, characters, and action all fused. The process with me is as purely automatic and spontaneous as dreaming; in fact it is really dreaming while you are awake."]

[5: "Here," says a well-known playwright, "is a common experience. You are struck by an idea with which you fall in love. 'Ha!' you say. 'What a superb scene where the man shall find the missing will under the sofa! If that doesn't make them sit up, what will?' You begin the play. The first act goes all right, and the second act goes all right. You come to the third act, and somehow it won't go at all. You battle with it for weeks in vain; and then it suddenly occurs to you, 'Why, I see what's wrong! It's that confounded scene where the man finds the will under the sofa! Out it must come!' You cut it out, and at once all goes smooth again. But you have thrown overboard the great effect that first tempted you."]

[6: The manuscripts of Dumas *fils* are said to contain, as a rule, about four times as much matter as the printed play! (Parigot: ***Genie et Metier***, p. 243). This probably means, however, that he preserved tentative and ultimately rejected scenes, which most playwrights destroy as they go along.]

[7: Lowell points out that this assertion of Heminge and Condell merely shows them to have been unfamiliar with the simple phenomenon known as a fair copy.]

[8: Since writing this I have learnt that my conjecture is correct, at any rate as regards some of M. Hervieu's plays.]

[9: See Chapters XIII and XVI.]

[10: This view is expressed with great emphasis by Dumas *fils* in the preface to ***La Princesse Georges***. "You should not begin your work," he says, "until you have your concluding scene, movement and speech clear in your mind. How can you tell what road you ought to take until you know where you are going?" It is perhaps a more apparent than real contradiction of this rule that, until *Iris* was three parts finished, Sir Arthur Pinero intended the play to end with the throttling of Iris by Maldonado. The actual end is tantamount to a murder, though Iris is not actually killed.]

[11: See Chapter XVIII.]

[12: See Chapter XX.]

[13: Most of the dramatists whom I have consulted are opposed to the principle of "roughing out" the big scenes first, and then imbedding them, as it were, in their context. Sir Arthur Pinero goes the length of saying: "I can never go on to page 2 until I am sure that page 1 is as right as I can make it. Indeed, when an act is finished, I send it at once to the printers, confident that I shall not have to go back upon it." Mr. Alfred Sutro says: "I write a play straight ahead from beginning to end, taking practically as long over the first act as over the last three." And Mr. Granville Barker: "I always write the beginning of a play first and the end last: but as to writing 'straight ahead'--it sounds like what one may be able to do in Heaven." But almost all dramatists, I take it, jot down brief passages of dialogue which they may or may not eventually work into the texture of their play.]

[14: One is not surprised to learn that Sardou "did his stage-management as he went along," and always knew exactly the position of his characters from moment to moment.]

[15: And aurally, it may be added. Sarcey comments on the impossibility of a scene in Zola's **Pot Bouille** in which the so-called "lovers," Octave Mouret and Blanche, throw open the window of the garret in which they are quarrelling, and hear the servants in the courtyard outside discussing their intrigue. In order that the comments of the servants might reach the ears of the audience, they had to be shouted in a way (says M. Sarcey) that was fatal to the desired illusion.]

CHAPTER V
DRAMATIS PERSONAE

The theme being chosen, the next step will probably be to determine what characters shall be employed in developing it. Most playwrights, I take it, draw up a provisional Dramatis Personae before beginning the serious work of construction. Ibsen seems always to have done so; but, in some of his plays, the list of persons was at first considerably larger than it ultimately became. The frugal poet sometimes saved up the characters rejected from one play, and used them in another. Thus Boletta and Hilda Wangel were originally intended to have been the daughters of Rosmer and Beata; and the delightful Foldal of ***John Gabriel Borkman*** was a character left over from ***The Lady from the Sea***.

The playwright cannot proceed far in planning out his work without determining, roughly at any rate, what auxiliary characters he means to employ. There are in every play essential characters, without whom the theme is unthinkable, and auxiliary characters, not indispensable to the theme, but simply convenient for filling in the canvas and carrying on the action. It is not always possible to decide whether a character is essential or auxiliary--it depends upon how we define the theme. In ***Hamlet***, for example, Hamlet, Claudius, and Gertrude are manifestly essential: for the theme is the hesitancy of a young man of a certain temperament in taking vengeance upon the seducer of his mother and murderer of his father. But is Ophelia essential, or merely auxiliary? Essential, if we consider Hamlet's pessimistic feeling as to woman and the "breeding of sinners" a necessary part of his character; auxiliary, if we take the view that without this feeling he would still have been Hamlet, and the action, to all intents and purposes, the same. The remaining characters, on the other hand, are clearly auxiliary. This is true even of the Ghost: for

Hamlet might have learnt of his father's murder in fifty other ways.

Polonius, Laertes, Horatio, and the rest might all have been utterly different, or might never have existed at all, and yet the essence of the play might have remained intact.

It would be perfectly possible to write a **Hamlet** after the manner of Racine, in which there should be only six personages instead of Shakespeare's six-and-twenty: and in this estimate I assume Ophelia to be an essential character. The dramatis personae would be: Hamlet, his confidant; Ophelia, her confidant; and the King and Queen, who would serve as confidants to each other. Indeed, an economy of one person might be affected by making the Queen (as she naturally might) play the part of confidant to Ophelia.

Shakespeare, to be sure, did not deliberately choose between his own method and that of Racine. Classic concentration was wholly unsuited to the physical conditions of the Elizabethan stage, on which external movement and bustle were imperatively demanded. But the modern playwright has a wide latitude of choice in this purely technical matter. He may work out his plot with the smallest possible number of characters, or he may introduce a crowd of auxiliary personages. The good craftsman will be guided by the nature of his theme. In a broad social study or a picturesque romance, you may have as many auxiliary figures as you please. In a subtle comedy, or a psychological tragedy, the essential characters should have the stage as much as possible to themselves. In Becque's **La Parisienne** there are only four characters and a servant; in Rostand's **Cyrano de Bergerac** there are fifty-four personages named in the playbill, to say nothing of supernumeraries. In **Peer Gynt**, a satiric phantasmagory, Ibsen introduces some fifty individual characters, with numberless supernumeraries; in **An Enemy of the People**, a social comedy, he has eleven characters and a crowd; for **Ghosts** and **Rosmersholm**, psychological tragedies, six persons apiece are sufficient.

It can scarcely be necessary, at this time of day, to say much on the subject of nomenclature. One does occasionally, in manuscripts of a quite hopeless type, find the millionaire's daughter figuring as "Miss Aurea Golden," and her poor but sprightly cousin as "Miss Lalage Gay"; but the veriest tyro realizes, as a rule, that this sort of punning characterization went out with the eighteenth century, or survived into the nineteenth century only as a flagrant anachronism, like knee-breeches and hair-powder.

A curious essay might be written on the reasons why such names as Sir John Brute, Sir Tunbelly Clumsy, Sir Peter Teazle, Sir Anthony Absolute, Sir Lucius O'Trigger, Lord Foppington, Lord Rake, Colonel Bully, Lovewell, Heartfree, Gripe, Shark and the rest were regarded as a matter of course in "the comedy of manners," but have become offensive to-day, except in deliberate imitations of the eighteenth-century style. The explanation does not lie merely in the contrast between "conventional" comedy and "realistic" drama. Our forefathers (whatever Lamb may say) did not consciously place their comedy in a realm of convention, but generally considered themselves, and sometimes were, realists. The fashion of label-names, if we may call them so, came down from the Elizabethans, who, again, borrowed it from the Mediaeval Moralities.[1] Shakespeare himself gave us Master Slender and Justice Shallow; but it was in the Jonsonian comedy of types that the practice of advertising a "humour" or "passion" in a name (English or Italian) established itself most firmly. Hence such strange appellatives as Sir Epicure Mammon, Sir Amorous La Foole, Morose, Wellbred, Downright, Fastidius Brisk, Volpone, Corbaccio, Sordido, and Fallace. After the Restoration, Jonson, Beaumont and Fletcher, and Massinger were, for a time, more popular than Shakespeare; so that the label-names seemed to have the sanction of the giants that were before the Flood. Even when comedy began to deal with individuals rather than mere incarnations of a single "humour," the practice of giving them obvious pseudonyms held its ground. Probably it was reinforced by the analogous practice which obtained in journalism, in which real persons were constantly alluded to (and libelled) under fictitious designations, more or less transparent to the initiated. Thus a label-name did not carry with it a sense of unreality, but rather, perhaps, a vague suggestion of covert reference to a real person. I must not here attempt to trace the stages by which the fashion went out. It could doubtless be shown that the process of change ran parallel to the shrinkage of the "apron" and the transformation of the platform-stage into the picture-stage. That transformation was completed about the middle of the nineteenth century; and it was about that time that label-names made their latest appearances in works of any artistic pretension--witness the Lady Gay Spanker of **London Assurance**, and the Captain Dudley (or "Deadly") Smooth of **Money**. Faint traces of the practice survive in T.W. Robertson, as in his master, Thackeray. But it was in his earliest play of any note that he called a journalist Stylus. In his later comedies the names are admirably chosen: they are characteristic without eccentricity or punning. One feels that Eccles in *Caste* could not possibly have borne any other name. How much less living would he be had he been called Mr. Soaker or Mr. Tosspot!

Characteristic without eccentricity--that is what a name ought to be. As the characteristic quality depends upon a hundred indefinable, subconscious associations, it is clearly impossible to suggest any principle of choice. The only general rule that can be laid down is that the key of the nomenclature, so to speak, may rightly vary with the key of the play--that farcical names are, within limits, admissible in farce, eccentric names in eccentric comedy, while soberly appropriate names are alone in place in serious plays. Some dramatists are habitually happy in their nomenclature, others much less so. Ibsen would often change a name three or four times in the course of writing a play, until at last he arrived at one which seemed absolutely to fit the character; but the appropriateness of his names is naturally lost upon foreign audiences.

One word may perhaps be said on the recent fashion--not to say fad--of suppressing in the printed play the traditional list of "Dramatis Personae." Bjoernson, in some of his later plays, was, so far as I am aware, the first of the moderns to adopt this plan. I do not know whether his example has influenced certain English playwrights, or whether they arrived independently at the same austere principle, by sheer force of individual genius. The matter is a trifling one--so trifling that the departure from established practice has something of the air of a pedantry. It is not, on the whole, to be approved. It adds perceptibly to the difficulty which some readers experience in picking up the threads of a play; and it deprives other readers of a real and appreciable pleasure of anticipation. There is a peculiar and not irrational charm in looking down a list of quite unknown names, and thinking: "In the course of three hours, I shall know these people: I shall have read their hearts: I shall have lived with them through a great crisis in their lives: some of them may be my friends for ever." It is one of the glories and privileges of the dramatist's calling that he can arouse in us this eager and poignant expectation; and I cannot commend his wisdom in deliberately taking the edge off it, and making us feel as though we were not sitting down to a play, but to a sort of conversational novel. A list of characters, it is true, may also affect one with acute anticipations of boredom;

but I have never yet found a play less tedious by reason of the suppression of the "Dramatis Personae."

* * * * *

Note:

[1: Partially, too, they were under the influence of antiquity; but the ancients were very discreet in their use of significant names. Only in satyr-plays, in the comic epics, and for a few extravagant characters in comedy (such as the boastful soldier) were grotesque appellations employed. For the rest, the Greek habit of nomenclature made it possible to use significant names which were at the same time probable enough in daily life. For example, a slave might be called Onesimus, "useful," or a soldier Polemon, to imply his warlike function; but both names would be familiar to the audience in actual use.]

BOOK II THE BEGINNING

CHAPTER VI
THE POINT OF ATTACK: SHAKESPEARE AND IBSEN

Though, as we have already noted, the writing of plays does not always follow the chronological sequence of events, in discussing the process of their evolution we are bound to assume that the playwright begins at the beginning, and proceeds in orderly fashion, by way of the middle, to the end. It was one of Aristotle's requirements that a play should have a beginning, middle and end; and though it may seem that it scarcely needed an Aristotle to lay down so self-evident a proposition, the fact is that playwrights are more than sufficiently apt to ignore or despise the rule.[1] Especially is there a tendency to rebel against the requirement that a play should have an end. We have seen a good many plays of late which do not end, but simply leave off: at their head we might perhaps place Ibsen's **Ghosts**. But let us not anticipate. For the moment, what we have to inquire is where, and how, a play ought to begin.

In life there are no such things as beginnings. Even a man's birth is a quite arbitrary point at which to launch his biography; for the determining factors in his career are to be found in persons, events, and conditions that existed before he was ever thought of. For the biographer, however, and for the novelist as a writer of fictitious biography, birth forms a good conventional starting-point. He can give a chapter or so to "Ancestry," and then relate the adventures of his hero from the cradle onwards. But the dramatist, as we have seen, deals, not with protracted sequences of events, but with short, sharp crises. The question for him, therefore, is: at what moment of the crisis, or of its antecedents, he had better ring up his curtain? At this point he is like the photographer studying his "finder" in order to determine how much of a given prospect he can "get in."

The answer to the question depends on many things, but chiefly on the nature of the crisis and the nature of the impression which the playwright desires to make upon his audience. If his play be a comedy, and if his object be gently and quietly to interest and entertain, the chances are that he begins by showing us his personages in their normal state, concisely indicates their characters, circumstances and relations, and then lets the crisis develop from the outset before our eyes. If, on the other hand, his play be of a more stirring description, and he wants to seize the spectator's attention firmly from the start, he will probably go straight at his crisis, plunging, perhaps, into the very middle of it, even at the cost of having afterwards to go back in order to put the audience in possession of the antecedent circumstances. In a third type of play, common of late years, and especially affected by Ibsen, the curtain rises on a surface aspect of profound peace, which is presently found to be but a thin crust over an absolutely volcanic condition of affairs, the origin of which has to be traced backwards, it may be for many years.

Let us glance at a few of Shakespeare's openings, and consider at what points he attacks his various themes. Of his comedies, all except one begin with a simple conversation, showing a state of affairs from which the crisis develops with more or less rapidity, but in which it is as yet imperceptibly latent. In no case does he plunge into the middle of his subject, leaving its antecedents to be stated in what is technically called an "exposition." Neither in tragedy nor in comedy, indeed, was this Shakespeare's method. In his historical plays he relied to some extent on his hearers' knowledge of history, whether gathered from books or from previous plays of the historical series; and where such knowledge was not to be looked for, he would expound the situation in good set terms, like those of a Euripidean Prologue. But the chronicle-play is a species apart, and practically an extinct species: we need not pause to study its methods. In his fictitious plays, with two notable exceptions, it was Shakespeare's constant practice to bring the whole action within the frame of the picture, opening at such a point that no retrospect should be necessary, beyond what could be conveyed in a few casual words. The exceptions are ***The Tempest*** and *Hamlet*, to which we shall return in due course.

How does *The Merchant of Venice* open? With a long conversation exhibiting the character of Antonio, the friendship between him and Bassanio, the latter's financial straits, and his purpose of wooing Portia. The second scene displays the character of Portia, and informs us of her father's device with regard to her marriage; but this information is conveyed in three or four lines. Not till the third scene do we see or hear of Shylock, and not until very near the end of the act is there any foreshadowing of what is to be the main crisis of the play. Not a single antecedent event has to be narrated to us; for the mere fact that Antonio has been uncivil to Shylock, and shown disapproval of his business methods, can scarcely be regarded as a preliminary outside the frame of the picture.

In *As You Like It* there are no preliminaries to be stated beyond the facts that Orlando is at enmity with his elder brother, and that Duke Frederick has usurped the coronet and dukedom of Rosalind's father. These facts being made apparent without any sort of formal exposition, the crisis of the play rapidly announces itself in the wrestling-match and its sequels. In *Much Ado About Nothing* there is even less of antecedent circumstance to be imparted. We learn in the first scene, indeed, that Beatrice and Benedick have already met and crossed swords; but this is not in the least essential to the action; the play might have been to all intents and purposes the same had they never heard of each other until after the rise of the curtain. In *Twelfth Night* there is a semblance of a retrospective exposition in the scene between Viola and the Captain; but it is of the simplest nature, and conveys no information beyond what, at a later period, would have been imparted on the playbill, thus--

"Orsino, Duke of Illyria, in love with Olivia. Olivia, an heiress, in mourning for her brother,"

and so forth. In *The Taming of the Shrew* there are no antecedents whatever to be stated. It is true that Lucentio, in the opening speech, is good enough to inform Tranio who he is and what he is doing there--facts with which Tranio is already perfectly acquainted. But this was merely a conventional opening, excused by the fashion of the time; it was in no sense a necessary exposition. For the rest, the crisis of the play--the battle between Katherine and Petruchio--begins, develops, and ends before our very eyes. In *The Winter's Tale*, a brief conversation between

Play-Making 61

Camillo and Archidamus informs us that the King of Bohemia is paying a visit to the King of Sicilia; and that is absolutely all we need to know. It was not even necessary that it should be conveyed to us in this way. The situation would be entirely comprehensible if the scene between Camillo and Archidamus were omitted.

It is needless to go through the whole list of comedies. The broad fact is that in all the plays commonly so described, excepting only *The Tempest*, the whole action comes within the frame of the picture. In *The Tempest* the poet employs a form of opening which otherwise he reserves for tragedies. The first scene is simply an animated tableau, calculated to arrest the spectator's attention, without conveying to him any knowledge either of situation or character. Such gleams of character as do, in fact, appear in the dialogue, are scarcely perceived in the hurly-burly of the storm. Then, in the calm which ensues, Prospero expounds to Miranda in great detail the antecedents of the crisis now developing. It might almost seem, indeed, that the poet, in this, his poetic last-will-and-testament, intended to warn his successors against the dangers of a long narrative exposition; for Prospero's story sends Miranda to sleep. Be this as it may, we have here a case in which Shakespeare deliberately adopted the plan of placing on the stage, not the whole crisis, but only its culmination, leaving its earlier stages to be conveyed in narrative.[2] It would have been very easy for him to have begun at the beginning and shown us in action the events narrated by Prospero. This course would have involved no greater leap, either in time or space, than he had perpetrated in the almost contemporary *Winter's Tale*; and it cannot be said that there would have been any difficulty in compressing into three acts, or even two, the essentials of the action of the play as we know it. His reasons for departing from his usual practice were probably connected with the particular occasion for which the play was written. He wanted to produce a masque rather than a drama. We must not, therefore, attach too much significance to the fact that in almost the only play in which Shakespeare seems to have built entirely out of his own head, with no previous play or novel to influence him, he adopted the plan of going straight to the catastrophe, in which he had been anticipated by Sophocles (Oedipus Rex), and was to be followed by Ibsen (Ghosts, *Rosmersholm*, etc.).

Coming now to the five great tragedies, we find that in four of them Shakespeare began, as in *The Tempest*, with a picturesque and stirring episode calculated to arrest the spectator's attention and awaken his interest, while conveying to him little or no information. The opening scene of **Romeo and Juliet** is simply a brawl, bringing home to us vividly the family feud which is the root of the tragedy, but informing us of nothing beyond the fact that such a feud exists. This is, indeed, absolutely all that we require to know. There is not a single preliminary circumstance, outside the limits of the play, that has to be explained to us. The whole tragedy germinates and culminates within what the prologue calls "the two hours' traffick of the stage." The opening colloquy of the Witches in **Macbeth**, strikes the eerie keynote, but does nothing more. Then, in the second scene, we learn that there has been a great battle and that a nobleman named Macbeth has won a victory which covers him with laurels. This can in no sense be called an exposition. It is the account of a single event, not of a sequence; and that event is contemporary, not antecedent. In the third scene, the meeting of Macbeth and Banquo with the Witches, we have what may be called an exposition reversed; not a narrative of the past, but a foreshadowing of the future. Here we touch on one of the subtlest of the playwright's problems--the art of arousing anticipation in just the right measure. But that is not the matter at present in hand.[3]

In the opening scene of **Othello** it is true that some talk passes between Iago and Roderigo before they raise the alarm and awaken Brabantio; but it is carefully non-expository talk; it expounds nothing but Iago's character. Far from being a real exception to the rule that Shakespeare liked to open his tragedies with a very crisply dramatic episode, **Othello** may rather be called its most conspicuous example. The rousing of Brabantio is immediately followed by the encounter between his men and Othello's, which so finely brings out the lofty character of the Moor; and only in the third scene, that of the Doge's Council, do we pass from shouts and swords to quiet discussion and, in a sense, exposition. Othello's great speech, while a vital portion of the drama, is in so far an exposition that it refers to events which do not come absolutely within the frame of the picture. But they are very recent, very simple, events. If Othello's speech were omitted, or cut down to half a dozen lines, we should know much less of his character and Desdemona's, but the mere action of the play would remain perfectly comprehensible.

King Lear necessarily opens with a great act of state, the partition of the kingdom. A few words between Kent and Gloucester show us what is afoot, and then, at one plunge, we are in the thick of the drama. There was no opportunity here for one of those picturesque tableaux, exciting rather than informative, which initiate the other tragedies. It would have had to be artificially dragged in; and it was the less necessary, as the partition scene took on, in a very few lines, just that arresting, stimulating quality which the poet seems to have desired in the opening of a play of this class.

Finally, when we turn to *Hamlet*, we find a consummate example of the crisply-touched opening tableau, making a nervous rather than an intellectual appeal, informing us of nothing, but exciting a vivid, though quite vague, anticipation. The silent transit of the Ghost, desiring to speak, yet tongue-tied, is certainly one of Shakespeare's unrivalled masterpieces of dramatic craftsmanship. One could pretty safely wager that if the *Ur-Hamlet*, on which Shakespeare worked, were to come to light to-morrow, this particular trait would not be found in it. But, oddly enough, into the middle of this admirable opening tableau, Shakespeare inserts a formal exposition, introduced in the most conventional way. Marcellus, for some unexplained reason, is ignorant of what is evidently common knowledge as to the affairs of the realm, and asks to be informed; whereupon Horatio, in a speech of some twenty-five lines, sets forth the past relations between Norway and Denmark, and prepares us for the appearance of Fortinbras in the fourth act. In modern stage versions all this falls away, and nobody who has not studied the printed text is conscious of its absence. The commentators, indeed, have proved that Fortinbras is an immensely valuable element in the moral scheme of the play; but from the point of view of pure drama, there is not the slightest necessity for this Norwegian-Danish embroilment or its consequences.[4] The real exposition--for *Hamlet* differs from the other tragedies in requiring an exposition--comes in the great speech of the Ghost in Scene V. The contrast between this speech and Horatio's lecture in the first scene, exemplifies the difference between a dramatized and an undramatized exposition. The crisis, as we now learn, began months or years before the rise of the curtain. It began when Claudius inveigled the affections of Gertrude; and it would have been possible for the poet to have started from this point, and shown us in action all that he in fact conveys to us by way of narration. His reason for choosing the latter course is abundantly obvious.[5] Hamlet the Younger was to be the protagonist: the interest of the play was to centre in his mental processes. To have awakened our interest in Hamlet the Elder would, therefore, have been a superfluity and an irrelevance. Moreover (to say nothing of the fact that the Ghost was doubtless a popular figure in the old play, and demanded by the public) it was highly desirable that Hamlet's knowledge of the usurper's crime should come to him from a supernatural witness, who could not be cross-questioned or called upon to give material proof. This was the readiest as well as the most picturesque method of begetting in him that condition of doubt, real or affected, which was necessary to account for his behaviour. But to have shown us in action the matter of the Ghost's revelation would have been hopelessly to ruin its effect. A repetition in narrative of matters already seen in action is the grossest of technical blunders.[6] Hamlet senior, in other words, being indispensable in the spirit, was superfluous in the flesh. But there was another and equally cogent reason for beginning the play after the commission of the initial crime or crimes. To have done otherwise would have been to discount, not only the Ghost, but the play-scene. By a piece of consummate ingenuity, which may, of course, have been conceived by the earlier playwright, the initial incidents of the story are in fact presented to us, in the guise of a play within the play, and as a means to the achievement of one of the greatest dramatic effects in all literature. The moment the idea of the play-scene presented itself to the author's mind, it became absolutely unthinkable that he should, to put it vulgarly, "queer the pitch" for the Players by showing us the real facts of which their performance was to be the counterfeit presentment. The dramatic effect of the incidents was incalculably heightened when they were presented, as in a looking-glass, before the guilty pair, with the eye of the avenger boring into their souls. And have we not here, perhaps, a clue to one of the most frequent and essential meanings of the word "dramatic"? May we not say that the dramatic quality of an incident is proportionate to the variety[7] and intensity of the emotions involved in it?

All this may appear too obvious to be worth setting forth at such length. Very likely it never occurred to Shakespeare that it was possible to open the play at an earlier point; so that he can hardly be said to have exercised a deliberate choice in the matter. Nevertheless, the very obviousness of the considerations involved makes this a good example of the importance of discovering just the right point at which to raise the curtain. In the case of *The Tempest*, Shakespeare plunged into the middle of the crisis because his object was to produce a philosophico-dramatic entertainment rather than a play in the strict sense of the word. He wanted room for the enchantments of Ariel, the brutishnesses of Caliban, the humours of Stephano and Trinculo--all elements extrinsic to the actual story. But in **Hamlet** he adopted a similar course for purely dramatic reasons--in order to concentrate his effects and present the dramatic elements of his theme at their highest potency.

In sum, then, it was Shakespeare's usual practice, histories apart, to bring the whole action of his plays within the frame of the picture, leaving little or nothing to narrative exposition. The two notable exceptions to this rule are those we have just examined--Hamlet and **The Tempest**. Furthermore, he usually opened his comedies with quiet conversational passages, presenting the antecedents of the crisis with great deliberation. In his tragedies, on the other hand, he was apt to lead off with a crisp, somewhat startling passage of more or less vehement action, appealing rather to the nerves than to the intelligence--such a passage as Gustav Freytag, in his **Technik des Dramas**, happily entitles an ***einleitende Akkord***, an introductory chord. It may be added that this rule holds good both for **Coriolanus** and for **Julius Caesar**, in which the keynote is briskly struck in highly animated scenes of commotion among the Roman populace.

Let us now look at the practice of Ibsen, which offers a sharp contrast to that of Shakespeare. To put it briefly, the plays in which Ibsen gets his whole action within the frame of the picture are as exceptional as those in which Shakespeare does not do so.

Ibsen's practice in this matter has been compared with that of the Greek dramatists, who also were apt to attack their crisis in the middle, or even towards the end, rather than at the beginning. It must not be forgotten, however, that there is one great difference between his position and theirs. They could almost always rely upon a general knowledge, on the part of the audience, of the theme with which they were dealing. The purpose even of the Euripidean prologue is not so much to state unknown facts, as to recall facts vaguely remembered, to state the particular version of a legend which the poet proposes to adopt, and to define the point in the development of the legend at which he is about to set his figures in motion. Ibsen, on the other hand, drew upon no storehouse of tradition. He had to convey to his audience everything that he wanted them to know; and this was often a long and complex series of facts.

The earliest play in which Ibsen can be said to show maturity of craftsmanship is *The Vikings at Helgeland*. It is curious to note that both in *The Vikings* and in *The Pretenders*, two plays which are in some measure comparable with Shakespearean tragedies, he opens with a firmly-touched *einleitende Akkord*. In *The Vikings*, Ornulf and his sons encounter and fight with Sigurd and his men, very much after the fashion of the Montagues and Capulets in *Romeo and Juliet*. In *The Pretenders* the rival factions of Haakon and Skule stand outside the cathedral of Bergen, intently awaiting the result of the ordeal which is proceeding within; and though they do not there and then come to blows, the air is electrical with their conflicting ambitions and passions. His modern plays, on the other hand, Ibsen opens quietly enough, though usually with some more or less arresting little incident, calculated to arouse immediate curiosity. One may cite as characteristic examples the hurried colloquy between Engstrand and Regina in *Ghosts*; Rebecca and Madam Helseth in *Rosmersholm*, watching to see whether Rosmer will cross the mill-race; and in *The Master Builder*, old Brovik's querulous outburst, immediately followed by the entrance of Solness and his mysterious behaviour towards Kaia. The opening of *Hedda Gabler*, with its long conversation between Miss Tesman and the servant Bertha, comes as near as Ibsen ever did to the conventional exposition of the French stage, conducted by a footman and a parlour-maid engaged in dusting the furniture. On the other hand, there never was a more masterly opening, in its sheer simplicity, than Nora's entrance in *A Doll's House*, and the little silent scene that precedes the appearance of Helmer.

Regarding *The Vikings* as Ibsen's first mature production, and surveying the whole series of his subsequent works in which he had stage presentation directly in view,[8] we find that in only two out of the fifteen plays does the whole action come within the frame of the picture. These two are *The League of Youth* and *An Enemy of the People*. In neither of these have any antecedents to be stated; neither turns upon any disclosure of bygone events or emotions. We are, indeed, afforded brief glimpses into the past both of Stensgaard and of Stockmann; but the glimpses are incidental and inessential. It is certainly no mere coincidence that if one were asked to pick out the pieces of thinnest texture in all Ibsen's mature work, one would certainly select these two plays. Far be it from me to disparage *An Enemy of the People*; as a work of art it is incomparably greater than such a piece as ***Pillars of Society***; but it is not so richly woven, not, as it were, so deep in pile. Written in half the time Ibsen usually devoted to a play, it is an outburst of humorous indignation, a *jeu d'esprit*, one might almost say, though the *jeu* of a giant *esprit*.

Observing the effect of comparative tenuity in these two plays, we cannot but surmise that the secret of the depth and richness of texture so characteristic of Ibsen's work, lay in his art of closely interweaving a drama of the present with a drama of the past. ***An Enemy of the People*** is a straightforward, spirited melody; ***The Wild Duck*** and ***Rosmersholm*** are subtly and intricately harmonized.

Going a little more into detail, we find in Ibsen's work an extraordinary progress in the art of so unfolding the drama of the past as to make the gradual revelation no mere preface or prologue to the drama of the present, but an integral part of its action. It is true that in ***The Vikings*** he already showed himself a master in this art. The great revelation--the disclosure of the fact that Sigurd, not Gunnar, did the deed of prowess which Hioerdis demanded of the man who should be her mate--this crucial revelation is brought about in a scene of the utmost dramatic intensity. The whole drama of the past, indeed--both its facts and its emotions--may be said to be dragged to light in the very stress and pressure of the drama of the present. Not a single detail of it is narrated in cold blood, as, for example, Prospero relates to Miranda the story of their marooning, or Horatio expounds the Norwegian-Danish political situation. I am not holding up ***The Vikings*** as a great masterpiece; it has many weaknesses both of substance and of method; but in this particular art of indistinguishably blending the drama of the present with the drama of the past, it is already consummate. ***The Pretenders*** scarcely comes into the comparison. It is Ibsen's one chronicle-play; and, like Shakespeare, he did not shrink from employing a good deal of narrative, though his narratives, it must be said, are always introduced under such circumstances as to make them a vital part of the drama. It is when we come to the modern plays that we find the poet falling back upon conventional and somewhat clumsy methods of exposition, which he only by degrees, though by rapid degrees, unlearns.

The League of Youth, as we have seen, requires no exposition. All we have to learn is the existing relations of the characters, which appear quite naturally as the action proceeds. But let us look at ***Pillars of Society***. Here we have to be placed in possession of a whole antecedent drama: the intrigue of Karsten Bernick with Dina Dorf's mother, the threatened scandal, Johan Toennesen's vicarious acceptance of Bernick's responsibility, the subsidiary scandal of Lona Hessel's outburst on learning of Bernick's engagement to her half-sister, the report of an embezzlement committed by Johan before his departure for America. All this has to be conveyed to us in retrospect; or, rather, in the first place, we have to be informed of the false version of these incidents which is current in the little town, and on which Bernick's moral and commercial prestige is built up. What device, then, does Ibsen adopt to this end? He introduces a "sewing-bee" of tattling women, one of whom happens to be a stranger to the town, and unfamiliar with its gossip. Into her willing ear the others pour the popular version of the Bernick story; and, this impartment effected, the group of gossips disappears, to be heard of no more. These ladies perform the function, in fact, of the First, Second, and Third Gentlemen, so common in Elizabethan and pseudo-Elizabethan plays.[9] They are not quite so artless in their conventionality, for they bring with them the social atmosphere of the tattling little town, which is an essential factor in the drama. Moreover, their exposition is not a simple narrative of facts. It is to some extent subtilized by the circumstance that the facts are not facts, and that the gist of the drama is to lie in the gradual triumph of the truth over this tissue of falsehoods. Still, explain it as we may, the fact remains that in no later play does Ibsen initiate us into the preliminaries of his action by so hackneyed and unwieldy a device. It is no conventional canon, but a maxim of mere common sense, that the dramatist should be chary of introducing characters who have no personal share in the drama, and are mere mouthpieces for the conveyance of information. Nowhere else does Ibsen so flagrantly disregard so obvious a principle of dramatic economy.[10]

When we turn to his next play, ***A Doll's House***, we find that he has already made a great step in advance. He has progressed from the First, Second, and Third Gentlemen of the Elizabethans to the confidant[11] of the French classic drama. He even attempts, not very successfully, to disguise the confidant by giving her a personal interest, an effective share, in the drama. Nothing can really dissemble the fact that the long scene between Nora and Mrs. Linden, which occupies almost one-third of the first act, is simply a formal exposition, outside the action of the play. Just as it was providential that one of the house-wives of the sewing-bee in ***Pillars*** *of Society* should have been a stranger to the town, so it was the luckiest of chances (for the dramatist's convenience) that an old school-friend should have dropped in from the clouds precisely half-an-hour before the entrance of Krogstad brings to a sudden head the great crisis of Nora's life. This happy conjuncture of events is manifestly artificial: a trick of the dramatist's trade: a point at which his art does not conceal his art. Mrs. Linden does not, like the dames of the sewing-bee, fade out of the saga; she even, through her influence on Krogstad, plays a determining part in the development of the action. But to all intents and purposes she remains a mere confidant, a pretext for Nora's review of the history of her married life. There are two other specimens of the genus confidant in Ibsen's later plays. Arnholm, in *The Lady from the Sea*, is little more; Dr. Herdal, in *The Master Builder*, is that and nothing else. It may be alleged in his defence that the family physician is the professional confidant of real life.

In *Ghosts*, Ibsen makes a sudden leap to the extreme of his retrospective method. I am not one of those who consider this play Ibsen's masterpiece: I do not even place it, technically, in the first rank among his works. And why? Because there is here no reasonable equilibrium between the drama of the past and the drama of the present. The drama of the past is almost everything, the drama of the present next to nothing. As soon as we have probed to the depths the Alving marriage and its consequences, the play is over, and there is nothing left but for Regina to set off in pursuit of the joy of life, and for Oswald to collapse into imbecility. It is scarcely an exaggeration to call the play all exposition and no drama. Here for the first time, however, Ibsen perfected his peculiar gift of imparting tense dramatic interest to the unveiling of the past. While in one sense the play is all exposition, in another sense it may quite as truly be said to contain no exposition; for it contains no narrative delivered in cold blood, in mere calm retrospection, as a necessary preliminary to the drama which is in the meantime waiting at the door. In other words, the exposition is all drama, it *is* the drama. The persons who are tearing the veils from the past, and for whom the veils are being torn, are intensely concerned in the process, which actually constitutes the dramatic crisis. The discovery of this method, or its rediscovery in modern drama,[12] was Ibsen's great technical achievement. In his best work, the progress of the unveiling occasions a marked development, or series of changes, in the actual and present relations of the characters. The drama of the past and the drama of the present proceed, so to speak, in interlacing rhythms, or, as I said before, in a rich, complex harmony. In *Ghosts* this harmony is not so rich as in some later plays, because the drama of the present is disproportionately meagre. None the less, or all the more, is it a conspicuous example of Ibsen's method of raising his curtain, not at the beginning of the crisis, but rather at the beginning of the catastrophe.

In *An Enemy of the People*, as already stated, he momentarily deserted that method, and gave us an action which begins, develops, and ends entirely within the frame of the picture. But in the two following plays, *The Wild Duck* and *Rosmersholm*, he touched the highest point of technical mastery in his interweaving of the past with the present. I shall not attempt any analysis of the fabric of these plays. The process would be long, tedious, and unhelpful; for no one could hope to employ a method of such complexity without something of Ibsen's genius; and genius will evolve its methods for itself. Let me only ask the reader to compare the scene between old Werle and Gregers in the first act of *The Wild Duck* with the scene between Nora and Mrs. Linden in the first act of *A Doll's House*, and mark the technical advance. Both scenes are, in a sense, scenes of exposition. Both are mainly designed to place us in possession of a sequence of bygone facts. But while the *Doll's House* scene is a piece of quiet gossip, brought about (as we have noted) by rather artificial means, and with no dramatic tension in it, the *Wild Duck* scene is a piece of tense, one might almost say fierce, drama, fulfilling the Brunetiere definition in that it shows us two characters, a father and son, at open war with each other. The one scene is outside the real action, the other is an integral part of it. The one belongs to Ibsen's tentative period, the other ushers in, one might almost say, his period of consummate mastery.[13]

Rosmersholm is so obviously nothing but the catastrophe of an antecedent drama that an attempt has actually been made to rectify Ibsen's supposed mistake, and to write the tragedy of the deceased Beata. It was made by an unskilful hand; but even a skilful hand would scarcely have done more than prove how rightly Ibsen judged that the recoil of Rebecca's crime upon herself and Rosmer would prove more interesting, and in a very real sense more dramatic, than the somewhat vulgar process of the crime itself. The play is not so profound in its humanity as *The Wild*

Duck, but it is Ibsen's masterpiece in the art of withdrawing veil after veil. From the technical point of view, it will repay the closest study.

We need not look closely at the remaining plays. ***Hedda Gabler*** is perhaps that in which a sound proportion between the past and the present is most successfully preserved. The interest of the present action is throughout very vivid; but it is all rooted in facts and relations of the past, which are elicited under circumstances of high dramatic tension. Here again it is instructive to compare the scene between Hedda and Thea, in the first act, with the scene between Nora and Mrs. Linden. Both are scenes of exposition: and each is, in its way, character-revealing; but the earlier scene is a passage of quite unemotional narrative; the later is a passage of palpitating drama. In the plays subsequent to ***Hedda Gabler***, it cannot be denied that the past took the upper hand of the present to a degree which could only be justified by the genius of an Ibsen. Three-fourths of the action of ***The Master Builder***, ***Little Eyolf***, ***John Gabriel Borkman***, and ***When We Dead Awaken***, consists of what may be called a passionate analysis of the past. Ibsen had the art of making such an analysis absorbingly interesting; but it is not a formula to be commended for the practical purposes of the everyday stage.

*   *   *   *   *

Notes:

[1: Writing of ***Le Supplice d'une Femme***, Alexandre Dumas *fils* said: "This situation I declare to be one of the most dramatic and interesting in all drama. But a situation is not an idea. An idea, has a beginning, a middle and an end: an exposition, a development, a conclusion. Any one can relate a dramatic situation: the art lies in preparing it, getting it accepted, rendering it possible, especially in untying the knot."]

[2: This is what we regard as peculiarly the method of Ibsen. There is, however, this essential difference, that, instead of narrating his preliminaries in cold blood, Ibsen, in his best work, ***dramatizes*** the narration.]

[3: See Chapter XII.]

[4: This must not be taken to imply that, in a good stage-version of the play,

Fortinbras should be altogether omitted. Mr. Forbes Robertson, in his Lyceum revival of 1897, found several advantages in his retention. Among the rest, it permitted the retention of one of Hamlet's most characteristic soliloquies.]

[5: I omit all speculation as to the form which the story assumed in the *Ur-Hamlet*. We have no evidence on the point; and, as the poet was no doubt free to remodel the material as he thought fit, even in following his original he was making a deliberate artistic choice.]

[6: Shakespeare committed it in **Romeo and Juliet**, where he made Friar Laurence, in the concluding scene, retell the whole story of the tragedy. Even in so early a play, such a manifest redundancy seems unaccountable. A narrative of things already seen may, of course, be a trait of character in the person delivering it; but, in that case, it will generally be mendacious (for instance, Falstaff and the men in buckram). Or it may be introduced for the sake of its effect upon the characters to whom the narration is addressed. But in these cases its purpose is no longer to convey information to the audience--it belongs, not to the "intelligence department," but to the department of analysis.]

[7: I say "variety" rather than complexity because I take it that the emotions of all concerned are here too intense to be very complex. The effect of the scene would appear to lie in the rapidly increasing intensity of comparatively simple emotions in Hamlet, in the King, in the Queen, and in the amazed and bewildered courtiers.]

[8: This excludes **Love's Comedy, Brand, Peer Gynt**, and **Emperor and Galilean**.]

[9: See, for example, **King Henry VIII**, Act IV, and the opening scene of Tennyson's **Queen Mary**.]

[10: This rule of economy does not necessarily exclude a group of characters performing something like the function of the antique Chorus; that is to say, commenting upon the action from a more or less disinterested point of view. The function of **Kaffee-Klatsch** in **Pillars of Society** is not at all that of the Chorus, but rather that of the Euripidean Prologue, somewhat thinly disguised.]

[11: It is perhaps worth nothing that Gabriele d'Annunzio in **La Gioconda**, reverts to, and outdoes, the French classic convention, by giving us three actors and four confidants. The play consists of a crisis in three lives, passively, though sympathetically, contemplated by what is in effect a Chorus of two men and two women.

It would be interesting to inquire why, in this particular play, such an abuse of the confidant seems quite admissible, if not conspicuously right.]

[12: Dryden, in his *Essay of Dramatic Poesy*, represents this method as being characteristic of Greek tragedy as a whole. The tragic poet, he says, "set the audience, as it were, at the post where the race is to be concluded; and, saving them the tedious expectation of seeing the poet set out and ride the beginning of the course, they suffer you not to behold him, till he is in sight of the goal and just upon you." Dryden seems to think that the method was forced upon them by "the rule of time."]

[13: It is a rash enterprise to reconstruct Ibsen, but one cannot help wondering how he would have planned *A Doll's House* had he written it in the 'eighties instead of the 'seventies. One can imagine a long opening scene between Helmer and Nora in which a great deal of the necessary information might have been conveyed; while it would have heightened by contrast the effect of the great final duologue as we now possess it. Such information as could not possibly have been conveyed in dialogue with Helmer might, one would think, have been left for Nora's first scene with Krogstad, the effect of which it would have enhanced. Perhaps Mrs. Linden might with advantage have been retained, though not in her present character of confidant, in order to show Nora in relation to another woman.]

CHAPTER VII
EXPOSITION: ITS END AND ITS MEANS

We have passed in rapid survey the practices of Shakespeare and Ibsen in respect of their point and method of attack upon their themes. What practical lessons can we now deduce from this examination? One thing is clear: namely, that there is no inherent superiority in one method over another. There are masterpieces in which the whole crisis falls within the frame of the picture, and masterpieces in which the greater part of the crisis has to be conveyed to us in retrospect, only the catastrophe being transacted before our eyes. Genius can manifest itself equally in either form.

But each form has its peculiar advantages. You cannot, in a retrospective play like ***Rosmersholm***, attain anything like the magnificent onward rush of Othello, which moves--

"Like to the Pontick sea   Whose icy current and compulsive course Ne'er feels retiring ebb, but keeps due on   To the Propontick and the Hellespont."

The movement of ***Rosmersholm*** is rather like that of a winding river, which flows with a full and steady current, but seems sometimes to be almost retracing its course. If, then, you aim at rapidity of movement, you will choose a theme which leaves little or nothing to retrospect; and conversely, if you have a theme the whole of which falls easily and conveniently within the frame of the picture, you will probably take advantage of the fact to give your play animated and rapid movement.

There is an undeniable attraction in a play which constitutes, so to speak, one brisk and continuous adventure, begun, developed, and ended before our eyes. For light comedy in particular is this a desirable form, and for romantic plays in which no very searching character-study is attempted. ***The Taming of the Shrew*** no doubt passed for a light comedy in Shakespeare's day, though we describe it by a briefer name. Its rapid, bustling action is possible because we are always ready to take the character of a shrew for granted. It would have been a very different play had the poet required to account for Katharine's peculiarities of temper by a retrospective study of her heredity and upbringing. Many eighteenth-century comedies are single-adventure plays, or dual-adventure plays, in the sense that the main action sometimes stands aside to let an underplot take the stage. Both ***She Stoops to Conquer*** and ***The Rivals*** are good examples of the rapid working-out of an intrigue, engendered, developed, and resolved all within the frame of the picture. Single-adventure plays of a more modern type are the elder Dumas's ***Mademoiselle de Belle-Isle***, the younger Dumas's ***Francillon***, Sardou's ***Divorcons***, Sir Arthur Pinero's ***Gay Lord Quex***, Mr. Shaw's ***Devil's Disciple***, Oscar Wilde's ***Importance of Being Earnest***, Mr. Galsworthy's ***Silver Box***. Widely as these plays differ in type and tone, they are alike in this, that they do not attempt to present very complex character-studies, or to probe the deeps of human experience. The last play cited, ***The Silver Box***, may perhaps be thought an exception to this rule; but, though the experience of the hapless charwoman is pitiful enough, hers is a simple soul, so inured to suffering that a little more or less is no such great matter. The play is an admirable genre-picture rather than a searching tragedy.

  The point to be observed is that, under modern conditions, it is difficult to produce a play of very complex psychological, moral, or emotional substance, in which the whole crisis comes within the frame of the picture. The method of attacking the crisis in the middle or towards the end is really a device for relaxing, in some measure, the narrow bounds of theatrical representation, and enabling the playwright to deal with a larger segment of human experience. It may be asked why modern conditions should in this respect differ from Elizabethan conditions, and why, if Shakespeare could produce such profound and complex tragedies as ***Othello*** and ***King Lear*** without a word of exposition or retrospect, the modern dramatist should not go and do likewise? The answer to this question is not simply that the modern dramatist is seldom a Shakespeare. That is true, but we must look deeper than that. There are, in fact, several points to be taken into consideration. For one thing--this is a minor point--Shakespeare had really far more elbow-room than the playwright of to-day. **Othello** and **King Lear**, to say nothing of **Hamlet**, are exceedingly long plays. Something like a third of them is omitted in modern representation; and when we speak of their richness and complexity of characterization, we do not think simply of the plays as we see them compressed into acting limits, but of the plays as we know them in the study. It is possible, no doubt, for modern playwrights to let themselves go in the matter of length, and then print their plays with brackets or other marks to show the "passages omitted in representation." This is, however, essentially an inartistic practice, and one cannot regret that it has gone out of fashion. Another point to be considered is this: are Othello and Lear really very complex character-studies? They are extremely vivid: they are projected with enormous energy, in actions whose violence affords scope for the most vehement self-expression; but are they not, in reality, colossally simple rather than complex? It is true that in Lear the phenomena of insanity are reproduced with astonishing minuteness and truth; but this does not imply any elaborate analysis or demand any great space. Hamlet is complex; and were I "talking for victory," I should point out that **Hamlet** is, of all the tragedies, precisely the one which does not come within the frame of the picture. But the true secret of the matter does not lie here: it lies in the fact that Hamlet unpacks his heart to us in a series of soliloquies--a device employed scarcely at all in the portrayal of Othello and Lear, and denied to the modern dramatist.[1] Yet again, the social position and environment of the great Shakespearean characters is taken for granted. No time is spent in "placing" them in a given stratum of society, or in establishing their heredity, traditions, education, and so forth. And, finally, the very copiousness of expression permitted by the rhetorical Elizabethan form came to Shakespeare's aid. The modern dramatist is hampered by all sorts of reticences. He has often to work rather in indirect suggestion than in direct expression. He has, in short, to submit to a hundred hampering conditions from which Shakespeare was exempt; wherefore, even if he had Shakespeare's genius, he would find it difficult to produce a very profound effect in a crisis worked out from first to last before the eyes of the audience.

Nevertheless, as before stated, such a crisis has a charm of its own. There is a peculiar interest in watching the rise and development out of nothing, as it were, of a dramatic complication. For this class of play (despite the Shakespearean precedents) a quiet opening is often advisable, rather than a strong *einleitende Akkord*.

"From calm, through storm, to calm," is its characteristic formula; whether the concluding calm be one of life and serenity or of despair and death. To my personal taste, one of the keenest forms of theatrical enjoyment is that of seeing the curtain go up on a picture of perfect tranquillity, wondering from what quarter the drama is going to arise, and then watching it gather on the horizon like a cloud no bigger than a man's hand. Of this type of opening, **An Enemy of the People** provides us with a classic example; and among English plays we may cite Mr. Shaw's **Candida**, Mr. Barker's **Waste**, and Mr. Besier's **Don**, in which so sudden and unlooked-for a cyclone swoops down upon the calm of an English vicarage. An admirable instance of a fantastic type may be found in **Prunella**, by Messrs. Barker and Housman.[2]

There is much to be said, however, in favour of the opening which does not present an aspect of delusive calm, but shows the atmosphere already charged with electricity. Compare, for instance, the opening of *The Case of Rebellious Susan*, by Mr. Henry Arthur Jones, with that of a French play of very similar theme-- Dumas's **Francillon**. In the latter, we see the storm-cloud slowly gathering up on the horizon; in the former, it is already on the point of breaking, right overhead. Mr. Jones places us at the beginning, where Dumas leaves us at the end, of his first act. It is true that at the end of Mr. Jones's act he has not advanced any further than Dumas. The French author shows his heroine gradually working up to a nervous crisis, the English author introduces his heroine already at the height of her paroxysm, and the act consists of the unavailing efforts of her friends to smooth her down. The upshot is the same; but in Mr. Jones's act we are, as the French say, "in full drama" all the time, while in Dumas's we await the coming of the drama, and only by exerting all his wit, not to say over-exerting it, does he prevent our feeling impatient. I am not claiming superiority for either method; I merely point to a good example of two different ways of attacking the same problem.

In *The Benefit of the Doubt*, by Sir Arthur Pinero, we have a crisply dramatic opening of the very best type. A few words from a contemporary criticism may serve to indicate the effect it produced on a first-night audience--

> We are in the thick of the action at once, or at least in the thick of the interest, so that the exposition, instead of being, so to speak, a mere platform from which the train is presently to start, becomes an inseparable part of the movement. The sense of dramatic irony is strongly and yet delicately suggested. We foresee a

"peripety," apparent prosperity suddenly crumbling into disaster, within the act itself; and, when it comes, it awakens our sympathy and redoubles our interest.

Almost the same words might be applied to the opening of **The Climbers**, by the late Clyde Fitch, one of the many individual scenes which make one deeply regret that Mr. Fitch did not live to do full justice to his remarkable talent.

One of the ablest of recent openings is that of Mr. Galsworthy's **Silver Box**. The curtain rises upon a solid, dull, upper-middle-class dining-room, empty and silent, the electric lights burning, the tray with whiskey, siphon and cigarette-box marking the midnight hour. Then we have the stumbling, fumbling entrance of Jack Barthwick, beatifically drunk, his maudlin babble, and his ill-omened hospitality to the haggard loafer who follows at his heels. Another example of a high-pitched opening scene may be found in Mr. Perceval Landon's **The House Opposite**. Here we have a midnight parting between a married woman and her lover, in the middle of which the man, glancing at the lighted window of the house opposite, sees a figure moving in such a way as to suggest that a crime is being perpetrated. As a matter of fact, an old man is murdered, and his housekeeper is accused of the crime. The hero, if so he can be called, knows that it was a man, not a woman, who was in the victim's room that night; and the problem is: how can he give his evidence without betraying a woman's secret by admitting his presence in her house at midnight? I neither praise nor blame this class of story; I merely cite the play as one in which we plunge straight into the crisis, without any introductory period of tranquillity.

The interest of Mr. Landon's play lay almost wholly in the story. There was just enough character in it to keep the story going, so to speak. The author might, on the other hand, have concentrated our attention on character, and made his play a soul-tragedy; but in that case it would doubtless have been necessary to take us some way backward in the heroine's antecedents and the history of her marriage. In other words, if the play had gone deeper into human nature, the preliminaries of the crisis would have had to be traced in some detail, possibly in a first act, introductory to the actual opening, but more probably, and better, in an exposition following the crisply touched *einleitende Akkord*. This brings us to the question how an exposition may best be managed.

It may not unreasonably be contended, I think, that, when an exposition cannot be thoroughly dramatized--that is, wrung out, in the stress of the action, from the characters primarily concerned--it may best be dismissed, rapidly and even conventionally, by any not too improbable device. That is the principle on which Sir Arthur Pinero has always proceeded, and for which he has been unduly censured, by critics who make no allowances for the narrow limits imposed by custom and the constitution of the modern audience upon the playwrights of to-day. In ***His House in Order*** (one of his greatest plays) Sir Arthur effects part of his exposition by the simple device of making Hilary Jesson a candidate for Parliament, and bringing on a reporter to interview his private secretary. The incident is perfectly natural and probable; all one can say of it is that it is perhaps an over-simplification of the dramatist's task.[3] ***The Second Mrs. Tanqueray*** requires an unusual amount of preliminary retrospect. We have to learn the history of Aubrey Tanqueray's first marriage, with the mother of Ellean, as well as the history of Paula Ray's past life. The mechanism employed to this end has been much criticized, but seems to me admirable. Aubrey gives a farewell dinner-party to his intimate friends, Misquith and Jayne. Cayley Drummle, too, is expected, but has not arrived when the play opens. Without naming the lady, Aubrey announces to his guests his approaching marriage. He proposes to go out with them, and has one or two notes to write before doing so. Moreover, he is not sorry to give them an opportunity to talk over the announcement he has made; so he retires to a side-table in the same room, to do his writing. Misquith and Jayne exchange a few speeches in an undertone, and then Cayley Drummle comes in, bringing the story of George Orreyd's marriage to the unmentionable Miss Hervey. This story is so unpleasant to Tanqueray that, to get out of the conversation, he returns to his writing; but still he cannot help listening to Cayley's comments on George Orreyd's "disappearance"; and at last the situation becomes so intolerable to him that he purposely leaves the room, bidding the other two "Tell Cayley the news." The technical manipulation of all this seems to me above reproach --dramatically effective and yet life-like in every detail. If one were bound to raise an objection, it would be to the coincidence which brings to Cayley's knowledge, on one and the same evening, two such exactly similar misalliances in his own circle of acquaintance. But these are just the coincidences that do constantly happen. Every one knows that life is full of them.

The exposition might, no doubt, have been more economically effected. Cayley Drummle might have figured as sole confidant and chorus; or even he might have been dispensed with, and all that was necessary might have appeared in colloquies between Aubrey and Paula on the one hand, Aubrey and Ellean on the other. But Cayley as sole confidant--the "Charles, his friend," of eighteenth-century comedy--would have been more plainly conventional than Cayley as one of a trio of Aubrey's old cronies, representing the society he is sacrificing in entering upon this experimental marriage; and to have conveyed the necessary information without any confidant or chorus at all would (one fancies) have strained probability, or, still worse, impaired consistency of character. Aubrey could not naturally discuss his late wife either with her successor or with her daughter; while, as for Paula's past, all he wanted was to avert his eyes from it. I do not say that these difficulties might not have been overcome; for, in the vocabulary of the truly ingenious dramatist there is no such word as impossible. But I do suggest that the result would scarcely have been worth the trouble, and that it is hyper-criticism which objects to an exposition so natural and probable as that of *The Second Mrs. Tanqueray*, simply on the ground that certain characters are introduced for the purpose of conveying certain information. It would be foolish to expect of every work of art an absolutely austere economy of means.

Sometimes, however, Sir Arthur Pinero injudiciously emphasizes the artifices employed to bring about an exposition. In *The Thunderbolt*, for instance, in order that the Mortimores' family solicitor may without reproach ask for information on matters with which a family solicitor ought to be fully conversant, it has to be explained that the senior partner of the firm, who had the Mortimore business specially in hand, has been called away to London, and that a junior partner has taken his place. Such a rubbing-in, as it were, of an obvious device ought at all hazards to be avoided. If the information cannot be otherwise imparted (as in this case it surely could), the solicitor had better be allowed to ask one or two improbable questions--it is the lesser evil of the two.

When the whole of a given subject cannot be got within the limits of presentation, is there any means of determining how much should be left for retrospect, and at what point the curtain ought to be raised? The principle would seem to be that slow and gradual processes, and especially separate lines of causation, should be left outside the frame of the picture, and that the curtain should be raised at the point where separate lines have converged, and where the crisis begins to move towards its solution with more or less rapidity and continuity. The ideas of rapidity and continuity may be conveniently summed up in the hackneyed and often misapplied term, unity of action. Though the unities of time and place are long ago exploded as binding principles--indeed, they never had any authority in English drama--yet it is true that a broken-backed action, whether in time or space, ought, so far as possible, to be avoided. An action with a gap of twenty years in it may be all very well in melodrama or romance, but scarcely in higher and more serious types of drama.[4] Especially is it to be desired that interest should be concentrated on one set of characters, and should not be frittered away on subsidiary or preliminary personages. Take, for instance, the case of *The Second Mrs. Tanqueray*. It would have been theoretically possible for Sir Arthur Pinero to have given us either (or both) of two preliminary scenes: he might have shown us the first Mrs. Tanqueray at home, and at the same time have introduced us more at large to the characters of Aubrey and Ellean; or he might have depicted for us one of the previous associations of Paula Ray--might perhaps have let us see her "keeping house" with Hugh Ardale. But either of these openings would have been disproportionate and superfluous. It would have excited, or tried to excite, our interest in something that was not the real theme of the play, and in characters which were to drop out before the real theme--the Aubrey-Paula marriage--was reached. Therefore the author, in all probability, never thought of beginning at either of these points. He passed instinctively to the point at which the two lines of causation converged, and from which the action could be carried continuously forward by one set of characters. He knew that we could learn in retrospect all that it was necessary for us to know of the first Mrs. Tanqueray, and that to introduce her in the flesh would be merely to lead the interest of the audience into a blind alley, and to break the back of his action. Again, in *His House in Order* it may seem that the intrigue between Maurewarde and the immaculate Annabel, with its tragic conclusion, would have made a stirring introductory act. But to have presented such an act would have been to destroy the unity of the play, which centres in the character of Nina. Annabel is "another story"; and to have told, or rather shown us, more of it than was absolutely necessary, would have been to distract our attention from the real theme of the play, while at the same time fatally curtailing the all-too-brief time available for the working-out of that theme. There are cases, no doubt, when verbal exposition may advantageously be avoided by means of a dramatized "Prologue"--a single act, constituting a little drama in itself, and generally separated by a considerable space of time from the action proper. But this method is scarcely to be commended, except, as aforesaid, for purposes of melodrama and romance. A "Prologue" is for such plays as ***The Prisoner of Zenda*** and ***The Only Way***, not for such plays as ***His House in Order***.

The question whether a legato or a staccato opening be the more desirable must be decided in accordance with the nature and opportunities of each theme. The only rule that can be stated is that, when the attention of the audience is required for an exposition of any length, some attempt ought to be made to awaken in advance their general interest in the theme and characters. It is dangerous to plunge straight into narrative, or unemotional discussion, without having first made the audience actively desire the information to be conveyed to them. Especially is it essential that the audience should know clearly who are the subjects of the discussion or narrative--that they should not be mere names to them. It is a grave flaw in the construction of Mr. Granville Barker's otherwise admirable play ***Waste***, that it should open with a long discussion, by people whom we scarcely know, of other people whom we do not know at all, whose names we may or may not have noted on the playbill.

Trebell, Lord Charles Cantelupe, and Blackborough ought certainly to have been presented to us in the flesh, however briefly and summarily, before we were asked to interest ourselves in their characters and the political situation arising from them.

There is, however, one limitation to this principle. A great effect is sometimes attained by retarding the entrance of a single leading figure for a whole act, or even two, while he is so constantly talked about as to beget in the audience a vivid desire to make his personal acquaintance. Thus Moliere's Tartufe does not come on the stage until the third act of the comedy which bears his name. Ibsen's John Gabriel Borkman is unseen until the second act, though (through his wife's ears) we have already heard him pacing up and down his room like a wolf in his cage. Dubedat, in ***The Doctor's Dilemma***, is not revealed to us in the flesh until the second act. But for this device to be successful, it is essential that only one leading character[5] should remain unseen, on whom the attention of the audience may, by that very fact, be riveted. In ***Waste***, for instance, all would have been well had it suited Mr.

Barker's purpose to leave Trebell invisible till the second act, while all the characters in the first act, clearly presented to us, canvassed him from their various points of view. Keen expectancy, in short, is the most desirable frame of mind in which an audience can be placed, so long as the expectancy be not ultimately disappointed. But there is no less desirable mental attitude than that of straining after gleams of guidance in an expository twilight.

The advantage of a staccato opening--or, to vary the metaphor, a brisk, highly aerated introductory passage--is clearly exemplified in ***A Doll's House***. It would have been quite possible for Ibsen to have sent up his curtain upon Nora and Mrs. Linden seated comfortably before the stove, and exchanging confidences as to their respective careers. Nothing indispensable would have been omitted; but how languid would have been the interest of the audience! As it is, a brief, bright scene has already introduced us, not only to Nora, but to Helmer, and aroused an eager desire for further insight into the affairs of this--to all appearance--radiantly happy household. Therefore, we settle down without impatience to listen to the fireside gossip of the two old school-fellows.

The problem of how to open a play is complicated in the English theatre by considerations wholly foreign to art. Until quite recently, it used to be held impossible for a playwright to raise his curtain upon his leading character or characters, because the actor-manager would thus be baulked of his carefully arranged "entrance" and "reception," and, furthermore, because twenty-five per cent of the audience would probably arrive about a quarter of an hour late, and would thus miss the opening scene or scenes. It used at one time to be the fashion to add to the advertisement of a play an entreaty that the audience should be punctually in their seats, "as the interest began with the rise of the curtain." One has seen this assertion made with regard to plays in which, as a matter of fact, the interest had not begun at the fall of the curtain. Nowadays, managers, and even leading ladies, are a good deal less insistent on their "reception" than they used to be. They realize that it may be a distinct advantage to hold the stage from the very outset. There are few more effective openings than that of ***The Second Mrs. Tanqueray***, where we find Aubrey Tanqueray seated squarely at his bachelor dinner-table with Misquith on his right and Jayne on his left. It may even be taken as a principle that, where it is desired to give to one character a special prominence and predominance, it ought, if possible, to be the first figure on which the eye of the audience falls. In a Sherlock Holmes play, for example, the curtain ought assuredly to rise on the great Sherlock enthroned in Baker Street, with Dr. Watson sitting at his feet. The solitary entrance of Richard III throws his figure into a relief which could by no other means have been attained. So, too, it would have been a mistake on Sophocles' part to let any one but the protagonist open the ***Oedipus Rex***.

So long as the fashion of late dinners continues, however, it must remain a measure of prudence to let nothing absolutely essential to the comprehension of a play be said or done during the first ten minutes after the rise of the curtain. Here, again, ***A Doll's House*** may be cited as a model, though Ibsen, certainly, had no thought of the British dinner-hour in planning the play. The opening scene is just what the ideal opening scene ought to be--invaluable, yet not indispensable. The late-comer who misses it deprives himself of a preliminary glimpse into the characters of Nora and Helmer and the relation between them; but he misses nothing that is absolutely essential to his comprehension of the play as a whole. This, then, would appear to be a sound maxim both of art and prudence: let your first ten minutes by all means be crisp, arresting, stimulating, but do not let them embody any absolutely vital matter, ignorance of which would leave the spectator in the dark as to the general design and purport of the play.

*   *   *   *   *

Notes:
[1: See Chapter XXIII.]
[2: Henri Becque's two best-known plays aptly exemplify the two types of opening. In ***Les Corbeaux*** we have almost an entire act of calm domesticity in which the only hint of coming trouble is an allusion to Vigneron's attacks of vertigo. In ***La Parisienne*** Clotilde and Lafont are in the thick of a vehement quarrel over a letter. It proceeds for ten minutes or so, at the end of which Clotilde says, "Prenez garde, voila mon mari!"--and we find that the two are not husband and wife, but wife and lover.]
[3: Mrs. Craigie ("John Oliver Hobbes") opened her very successful play, ***The***

Ambassador, with a scene between Juliet Desborough and her sister Alice, a nun, who apparently left her convent specially to hear her sister's confession, and then returned to it for ever. This was certainly not an economical form of exposition, but it was not unsuited to the type of play.]

[4: In that charming comedy, **Rosemary**, by Messrs. Parker and Carson, there is a gap of fifty years between the last act and its predecessor; but the so-called last act is only an "epi-monologue."]

[5: Or at most two closely connected characters: for instance, a husband and wife.]

CHAPTER VIII
THE FIRST ACT

Both in the theory and in practice, of late years, war has been declared in certain quarters against the division of a play into acts. Students of the Elizabethan stage have persuaded themselves, by what I believe to be a complete misreading of the evidence, that Shakespeare did not, as it were, "think in acts," but conceived his plays as continuous series of events, without any pause or intermission in their flow. It can, I think, be proved beyond any shadow of doubt that they are wrong in this; that the act division was perfectly familiar to Shakespeare, and was used by him to give to the action of his plays a rhythm which ought not, in representation, to be obscured or falsified. It is true that in the Elizabethan theatre there was no need of long interacts for the change of scenes, and that such interacts are an abuse that calls for remedy. But we have abundant evidence that the act division was sometimes marked on the Elizabethan stage, and have no reason to doubt that it was always more or less recognized, and was present to Shakespeare's mind no less than to Ibsen's or Pinero's.

Influenced in part, perhaps, by the Elizabethan theorists, but mainly by the freakishness of his own genius, Mr. Bernard Shaw has taken to writing plays in one continuous gush of dialogue, and has put forward, more or less seriously, the claim that he is thereby reviving the practice of the Greeks. In a prefatory note to **Getting Married**, he says--

"There is a point of some technical interest to be noted in this play. The customary division into acts and scenes has been disused, and a return made to unity of time and place, as observed in the ancient Greek drama. In the foregoing tragedy, *The Doctor's Dilemma*, there are five acts; the place is altered five times; and the time is spread over an undetermined period of more than a year. No doubt the strain on the attention of the audience and on the ingenuity of the playwright is much less; but I find in practice that the Greek form is inevitable when the drama reaches a certain point in poetic and intellectual evolution. Its adoption was not, on my part, a deliberate display of virtuosity in form, but simply the spontaneous falling of a play of ideas into the form most suitable to it, which turned out to be the classical form."

It is hard to say whether Mr. Shaw is here writing seriously or in a mood of solemn facetiousness. Perhaps he himself is not quite clear on the point. There can be no harm, at any rate, in assuming that he genuinely believes the unity of *Getting Married* to be "a return to the unity observed in," say, the *Oedipus Rex*, and examining a little into so pleasant an illusion.

It is, if I may so phrase it, a double-barrelled illusion. *Getting Married* has not the unity of the Greek drama, and the Greek drama has not the unity of *Getting Married*. Whatever "unity" is predicable of either form of art is a wholly different thing from whatever "unity" is predicable of the other. Mr. Shaw, in fact, is, consciously or unconsciously, playing with words, very much as Lamb did when he said to the sportsman, "Is that your own hare or a wig?" There are, roughly speaking, three sorts of unity: the unity of a plum-pudding, the unity of a string or chain, and, the unity of the Parthenon. Let us call them, respectively, unity of concoction, unity of concatenation, and structural or organic unity. The second form of unity is that of most novels and some plays. They present a series of events, more or less closely intertwined or interlinked with one another, but not built up into any symmetrical interdependence. This unity of longitudinal extension does not here concern us, for it is not that of either Shaw or Sophocles. Plum-pudding unity, on the other hand--the unity of a number of ingredients stirred up together, put in a cloth, boiled to a certain consistency, and then served up in a blue flame of lambent humour--that is precisely the unity of *Getting Married*. A jumble of ideas, prejudices, points of view, and whimsicalities on the subject of marriage is tied up in a cloth and boiled into a sort of glutinous fusion or confusion, so that when the cloth is taken off they do not at once lose the coherent rotundity conferred upon them by pressure from without. In a quite real sense, the comparison does more than justice to the technical qualities of the play; for in a good plum-pudding the due proportions of the ingredients are carefully studied, whereas Mr. Shaw flings in recklessly whatever comes into his head. At the same time it is undeniably true that he shows us a number of people in one room, talking continuously and without a single pause, on different aspects of a given theme. If this be unity, then he has achieved it. In the theatre, as a matter of fact, the plum-pudding was served up in three chunks instead of one; but this was a mere concession to human weakness. The play had all the globular unity of a pill, though it happened to be too big a pill to be swallowed at one gulp.

Turning now to the *Oedipus*--I choose that play as a typical example of Greek tragedy--what sort of unity do we find? It is the unity, not of a continuous mass or mash, but of carefully calculated proportion, order, interrelation of parts--the unity of a fine piece of architecture, or even of a living organism. The inorganic continuity of *Getting Married* it does not possess. If that be what we understand by unity, then Shaw has it and Sophocles has not. The *Oedipus* is as clearly divided into acts as is *Hamlet* or *Hedda Gabler*. In modern parlance, we should probably call it a play in five acts and an epilogue. It so happened that the Greek theatre did not possess a curtain, and did possess a Chorus; consequently, the Greek dramatist employed the Chorus, as we employ the curtain, to emphasize the successive stages of his action, to mark the rhythm of its progress, and, incidentally, to provide resting-places for the mind of the audience--intervals during which the strain upon their attention was relaxed, or at any rate varied. It is not even true that the Greeks habitually aimed at such continuity of time as we find in *Getting Married*. They treated time ideally, the imaginary duration of the story being, as a rule, widely different from the actual time of representation. In this respect the *Oedipus* is something of an exception, since the events might, at a pinch, be conceived as passing within the "two hours' traffick of the stage"; but in many cases a whole day, or even more, must be understood to be compressed within these two hours. It is true that the continuous presence of the Chorus made it impossible for the Greeks to overleap months and years, as we do on the modern stage; but they did not aim at that strict coincidence of imaginary with actual time which Mr. Shaw believes himself to have achieved.[1] Even he, however, subjects the events which take place behind the scenes to a good deal of "ideal" compression.

Of course, when Mr. Shaw protests that, in *Getting Married*, he did not indulge in a "deliberate display of virtuosity of form," that is only his fun. You cannot well have virtuosity of form where there is no form. What he did was to rely upon his virtuosity of dialogue to enable him to dispense with form. Whether he succeeded or not is a matter of opinion which does not at present concern us. The point to be noted is the essential difference between the formless continuity of ***Getting Married***, and the sedulous ordering and balancing of clearly differentiated parts, which went to the structure of a Greek tragedy. A dramatist who can so develop his story as to bring it within the quasi-Aristotelean "unities" performs a curious but not particularly difficult or valuable feat; but this does not, or ought not to, imply the abandonment of the act-division, which is no mere convention, but a valuable means of marking the rhythm of the story. When, on the other hand, you have no story to tell, the act-division is manifestly superfluous; but it needs no "virtuosity" to dispense with it.

It is a grave error, then, to suppose that the act is a mere division of convenience, imposed by the limited power of attention of the human mind, or by the need of the human body for occasional refreshment. A play with a well-marked, well-balanced act-structure is a higher artistic organism than a play with no act-structure, just as a vertebrate animal is higher than a mollusc. In every crisis of real life (unless it be so short as to be a mere incident) there is a rhythm of rise, progress, culmination and solution. We are not always, perhaps not often, conscious of these stages; but that is only because we do not reflect upon our experiences while they are passing, or map them out in memory when they are past. We do, however, constantly apply to real-life crises expressions borrowed more or less directly from the terminology of the drama. We say, somewhat incorrectly, "Things have come to a climax," meaning thereby a culmination; or we say, "The catastrophe is at hand," or, again, "What a fortunate ***denouement***!" Be this as it may, it is the business of the dramatist to analyse the crises with which he deals, and to present them to us in their rhythm of growth, culmination, solution. To this end the act-division is--not, perhaps, essential, since the rhythm may be marked even in a one-act play--but certainly of enormous and invaluable convenience. "Si l'acte n'existait pas, il faudrait l'inventer"; but as a matter of fact it has existed wherever, in the Western world, the drama has developed beyond its rudest beginnings.

It was doubtless the necessity for marking this rhythm that Aristotle had in mind when he said that a dramatic action must have a beginning, a middle and an end. Taken in its simplicity, this principle would indicate the three-act division as the ideal scheme for a play. As a matter of fact, many of the best modern plays in all languages fall into three acts; one has only to note ***Monsieur Alphonse, Francillon, La Parisienne, Amoureuse, A Doll's House, Ghosts, The Master Builder, Little Eyolf, Johannisfeuer, Caste, Candida, The Benefit of the Doubt, The Importance of Being Earnest, The Silver Box***; and, furthermore, many old plays which are nominally in five acts really fall into a triple rhythm, and might better have been divided into three. Alexandrian precept, handed on by Horace, gave to the five act division a purely arbitrary sanction, which induced playwrights to mask the natural rhythm of their themes beneath this artificial one.[2] But in truth the three-act division ought no more to be elevated into an absolute rule than the five-act division. We have seen that a play consists, or ought to consist, of a great crisis, worked out through a series of minor crises. An act, then, ought to consist either of a minor crisis, carried to its temporary solution, or of a well-marked group of such crises; and there can be no rule as to the number of such crises which ought to present themselves in the development of a given theme. On the modern stage, five acts may be regarded as the maximum, simply by reason of the time-limit imposed by social custom on a performance. But one frequently sees a melodrama divided into "five acts and eight tableaux," or even more; which practically means that the play is in eight, or nine, or ten acts, but that there will be only the four conventional interacts in the course of the evening. The playwright should not let himself be constrained by custom to force his theme into the arbitrary mould of a stated number of acts. Three acts is a good number, four acts is a good number,[3] there is no positive objection to five acts. Should he find himself hankering after more acts, he will do well to consider whether he be not, at one point or another, failing in the art of condensation and trespassing on the domain of the novelist.

There is undoubted convenience in the rule of the modern stage: "One act, one scene." A change of scene in the middle of an act is not only materially difficult, but tends to impair the particular order of illusion at which the modern drama aims.[4] Roughly, indeed, an act may be defined as any part of a given crisis which works itself out at one time and in one place; but more fundamentally it is a segment of the action during which the author desires to hold the attention of his audience unbroken and unrelaxed. It is no mere convention, however, which decrees that the flight of time is best indicated by an interact. When the curtain is down, the action on the stage remains, as it were, in suspense. The audience lets its attention revert to the affairs of real life; and it is quite willing, when the mimic world is once more revealed, to suppose that any reasonable space of time has elapsed while its thoughts were occupied with other matters. It is much more difficult for it to accept a wholly imaginary lapse of time while its attention is centred on the mimic world. Some playwrights have of late years adopted the device of dropping their curtain once, or even twice, in the middle of an act, to indicate an interval of a few minutes, or even of an hour--for instance, of the time between "going in to dinner" and the return of the ladies to the drawing-room. Sir Arthur Pinero employs this device with good effect in *Iris*; so does Mr. Granville Barker in *Waste*, and Mr. Galsworthy in *The Silver Box*. It is certainly far preferable to that "ideal" treatment of time which was common in the French drama of the nineteenth century, and survives to this day in plays adapted or imitated from the French.

I remember seeing in London, not very long ago, a one-act play on the subject of Rouget de l'Isle. In the space of about half-an-hour, he handed the manuscript of the "Marseillaise" to an opera-singer whom he adored, she took it away and sang it at the Opera, it caught the popular ear from that one performance, and the dying Rouget heard it sung by the passing multitude in the streets within about fifteen minutes of the moment when it first left his hands. (The whole piece, I repeat, occupied about half-an-hour; but as a good deal of that time was devoted to preliminaries, not more than fifteen minutes can have elapsed between the time when the cantatrice left Rouget's garret and the time when all Paris was singing the "Marseillaise.") This is perhaps an extreme instance of the ideal treatment of time; but one could find numberless cases in the works of Scribe, Labiche, and others, in which the transactions of many hours are represented as occurring within the limits of a single act. Our modern practice eschews such licenses. It will often compress into an act of half-an-hour more events than would probably happen in real life in a similar space of time, but not such a train of occurrences as to transcend the limits of possibility. It must be remembered, however, that the standard of verisimilitude naturally and properly varies with the seriousness of the theme under treatment. Improbabilities are admissible in light comedy, and still more in farce, which would wreck the fortunes of a drama purporting to present a sober and faithful picture of real life.

Acts, then, mark the time-stages in the development of a given crisis; and each act ought to embody a minor crisis of its own, with a culmination and a temporary solution. It would be no gain, but a loss, if a whole two hours' or three hours' action could be carried through in one continuous movement, with no relaxation of the strain upon the attention of the audience, and without a single point at which the spectator might review what was past and anticipate what was to come. The act-division positively enhances the amount of pleasurable emotion through which the audience passes. Each act ought to stimulate and temporarily satisfy an interest of its own, while definitely advancing the main action. The psychological principle is evident enough; namely, that there is more sensation to be got out of three or four comparatively brief experiences, suited to our powers of perception, than out of one protracted experience, forced on us without relief, without contrast, in such a way as to fatigue and deaden our faculties. Who would not rather drink three, four, or five glasses of wine than put the bottle to his lips and let its contents pour down his throat in one long draught? Who would not rather see a stained-glass window broken into three, four, or five cunningly-proportioned "lights," than a great flat sheet of coloured glass, be its design never so effective?

It used to be the fashion in mid Victorian melodramas to give each act a more or less alluring title of its own. I am far from recommending the revival of this practice; but it might be no bad plan for a beginner, in sketching out a play, to have in his mind, or in his private notes, a descriptive head-line for each act, thereby assuring himself that each had a character of its own, and at the same time contributed its due share to the advancement of the whole design. Let us apply this principle to a Shakespearean play--for example, to ***Macbeth***. The act headings might run somewhat as follows--

ACT I.--TEMPTATION.

ACT II.--MURDER AND USURPATION.

ACT III.--THE FRENZY OF CRIME AND THE HAUNTING OF REMORSE.

ACT IV.--GATHERING RETRIBUTION.

ACT V.--RETRIBUTION CONSUMMATED.

Can it be doubted that Shakespeare had in his mind the rhythm marked by this act-division? I do not mean, of course, that these phrases, or anything like them, were present to his consciousness, but merely that he "thought in acts," and mentally assigned to each act its definite share in the development of the crisis.

Turning now to Ibsen, let us draw up an act-scheme for the simplest and most straightforward of his plays, *An Enemy of the People*. It might run as follows:

ACT I.--THE INCURABLE OPTIMIST.--Dr. Stockmann announces his discovery of the insanitary condition of the Baths.

ACT II.--THE COMPACT MAJORITY.--Dr. Stockmann finds that he will have to fight vested interests before the evils he has discovered can be remedied, but is assured that the Compact Majority is at his back.

ACT III.--THE TURN OF FORTUNE.--The Doctor falls from the pinnacle of his optimistic confidence, and learns that he will have the Compact Majority, not at, but on his back.

ACT IV.--THE COMPACT MAJORITY ON THE WARPATH.--The crowd, finding that its immediate interests are identical with those of the privileged few, joins with the bureaucracy in shouting down the truth, and organizing a conspiracy of silence.

ACT V.--OPTIMISM DISILLUSIONED BUT INDOMITABLE.--Dr. Stockmann, gagged and thrown back into poverty, is tempted to take flight, but determines to remain in his native place and fight for its moral, if not for its physical, sanitation.

Each of these acts is a little drama in itself, while each leads forward to the next, and marks a distinct phase in the development of the crisis.

When the younger Dumas asked his father, that master of dramatic movement, to initiate him into the secret of dramatic craftsmanship, the great Alexandre replied in this concise formula: "Let your first act be clear, your last act brief, and the whole interesting." Of the wisdom of the first clause there can be no manner of doubt. Whether incidentally or by way of formal exposition, the first act ought to show us clearly who the characters are, what are their relations and relationships, and what is the nature of the gathering crisis. It is very important that the attention of the audience should not be overstrained in following out needlessly complex genealogies and kinships. How often, at the end of a first act, does one turn to one's neighbour and say, "Are Edith and Adela sisters or only half-sisters?" or, "Did you gather what was the villain's claim to the title?" If a story cannot be made clear without an elaborate study of one or more family trees, beware of it. In all probability, it is of very little use for dramatic purposes. But before giving it up, see whether the relationships, and other relations, cannot be simplified. Complexities which at first seemed indispensable will often prove to be mere useless encumbrances.

In *Pillars of Society* Ibsen goes as far as any playwright ought to go in postulating fine degrees of kinship--and perhaps a little further. Karsten Bernick has married into a family whose gradations put something of a strain on the apprehension and memory of an audience. We have to bear in mind that Mrs. Bernick has (a) a half-sister, Lona Hessel; (b) a full brother, Johan Toennesen; (c) a cousin, Hilmar Toennesen. Then Bernick has an unmarried sister, Martha; another relationship, however simple, to be borne in mind. And, finally, when we see Dina Dorf living in Bernick's house, and know that Bernick has had an intrigue with her mother, we are apt to fall into the error of supposing her to be Bernick's daughter. There is only one line which proves that this is not so--a remark to the effect that, when Madam Dorf came to the town. Dina was already old enough to run about and play angels in the theatre. Any one who does not happen to hear or notice this remark, is almost certain to misapprehend Dina's parentage. Taking one thing with another, then, the Bernick family group is rather more complex than is strictly desirable. Ibsen's reasons for making Lona Hessel a half-sister instead of a full sister of Mrs. Bernick are evident enough. He wanted her to be a considerably older woman, of a very different type of character; and it was necessary, in order to explain Karsten's desertion of Lona for Betty, that the latter should be an heiress, while the former was penniless. These reasons are clear and apparently adequate; yet it may be doubted whether the dramatist did not lose more than he gained by introducing even this small degree of complexity. It was certainly not necessary to explain the difference of age and character between Lona and Betty; while as for the money, there would have been nothing improbable in supposing that a wealthy uncle had marked his disapproval of Lona's strong-mindedness by bequeathing all his property to her younger sister. Again, there is no reason why Hilmar should not have been a brother of Johan and Betty;[5] in which case we should have had the simple family group of two brothers and two sisters, instead of the comparatively complex relationship of a brother and sister, a half-sister and a cousin.

These may seem very trivial considerations: but nothing is really trivial when it comes to be placed under the powerful lens of theatrical presentation. Any given audience has only a certain measure of attention at command, and to claim attention for inessentials is to diminish the stock available for essentials. In only one other play does Ibsen introduce any complexity of relationship, and in that case it does not appear in the exposition, but is revealed at a critical moment towards the close. In *Little Eyolf*, Asta and Allmers are introduced to us at first as half-sister and half-brother; and only at the end of the second act does it appear that Asta's mother (Allmers' stepmother) was unfaithful to her husband, and that, Asta being the fruit of this infidelity, there is no blood kinship between her and Allmers. The danger of relying upon such complexities is shown by the fact that so acute a critic as M. Jules Lemaitre, in writing of *Little Eyolf*, mistook the situation, and thought that Asta fled from Allmers because he was her brother, whereas in fact she fled because he was not. I had the honour of calling M. Lemaitre's attention to this error, which he handsomely acknowledged.

Complexities of kinship are, of course, not the only complexities which should, so far as possible, be avoided. Every complexity of relation or of antecedent circumstance is in itself a weakness, which, if it cannot be eliminated, must, so to speak, be lived down. No dramatic critic, I think, can have failed to notice that the good plays are those of which the story can be clearly indicated in ten lines; while it very often takes a column to give even a confused idea of the plot of a bad play. Here, then, is a preliminary test which may be commended to the would-be playwright, in order to ascertain whether the subject he is contemplating is or is not a good one: can he state the gist of it in a hundred words or so, like the "argument" of a Boccaccian novella? The test, of course, is far from being infallible; for a theme may err on the side of over-simplicity or emptiness, no less than on the side of over-complexity. But it is, at any rate, negatively useful: if the playwright finds that he cannot make his story comprehensible without a long explanation of an intricate network of facts, he may be pretty sure that he has got hold of a bad theme, or of one that stands sorely in need of simplification.[6]

It is not sufficient, however, that a first act should fulfil Dumas's requirement by placing the situation clearly before us: it ought also to carry us some way towards the heart of the drama, or, at the very least, to point distinctly towards that quarter of the horizon where the clouds are gathering up. In a three-act play this is evidently demanded by the most elementary principles of proportion. It would be absurd to make one-third of the play merely introductory, and to compress the whole action into the remaining two-thirds. But even in a four- or five-act play, the interest of the audience ought to be strongly enlisted, and its anticipation headed in a definite direction, before the curtain falls for the first time. When we find a dramatist of repute neglecting this principle, we may suspect some reason with which art has no concern. Several of Sardou's social dramas begin with two acts of more or less smart and entertaining satire or caricature, and only at the end of the second or beginning of the third act (out of five) does the drama proper set in. What was the reason of this? Simply that under the system of royalties prevalent in France, it was greatly to the author's interest that his play should fill the whole evening. Sardou needed no more than three acts for the development of his drama; to have spread it out thinner would have been to weaken and injure it; wherefore he preferred to occupy an hour or so with clever dramatic journalism, rather than share the evening, and the fees, with another dramatist. So, at least, I have heard his practice explained; perhaps his own account of the matter may have been that he wanted to paint a broad social picture to serve as a background for his action.

The question how far an audience ought to be carried towards the heart of a dramatic action in the course of the first act is always and inevitably one of proportion. It is clear that too much ought not to be told, so as to leave the remaining acts meagre and spun-out; nor should any one scene be so intense in its interest as to outshine all subsequent scenes, and give to the rest of the play an effect of anti-climax. If the strange and fascinating creations of Ibsen's last years were to be judged by ordinary dramaturgic canons, we should have to admit that in **Little Eyolf** he was guilty of the latter fault, since in point of sheer "strength," in the common acceptation of the word, the situation at the end of the first act could scarcely be outdone, in that play or any other. The beginner, however, is far more likely to put too little than too much into his first act: he is more likely to leave our interest insufficiently stimulated than to carry us too far in the development of his theme. My own feeling is that, as a general rule, what Freytag calls the *erregende Moment* ought by all means to fall within the first act. What is the *erregende Moment*? One is inclined to render it "the firing of the fuse." In legal parlance, it might be interpreted as the joining of issue. It means the point at which the drama, hitherto latent, plainly declares itself. It means the germination of the crisis, the appearance on the horizon of the cloud no bigger than a man's hand. I suggest, then, that this *erregende Moment* ought always to come within the first act--if it is to come at all There are plays, as we have seen, which depict life on so even a plane that it is impossible to say at any given point, "Here the drama sets in," or "The interest is heightened there."

Pillars of Society is, in a sense, Ibsen's prentice-work in the form of drama which he afterwards perfected; wherefore it affords us numerous illustrations of the problems we have to consider. Does he, or does he not, give us in the first act sufficient insight into his story? I am inclined to answer the question in the negative. The first act puts us in possession of the current version of the Bernick-Toennesen family history, but it gives us no clear indication that this version is an elaborate tissue of falsehoods. It is true that Bernick's evident uneasiness and embarrassment at the mere idea of the reappearance of Lona and Johan may lead us to suspect that all is not as it seems; but simple annoyance at the inopportune arrival of the black sheep of the family might be sufficient to account for this. To all intents and purposes, we are completely in the dark as to the course the drama is about to take; and when, at the end of the first act, Lona Hessel marches in and flutters the social dovecote, we do not know in what light to regard her, or why we are supposed to sympathize with her. The fact that she is eccentric, and that she talks of "letting in fresh air," combines with our previous knowledge of the author's idiosyncrasy to assure us that she is his heroine; but so far as the evidence actually before us goes, we have no means of forming even the vaguest provisional judgment as to her true character. This is almost certainly a mistake in art. It is useless to urge that sympathy and antipathy are primitive emotions, and that we ought to be able to regard a character objectively, rating it as true or false, not as attractive or repellent. The answer to this is twofold. Firstly, the theatre has never been, and never will be, a moral dissecting room, nor has the theatrical audience anything in common with a class of students dispassionately following a professor's demonstration of cold scientific facts. Secondly, in the particular case in point, the dramatist makes a manifest appeal to our sympathies. There can be no doubt that we are intended to take Lona's part, as against the representatives of propriety and convention assembled at the sewing-bee; but we have been vouchsafed no rational reason for so doing. In other words, the author has not taken us far enough into his action to enable us to grasp the true import and significance of the situation. He relies for his effect either on the general principle that an eccentric character must be sympathetic, or on the knowledge possessed by those who have already seen or read the rest of the play. Either form of reliance is clearly inartistic. The former appeals to irrational prejudice; the latter ignores what we shall presently find to be a fundamental principle of the playwright's art--namely, that, with certain doubtful exceptions in the case of historical themes, he must never assume previous knowledge either of plot or character on the part of his public, but must always have in his mind's eye a first-night audience, which knows nothing but what he chooses to tell it.

My criticism of the first act of ***Pillars of Society*** may be summed up in saying that the author has omitted to place in it the ***erregende Moment***. The issue is not joined, the true substance of the drama is not clear to us, until, in the second act, Bernick makes sure there are no listeners, and then holds out both hands to Johan, saying: "Johan, now we are alone; now you must give me leave to thank you," and so forth. Why should not this scene have occurred in the first act? Materially, there is no reason whatever. It would need only the change of a few words to lift the scene bodily out of the second act and transfer it to the first. Why did Ibsen not do so? His reason is not hard to divine; he wished to concentrate into two great scenes, with scarcely a moment's interval between them, the revelation of Bernick's treachery, first to Johan, second to Lona. He gained his point: the sledge-hammer effect of these two scenes is undeniable. But it remains a question whether he did not make a disproportionate sacrifice; whether he did not empty his first act in order to overfill his second. I do not say he did: I merely propound the question for the student's consideration. One thing we must recognize in dramatic art as in all other human affairs; namely, that perfection, if not unattainable, is extremely rare. We have often to make a deliberate sacrifice at one point in order to gain some greater advantage at another; to incur imperfection here that we may achieve perfection there. It is no disparagement to the great masters to admit that they frequently show us rather what to avoid than what to do. Negative instruction, indeed, is in its essence more desirable than positive. The latter tends to make us mere imitators, whereas the former, in saving us from dangers, leaves our originality unimpaired.

It is curious to note that, in another play, Ibsen did actually transfer the *erregende Moment*, the joining of issue, from the second act to the first. In his early draft of **Rosmersholm**, the great scene in which Rosmer confesses to Kroll his change of views did not occur until the second act. There can be no doubt that the balance and proportion of the play gained enormously by the transference.

After all, however, the essential question is not how much or how little is conveyed to us in the first act, but whether our interest is thoroughly aroused, and, what is of equal importance, skilfully carried forward. Before going more at large into this very important detail of the playwright's craft, it may be well to say something of the nature of dramatic interest in general.

*   *   *   *   *

Notes:
[1: There are several cases in Greek drama in which a hero leaves the stage to fight a battle and returns victorious in a few minutes. See, for example, the ***Supplices*** of Euripides.]

[2: So far was Shakespeare from ignoring the act-division that it is a question whether his art did not sometimes suffer from the supposed necessity of letting a fourth act intervene between the culmination in the third act and the catastrophe in the fifth.]

[3: I think it may be said that the majority of modern serious plays are in four acts. It is a favourite number with Sir Arthur Pinero, Mr. Henry Arthur Jones, Mr. Clyde Fitch, and Mr. Alfred Sutro.]

[4: This must not be taken to mean that in no case is a change of scene within the act advisable. The point to be considered is whether the author does or does not want to give the audience time for reflection--time to return to the real world--between two episodes. If it is of great importance that they should not do so, then a rapid change of scene may be the less of two evils. In this case the lights should be kept lowered in order to show that no interact is intended; but the fashion of changing the scene on a pitch-dark stage, without dropping the curtain, is much to be deprecated. If the revolving stage should ever become a common institution in English-speaking countries, dramatists would doubtless be more tempted than they are at present to change their scenes within the act; but I doubt whether the tendency would be wholly advantageous. No absolute rule, however, can be laid down, and it may well be maintained that a true dramatic artist could only profit by the greater flexibility of his medium.]

[5: He was, in the first draft; and Lona Hessel was only a distant relative of Bernick's.]

[6: The Greeks, who knew most things, knew the value of manageable dimensions and simple structure in a work of art, and had a word to express that combination of qualities--the word *eusynopton*.]

CHAPTER IX
"CURIOSITY" AND "INTEREST"

The paradox of dramatic theory is this: while our aim is, of course, to write plays which shall achieve immortality, or shall at any rate become highly popular, and consequently familiar in advance to a considerable proportion of any given audience, we are all the time studying how to awaken and to sustain that interest, or, more precisely, that curiosity, which can be felt only by those who see the play for the first time, without any previous knowledge of its action. Under modern conditions especially, the spectators who come to the theatre with their minds an absolute blank as to what is awaiting them, are comparatively few; for newspaper criticism and society gossip very soon bruit abroad a general idea of the plot of any play which attains a reasonable measure of success. Why, then, should we assume, in the ideal spectator to whom we address ourselves, a state of mind which, we hope and trust, will not be the state of mind of the majority of actual spectators?

To this question there are several answers. The first and most obvious is that to one audience, at any rate, every play must be absolutely new, and that it is this first-night audience which in great measure determines its success or failure. Many plays have survived a first-night failure, and still more have gone off in a rapid decline after a first-night success. But these caprices of fortune are not to be counted on. The only prudent course is for the dramatist to direct all his thought and care towards conciliating or dominating an audience to which his theme is entirely unknown,[1] and so coming triumphant through his first-night ordeal. This principle is subject to a certain qualification in the case of historic and legendary themes. In treating such subjects, the dramatist is not relieved of the necessity of developing his story clearly and interestingly, but has, on the contrary, an additional charge imposed upon him--that of not flagrantly defying or disappointing popular knowledge or prejudice. Charles I must not die in a green old age, Oliver Cromwell must not display the manners and graces of Sir Charles Grandison, Charles II must not be represented as a model of domestic virtue. Historians may indict a hero or whitewash a villain at their leisure; but to the dramatist a hero must be (more or less) a hero, a villain (more or less) a villain, if accepted tradition so decrees it.[2] Thus popular knowledge can scarcely be said to lighten a dramatist's task, but rather to impose a new limitation upon him. In some cases, however, he can rely on a general knowledge of the historic background of a given period, which may save him some exposition. An English audience, for instance, does not require to be told what was the difference between Cavaliers and Roundheads; nor does any audience, I imagine, look for a historical disquisition on the Reign of Terror. The dramatist has only to bring on some ruffianly characters in Phrygian caps, who address each other as "Citizen" and "Citizeness," and at once the imagination of the audience will supply the roll of the tumbrels and the silhouette of the guillotine in the background.

To return to the general question: not only must the dramatist reckon with one all-important audience which is totally ignorant of the story he has to tell; he must also bear in mind that it is very easy to exaggerate the proportion of any given audience which will know his plot in advance, even when his play has been performed a thousand times. There are inexhaustible possibilities of ignorance in the theatrical public. A story is told, on pretty good authority, of a late eminent statesman who visited the Lyceum one night when Sir Henry Irving was appearing as Hamlet. After the third act he went to the actor's dressing-room, expressed great regret that duty called him back to Westminster, and begged Sir Henry to tell him how the play ended, as it had interested him greatly.[3] One of our most eminent novelists has assured me that he never saw or read *Macbeth* until he was present at (I think) Mr. Forbes Robertson's revival of the play, he being then nearer fifty than forty. These, no doubt, are "freak" instances; but in any given audience, even at the most hackneyed classical plays, there will be a certain percentage of children (who contribute as much as their elders to the general temper of an audience), and also a percentage of adult ignoramuses. And if this be so in the case of plays which have held the stage for generations, are studied in schools, and are every day cited as matters of common knowledge, how much more certain may we be that even the most popular modern play will have to appeal night after night to a considerable number of people who have no previous acquaintance with either its story or its characters! The playwright may absolutely count on having to make such an appeal; but he must remember at the same time that he can by no means count on keeping any individual effect, more especially any notable trick or device, a secret from the generality of his audience. Mr. J.M. Barrie (to take a recent instance) sedulously concealed, throughout the greater part of *Little Mary*, what was meant by that ever-recurring expression, and probably relied to some extent on an effect of amused surprise when the disclosure was made. On the first night, the effect came off happily enough; but on subsequent nights, there would rarely be a score of people in the house who did not know the secret. The great majority might know nothing else about the play, but that they knew. Similarly, in the case of any mechanical *truc*, as the French call it, or feat of theatrical sleight-of-hand, it is futile to trust to its taking unawares any audience after the first. Nine-tenths of all subsequent audiences are sure to be on the look-out for it, and to know, or think they know, "how it's done."[4] These are the things which theatrical gossip, printed and oral, most industriously disseminates. The fine details of a plot are much less easily conveyed and less likely to be remembered.

To sum up this branch of the argument: however oft-repeated and much-discussed a play may be, the playwright must assume that in every audience there will be an appreciable number of persons who know practically nothing about it, and whose enjoyment will depend, like that of the first-night audience, on the skill with which he develops his story. On the other hand, he can never rely on taking an audience by surprise at any particular point. The class of effect which depends on surprise is precisely the class of effect which is certain to be discounted.[5]

We come now to a third reason why a playwright is bound to assume that the audience to which he addresses himself has no previous knowledge of his fable. It is simply that no other assumption has, or can have, any logical basis. If the audience is not to be conceived as ignorant, how much is it to be assumed to know? There is clearly no possible answer to this question, except a purely arbitrary one, having no relation to the facts. In any audience after the first, there will doubtless be a hundred degrees of knowledge and of ignorance. Many people will know nothing at all about the play; some people will have seen or read it yesterday, and will thus know all there is to know; while between these extremes there will be every variety of clearness or vagueness of knowledge. Some people will have read and remembered a detailed newspaper notice; others will have read the same notice and forgotten almost all of it. Some will have heard a correct and vivid account of the play, others a vague and misleading summary. It would be absolutely impossible to enumerate all the degrees of previous knowledge which are pretty certain to be represented in an average audience; and to which degree of knowledge is the playwright to address himself? If he is to have any firm ground under his feet, he must clearly adopt the only logical course, and address himself to a spectator assumed to have no previous knowledge whatever. To proceed on any other assumption would not only be to ignore the all-powerful first-night audience, but to plunge into a veritable morass of inconsistencies, dubieties and slovenlinesses.

These considerations, however, have not yet taken us to the heart of the matter. We have seen that the dramatist has no rational course open to him but to assume complete ignorance in his audience; but we have also seen that, as a matter of fact, only one audience will be entirely in this condition, and that, the more successful the play is, the more widely will subsequent audiences tend to depart from it. Does it not follow that interest of plot, interest of curiosity as to coming events, is at best an evanescent factor in a play's attractiveness--of a certain importance, no doubt, on the first night, but less and less efficient the longer the play holds the stage?

In a sense, this is undoubtedly true. We see every day that a mere story-play--a play which appeals to us solely by reason of the adroit stimulation and satisfaction of curiosity--very rapidly exhausts its success. No one cares to see it a second time; and spectators who happen to have read the plot in advance, find its attraction discounted even on a first hearing. But if we jump to the conclusion that the skilful marshalling and development of the story is an unimportant detail, which matters little when once the first-night ordeal is past, we shall go very far astray. Experience shows us that dramatic *interest* is entirely distinct from mere *curiosity*, and survives when curiosity is dead. Though a skilfully-told story is not of itself enough to secure long life for a play, it materially and permanently enhances the attractions of a play which has other and higher claims to longevity. Character, poetry, philosophy, atmosphere, are all very good in their way; but they all show to greater advantage by aid of a well-ordered fable. In a picture, I take it, drawing is not everything; but drawing will always count for much.

This separation of interest from curiosity is partly explicable by one very simple reflection. However well we may know a play beforehand, we seldom know it by heart or nearly by heart; so that, though we may anticipate a development in general outline, we do not clearly foresee the ordering of its details, which, therefore, may give us almost the same sort of pleasure that it gave us when the story was new to us. Most playgoers will, I think, bear me out in saying that we constantly find a great scene or act to be in reality richer in invention and more ingenious in arrangement than we remembered it to be.

We come, now, to another point that must not be overlooked. It needs no subtle introspection to assure us that we, the audience, do our own little bit of acting, and instinctively place ourselves at the point of view of a spectator before whose eyes the drama is unrolling itself for the first time. If the play has any richness of texture, we have many sensations that he cannot have. We are conscious of ironies and subtleties which necessarily escape him, or which he can but dimly divine. But in regard to the actual development of the story, we imagine ourselves back into his condition of ignorance, with this difference, that we can more fully appreciate the dramatist's skill, and more clearly resent his clumsiness or slovenliness. Our sensations, in short, are not simply conditioned by our knowledge or ignorance of what is to come. The mood of dramatic receptivity is a complex one. We instinctively and without any effort remember that the dramatist is bound by the rules of the game, or, in other words, by the inherent conditions of his craft, to unfold his tale before an audience to which it is unknown; and it is with implicit reference to these conditions that we enjoy and appreciate his skill. Even the most unsophisticated audience realizes in some measure that the playwright is an artist presenting a picture of life under such-and-such assumptions and limitations, and appraises his skill by its own vague and instinctive standards. As our culture increases, we more and more consistently adopt this attitude, and take pleasure in a playwright's marshalling of material in proportion to its absolute skill, even if that skill no longer produces its direct and pristine effect upon us. In many cases, indeed, our pleasure consists of a delicate blending of surprise with realized anticipation. We foresaw, and are pleased to recognize, the art of the whole achievement, while details which had grown dim to us give us each its little thrill of fresh admiration. Regarded in this aspect, a great play is like a great piece of music: we can hear it again and again with ever-new realization of its subtle beauties, its complex harmonies, and with unfailing interest in the merits and demerits of each particular rendering.

But we must look deeper than this if we would fully understand the true nature of dramatic interest. The last paragraph has brought us to the verge of the inmost secret, but we have yet to take the final step. We have yet to realize that, in truly great drama, the foreknowledge possessed by the audience is not a disadvantage with certain incidental mitigations and compensations, but is the source of the highest pleasure which the theatre is capable of affording us. In order to illustrate my meaning, I propose to analyse a particular scene, not, certainly, among the loftiest in dramatic literature, but particularly suited to my purpose, inasmuch as it is familiar to every one, and at the same time full of the essential qualities of drama. I mean the Screen Scene in *The School for Scandal*.

In her "English Men of Letters" volume on Sheridan, Mrs. Oliphant discusses this scene. Speaking in particular of the moment at which the screen is overturned, revealing Lady Teazle behind it, she says--

"It would no doubt have been higher art could the dramatist have deceived his audience as well as the personages of the play, and made us also parties in the surprise of the discovery."

There could scarcely be a completer reversal of the truth than this "hopeless comment," as Professor Brander Matthews has justly called it. The whole effect of the long and highly-elaborated scene depends upon our knowledge that Lady Teazle is behind the screen. Had the audience either not known that there was anybody there, or supposed it to be the "little French milliner," where would have been the breathless interest which has held us through a whole series of preceding scenes? When Sir Peter reveals to Joseph his generous intentions towards his wife, the point lies in the fact that Lady Teazle overhears; and this is doubly the case when he alludes to Joseph as a suitor for the hand of Maria. So, too, with the following scene between Joseph and Charles; in itself it would be flat enough; the fact that Sir Peter is listening lends it a certain piquancy; but this is ten times multiplied by the fact that Lady Teazle, too, hears all that passes. When Joseph is called from the room by the arrival of the pretended Old Stanley, there would be no interest in his embarrassment if we believed the person behind the screen to be the French milliner. And when Sir Peter yields to the temptation to let Charles into the secret of his brother's frailty, and we feel every moment more certain that the screen will be overthrown, where would be the excitement, the tension, if we did not know who was behind it? The real drama, in fact, passes behind the screen. It lies in the terror, humiliation, and disillusionment which we know to be coursing each other through Lady Teazle's soul. And all this Mrs. Oliphant would have sacrificed for a single moment of crude surprise!

Now let us hear Professor Matthews's analysis of the effect of the scene. He says:

"The playgoer's interest is really not so much as to what is to happen as the way in which this event is going to affect the characters involved. He thinks it likely enough that Sir Peter will discover that Lady Teazle is paying a visit to Joseph Surface; but what he is really anxious to learn is the way the husband will take it. What will Lady Teazle have to say when she is discovered where she has no business to be? How will Sir Peter receive her excuses? What will the effect be on the future conduct of both husband and wife? These are the questions which the spectators are eager to have answered."

This is an admirable exposition of the frame of mind of the Drury Lane audience of May 8, 1777. who first saw the screen overturned. But in the thousands of audiences who have since witnessed the play, how many individuals, on an average, had any doubt as to what Lady Teazle would have to say, and how Sir Peter would receive her excuses? It would probably be safe to guess that, for a century past, two-thirds of every audience have clearly foreknown the outcome of the situation. Professor Matthews himself has edited Sheridan's plays, and probably knows ***The School for Scandal*** almost by heart; yet we may be pretty sure that any reasonably good performance of the Screen Scene will to-day give him pleasure not so very much inferior to that which he felt the first time he saw it. In this pleasure, it is manifest that mere curiosity as to the immediate and subsequent conduct of Sir Peter and Lady Teazle can have no part. There is absolutely no question which Professor Matthews, or any playgoer who shares his point of view, is "eager to have answered."

Assuming, then, that we are all familiar with the Screen Scene, and assuming that we, nevertheless, take pleasure in seeing it reasonably well acted,[6] let us try to discover of what elements that pleasure is composed. It is, no doubt, somewhat complex. For one thing, we have pleasure in meeting old friends. Sir Peter, Lady Teazle, Charles, even Joseph, are agreeable creatures who have all sorts of pleasant associations for us. Again, we love to encounter not only familiar characters but familiar jokes. Like Goldsmith's Diggory, we can never help laughing at the story of "ould Grouse in the gunroom." The best order of dramatic wit does not become stale, but rather grows upon us. We relish it at least as much at the tenth repetition as at the first. But while these considerations may partly account for the pleasure we take in seeing the play as a whole, they do not explain why the Screen Scene in particular should interest and excite us. Another source of pleasure, as before indicated, may be renewed recognition of the ingenuity with which the scene is pieced together. However familiar we may be with it, short of actually knowing it by heart, we do not recall the details of its dovetailing, and it is a delight to realize afresh the neatness of the manipulation by which the tension is heightened from speech to speech and from incident to incident. If it be objected that this is a pleasure which the critic alone is capable of experiencing, I venture to disagree. The most unsophisticated playgoer feels the effect of neat workmanship, though he may not be able to put his satisfaction into words. It is evident, however, that the mere intellectual recognition of fine workmanship is not sufficient to account for the emotions with which we witness the Screen Scene. A similar, though, of course, not quite identical, effect is produced by scenes of the utmost simplicity, in which there is no room for delicacy of dovetailing or neatness of manipulation.

Where, then, are we to seek for the fundamental constituent in dramatic interest, as distinct from mere curiosity? Perhaps Mrs. Oliphant's glaring error may put us on the track of the truth. Mrs. Oliphant thought that Sheridan would have shown higher art had he kept the audience, as well as Sir Peter and Charles, ignorant of Lady Teazle's presence behind the screen. But this, as we saw, is precisely the reverse of the truth: the whole interest of the scene arises from our knowledge of Lady Teazle's presence. Had Sheridan fallen into Mrs. Oliphant's mistake, the little shock of surprise which the first-night audience would have felt when the screen was thrown down would have been no compensation at all for the comparative tameness and pointlessness of the preceding passages. Thus we see that the greater part of our pleasure arises precisely from the fact that we know what Sir Peter and Charles do not know, or, in other words, that we have a clear vision of all the circumstances, relations, and implications of a certain conjuncture of affairs, in which two, at least, of the persons concerned are ignorantly and blindly moving towards issues of which they do not dream. We are, in fact, in the position of superior intelligences contemplating, with miraculous clairvoyance, the stumblings and tumblings of poor blind mortals straying through the labyrinth of life. Our seat in the theatre is like a throne on the Epicurean Olympus, whence we can view with perfect intelligence, but without participation or responsibility, the intricate reactions of human destiny. And this sense of superiority does not pall upon us. When Othello comes on the scene, radiant and confident in Desdemona's love, our knowledge of the fate awaiting him makes him a hundred times more interesting than could any mere curiosity as to what was about to happen. It is our prevision of Nora's exit at the end of the last act that lends its dramatic poignancy to her entrance at the beginning of the first.

There is nothing absolutely new in this theory.[7] "The irony of fate" has long been recognized as one of the main elements of dramatic effect. It has been especially dwelt upon in relation to Greek tragedy, of which the themes were all known in advance even to "first-day" audiences. We should take but little interest in seeing the purple carpet spread for Agamemnon's triumphal entry into his ancestral halls, if it were not for our foreknowledge of the net and the axe prepared for him. But, familiar as is this principle, I am not aware that it has hitherto been extended, as I suggest that it should be, to cover the whole field of dramatic interest. I suggest that the theorists have hitherto dwelt far too much on curiosity[8]--which may be defined as the interest of ignorance--and far too little on the feeling of superiority, of clairvoyance, with which we contemplate a foreknown action, whether of a comic or of a tragic cast. Of course the action must be, essentially if not in every detail, true to nature. We can derive no sense of superiority from our foreknowledge of an arbitrary or preposterous action; and that, I take it, is the reason why a good many plays have an initial success of curiosity, but cease to attract when their plot becomes familiar. Again, we take no pleasure in foreknowing the fate of wholly uninteresting people; which is as much as to say that character is indispensable to enduring interest in drama. With these provisos, I suggest a reconstruction of our theories of dramatic interest, in which mere first-night curiosity shall be relegated to the subordinate place which by right belongs to it.

Nevertheless, we must come back to the point that there is always the ordeal of the first night to be faced, and that the plays are comparatively few which have lived-down a bad first-night. It is true that specifically first-night merit is a trivial matter compared with what may be called thousandth-performance merit; but it is equally true that there is no inconsistency between the two orders of merit, and that a play will never be less esteemed on its thousandth performance for having achieved a conspicuous first-night success. The practical lesson which seems to emerge from these considerations is that a wise theatrical policy would seek to diminish the all-importance of the first-night, and to give a play a greater chance of recovery than it has under present conditions, from the depressing effect of an inauspicious production. This is the more desirable as its initial misadventure may very likely be due to external and fortuitous circumstances, wholly unconnected with its inherent qualities.

At the same time, we are bound to recognize that, from the very nature of the case, our present inquiry must be far more concerned with first-night than with thousandth-performance merit. Craftsmanship can, within limits, be acquired, genius cannot; and it is craftsmanship that pilots us through the perils of the first performance, genius that carries us on to the apotheosis of the thousandth. Therefore, our primary concern must be with the arousing and sustaining of curiosity, though we should never forget that it is only a means to the ultimate enlistment of the higher and more abiding forms of interest.

*   *   *   *   *

Notes:
[1: The view that the dramatist has only to think of pleasing himself is elsewhere dealt with.]

[2: Two dramatists who have read these pages in proof, exclaim at this passage. The one says, "No, no!" the other asks, "Why?" I can only reiterate that, where there exists a strong and generally accepted tradition, the dramatist not only runs counter to it at his peril, but goes outside the true domain of his art in so doing. New truth, in history, must be established either by new documents, or by a careful and detailed re-interpretation of old documents; but the stage is not the place either for the production of documents or for historical exegesis. It is needless to say that where the popular mind is unbiased, the dramatist's hands are free. For instance, I presume that one might, in England, take any view one pleased of the character of Mary. Queen of Scots; but a highly unfavourable view would scarcely be accepted by Scottish audiences. Similarly, it would be both dangerous and unprofitable to present on the English stage any very damaging "scandal about Queen Elizabeth." Historical criticism, I understand, does not accept the view that Robespierre was mainly responsible for the Reign of Terror, and that his death betokened a general revolt against his sanguinary tyranny; but it would be very hard for any dramatist to secure general acceptance for a more accurate reading of his character and function. Some further remarks on this subject will be found in Chapter XIII.]

[3: A malicious anecdote to a similar effect was current in the early days of Sir Henry Irving's career. It was said that at Bristol one night, when Mr. Irving, as Hamlet, "took his call" after the first act, a man turned to his neighbour in the pit and said, "Can you tell me, sir, does that young man appear much in this play?" His neighbour informed him that Hamlet was rather largely concerned in the action, whereupon the inquirer remarked, "Oh! Then I'm off!"]

[4: If it be well done, it may remain highly effective in spite of being discounted by previous knowledge. For instance, the clock-trick in **Raffles** was none the less amusing because every one was on the look-out for it.]

[5: The question whether it is ever politic for a playwright to keep a secret from his audience is discussed elsewhere. What I have here in mind is not an ordinary secret, but a more or less tricky effect of surprise.]

[6: The pleasure received from exceptionally good acting is, of course, a different matter. I assume that the acting is merely competent enough to pass muster without irritating us, and so distracting our attention.]

[7: I myself expressed it in slightly different terms nearly ten years ago. "Curiosity," I said, "is the accidental relish of a single night; whereas the essential and abiding pleasure of the theatre lies in foreknowledge. In relation to the characters in the drama, the audience are as gods looking before and after. Sitting in the theatre, we taste, for a moment, the glory of omniscience. With vision unsealed, we watch the gropings of purblind mortals after happiness, and smile at their stumblings, their blunders, their futile quests, their misplaced exultations, their groundless panics. To keep a secret from us is to reduce us to their level, and deprive us of our clairvoyant aloofness. There may be a pleasure in that too; we may join with zest in the game of blind-man's-buff; but the theatre is in its essence a place where we are privileged to take off the bandage we wear in daily life, and to contemplate, with laughter or with tears, the blindfold gambols of our neighbours."]

[8: Here an acute critic writes: "On the whole I agree; but I do think there is dramatic interest to be had out of curiosity, through the identification, so to speak, of the audience with the discovering persons on the stage. It is an interest of sympathy, not to be despised, rather than an interest of actual curiosity."]

CHAPTER X
FORESHADOWING, NOT FORESTALLING

We return now to the point at which the foregoing disquisition--it is not a digression--became necessary. We had arrived at the general principle that the playwright's chief aim in his first act ought to be to arouse and carry forward the interest of the audience. This may seem a tolerably obvious statement; but it is worth while to examine a little more closely into its implications.

As to arousing the interest of the audience, it is clear that very little specific advice can be given. One can only say, "Find an interesting theme, state its preliminaries clearly and crisply, and let issue be joined without too much delay." There can be no rules for finding an interesting theme, any more than for catching the Blue Bird. At a later stage we may perhaps attempt a summary enumeration of themes which are not interesting, which have exhausted any interest they ever possessed, and "repay careful avoidance." But such an enumeration would be out of place here, where we are studying principles of form apart from details of matter.

The arousing of interest, however, is one thing, the carrying-forward of interest is another; and on the latter point there are one or two things that may profitably be said. Each act, as we have seen, should consist of, or at all events contain, a subordinate crisis, contributory to the main crisis of the play: and the art of act-construction lies in giving to each act an individuality and interest of its own, without so rounding it off as to obscure even for a moment its subsidiary, and, in the case of the first act, its introductory, relation to the whole. This is a point which many dramatists ignore or undervalue. Very often, when the curtain falls on a first or a second act, one says, "This is a fairly good act in itself; but whither does it lead?

what is to come of it all?" It awakens no definite anticipation, and for two pins one would take up one's hat and go home. The author has neglected the art of carrying-forward the interest.

It is curious to note that in the most unsophisticated forms of melodrama this art is deliberately ignored. In plays of the type of *The Worst Woman in London*, it appears to be an absolute canon of art that every act must have a "happy ending"--that the curtain must always fall on the hero, or, preferably, the comic man, in an attitude of triumph, while the villain and villainess cower before him in baffled impotence. We have perfect faith, of course, that the villain will come up smiling in the next act, and proceed with his nefarious practices; but, for the moment, virtue has it all its own way. This, however, is a very artless formula which has somehow developed of recent years; and it is doubtful whether even the audiences to which these plays appeal would not in reality prefer something a little less inept in the matter of construction. As soon as we get above this level, at all events, the fostering of anticipation becomes a matter of the first importance. The problem is, not to cut short the spectator's interest, or to leave it fluttering at a loose end, but to provide it either with a clearly-foreseen point in the next act towards which it can reach onwards, or with a definite enigma, the solution of which is impatiently awaited. In general terms, a bridge should be provided between one act and another, along which the spectator's mind cannot but travel with eager anticipation. And this is particularly important, or particularly apt to be neglected, at the end of the first act. At a later point, if the interest does not naturally and inevitably carry itself forward, the case is hopeless indeed.

To illustrate what is meant by the carrying-forward of interest, let me cite one or two instances in which it is achieved with conspicuous success.

In Oscar Wilde's first modern comedy, *Lady Windermere's Fan*, the heroine, Lady Windermere, has learnt that her husband has of late been seen to call very frequently at the house of a certain Mrs. Erlynne, whom nobody knows. Her suspicions thus aroused, she searches her husband's desk, discovers a private and locked bank-book, cuts it open, and finds that one large cheque after another has been drawn in favour of the lady in question. At this inopportune moment, Lord Windermere appears with a request that Mrs. Erlynne shall be invited to their reception that evening. Lady Windermere indignantly refuses, her husband insists, and, finally, with his own hand, fills in an invitation-card and sends it by messenger to Mrs. Erlynne. Here some playwrights might have been content to finish the act. It is sufficiently evident that Lady Windermere will not submit to the apparent insult, and that something exciting may be looked for at the reception in the following act. But Oscar Wilde was not content with this vague expectancy. He first defined it, and then he underlined the definition, in a perfectly natural and yet ingenious and skilful way. The day happens to be Lady Windermere's birthday, and at the beginning of the act her husband has given her a beautiful ostrich-feather fan. When he sends off the invitation, she turns upon him and says, "If that woman crosses my threshold, I shall strike her across the face with this fan." Here, again, many a dramatist might be content to bring down his curtain. The announcement of Lady Windermere's resolve carries forward the interest quite clearly enough for all practical purposes. But even this did not satisfy Wilde. He imagined a refinement, simple, probable, and yet immensely effective, which put an extraordinarily keen edge upon the expectancy of the audience. He made Lady Windermere ring for her butler, and say: "Parker, be sure you pronounce the names of the guests very distinctly to-night. Sometimes you speak so fast that I miss them. I am particularly anxious to hear the names quite clearly, so as to make no mistake." I well remember the effect which this little touch produced on the first night. The situation was, in itself, open to grave objections. There is no plausible excuse for Lord Windermere's obstinacy in forcing Mrs. Erlynne upon his wife, and risking a violent scandal in order to postpone an explanation which he must know to be ultimately inevitable. Though one had not as yet learnt the precise facts of the case, one felt pretty confident that his lordship's conduct would scarcely justify itself. But interest is largely independent of critical judgment, and, for my own part, I can aver that, when the curtain fell on the first act, a five-pound note would not have bribed me to leave the theatre without assisting at Lady Windermere's reception in the second act. That is the frame of mind which the author should try to beget in his audience; and Oscar Wilde, then almost a novice, had, in this one little passage between Lady Windermere and the butler, shown himself a master of the art of dramatic story-telling. The dramatist has higher functions than mere story-telling; but this is fundamental, and the true artist is the last to despise it.[1]

For another example of a first act brought to what one may call a judiciously tantalizing conclusion, I turn to Mr. R.C. Carton's comedy **Wheels within Wheels.** Lord Eric Chantrell has just returned from abroad after many years' absence. He drives straight to the bachelor flat of his old chum, Egerton Vartrey. At the flat he finds only his friend's valet, Vartrey himself has been summoned to Scotland that very evening, and the valet is on the point of following him. He knows, however, that his master would wish his old friend to make himself at home in the flat; so he presently goes off, leaving the newcomer installed for the night. Lord Eric goes to the bedroom to change his clothes; and, the stage being thus left vacant, we hear a latch-key turning in the outer door. A lady in evening dress enters, goes up to the bureau at the back of the stage, and calmly proceeds to break it open and ransack it. While she is thus burglariously employed, Lord Eric enters, and cannot refrain from a slight expression of surprise. The lady takes the situation with humorous calmness, they fall into conversation, and it is manifest that at every word Lord Eric is more and more fascinated by the fair house-breaker. She learns who he is, and evidently knows all about him; but she is careful to give him no inkling of her own identity. At last she takes her leave, and he expresses such an eager hope of being allowed to renew their acquaintance, that it amounts to a declaration of a peculiar interest in her. Thereupon she addresses him to this effect: "Has it occurred to you to wonder how I got into your friend's rooms? I will show you how"--and, producing a latch-key, she holds it up, with all its questionable implications, before his eyes. Then she lays it on the table, says: "I leave you to draw your own conclusions" and departs. A better opening for a light social comedy could scarcely be devised. We have no difficulty in guessing that the lady, who is not quite young, and has clearly a strong sense of humour, is freakishly turning appearances against herself, by way of throwing a dash of cold water on Lord Eric's sudden flame of devotion. But we long for a clear explanation of the whole quaint little episode; and here, again, no reasonable offer would tempt us to leave the theatre before our curiosity is satisfied. The remainder of the play, though amusing, is unfortunately not up to the level of the first act; else **Wheels within Wheels** would be a little classic of light comedy.

For a third example of interest carefully carried forward, I turn to a recent Norwegian play, **The Idyll**, by Peter Egge. At the very rise of the curtain, we find Inga Gar, wife of an author and journalist, Dr. Gar, reading, with evident tokens of annoyance and distaste, a new book of poems by one Rolfe Ringve. Before her marriage, Inga was an actress of no great talent; Ringve made himself conspicuous by praising her far beyond her merits; and when, at last, an engagement between them was announced, people shrugged their shoulders and said: "They are going to regularize the situation." As a matter of fact (of this we have early assurance), though Ringve has been her ardent lover, Inga has neither loved him nor been his mistress. Ringve being called abroad, she has, during his absence, broken off her engagement to him, and has then, about a year before the play opens, married Dr. Gar, to whom she is devoted. While Gar is away on a short lecture tour, Ringve has published the book of love-poems which we find her reading. They are very remarkable poems; they have already made a great stir in the literary world; and interest is all the keener for the fact that they are evidently inspired by his passion for Inga, and are couched in such a tone of intimacy as to create a highly injurious impression of the relations between them. Gar, having just come home, has no suspicion of the nature of the book; and when an editor, who cherishes a grudge against him, conceives the malicious idea of asking him to review Ringve's masterpiece, he consents with alacrity. One or two small incidents have in the meantime shown us that there is a little rift in the idyllic happiness of Inga and Gar, arising from her inveterate habit of telling trifling fibs to avoid facing the petty annoyances of life. For instance, when Gar asks her casually whether she has read Ringve's poems, a foolish denial slips out, though she knows that the cut pages of the book will give her the lie. These incidents point to a state of unstable equilibrium in the relations between husband and wife; wherefore, when we see Gar, at the end of the act, preparing to read Ringve's poems, our curiosity is very keen as to how he will take them. We feel the next hour to be big with fate for these two people; and we long for the curtain to rise again upon the threatened household. The fuse has been fired; we are all agog for the explosion.

In Herr Egge's place, I should have been inclined to have dropped my curtain upon Gar, with the light of the reading-lamp full upon him, in the act of opening the book, and then to have shown him, at the beginning of the second act, in exactly the same position. With more delicate art, perhaps, the author interposes a little domestic incident at the end of the first act, while leaving it clearly impressed on our minds that the reading of the poems is only postponed by a few minutes. That is the essential point: the actual moment upon which the curtain falls is of minor importance. What is of vast importance, on the other hand, is that the expectation of the audience should not be baffled, and that the curtain should rise upon the immediate sequel to the reading of the poems. This is, in the exact sense of the words, *a scene a faire*--an obligatory scene. The author has aroused in us a reasonable expectation of it, and should he choose to balk us--to raise his curtain, say, a week, or a month, later--we should feel that we had been trifled with. The general theory of the *scene a faire* will presently come up for discussion. In the meantime, I merely make the obvious remark that it is worse than useless to awaken a definite expectation in the breast of the audience, and then to disappoint it.[2]

The works of Sir Arthur Pinero afford many examples of interest very skilfully carried forward. In his farces--let no one despise the technical lessons to be learnt from a good farce--there is always an *adventure* afoot, whose development we eagerly anticipate. When the curtain falls on the first act of *The Magistrate*, we foresee the meeting of all the characters at the Hotel des Princes, and are impatient to assist at it. In *The Schoolmistress*, we would not for worlds miss Peggy Hesseltine's party, which we know awaits us in Act II. An excellent example, of a more serious order, is to be found in *The Benefit of the Doubt*. When poor Theo, rebuffed by her husband's chilly scepticism, goes off on some manifestly harebrained errand, we divine, as do her relatives, that she is about to commit social suicide by seeking out John Allingham; and we feel more than curiosity as to the event--we feel active concern, almost anxiety, as though our own personal interests were involved. Our anticipation is heightened, too, when we see Sir Fletcher Portwood and Mrs. Cloys set off upon her track. This gives us a definite point to which to look forward, while leaving the actual course of events entirely undefined. It fulfils one of the great ends of craftsmanship, in foreshadowing without forestalling an intensely interesting conjuncture of affairs.

I have laid stress on the importance of carrying forward the interest of the audience because it is a detail that is often overlooked. There is, as a rule, no difficulty in the matter, always assuming that the theme be not inherently devoid of interest. One could mention many plays in which the author has, from sheer inadvertence, failed to carry forward the interest of the first act, though a very little readjustment, or a trifling exercise of invention, would have enabled him to do so. *Pillars of*

Society, indeed, may be taken as an instance, though not a very flagrant one. Such interest as we feel at the end of the first act is vague and unfocused. We are sure that something is to come of the return of Lona and Johan, but we have no inkling as to what that something may be. If we guess that the so-called black sheep of the family will prove to be the white sheep, it is only because we know that it is Ibsen's habit to attack respectability and criticize accepted moral values--it is not because of anything that he has told us, or hinted to us, in the play itself. In no other case does he leave our interest at such a loose end as in this, his prentice-work in modern drama. In ***The League of Youth***, an earlier play, but of an altogether lighter type, the interest is much more definitely carried forward at the end of the first act. Stensgaard has attacked Chamberlain Bratsberg in a rousing speech, and the Chamberlain has been induced to believe that the attack was directed not against himself, but against his enemy Monsen. Consequently he invites Stensgaard to his great dinner-party, and this invitation Stensgaard regards as a cowardly attempt at conciliation. We clearly see a crisis looming ahead, when this misunderstanding shall be cleared up; and we consequently look forward with lively interest to the dinner-party of the second act--which ends, as a matter of fact, in a brilliant scene of comedy.

The principle, to recapitulate, is simply this: a good first act should never end in a blank wall. There should always be a window in it, with at least a glimpse of something attractive beyond. In ***Pillars of Society*** there is a window, indeed; but it is of ground glass.

*   *   *   *   *

Notes:

[1: That great story-teller, Alexandra Dumas *pere,* those a straightforward way of carrying forward the interest at the end of the first act of ***Henri III et sa Cour.*** The Due de Guise, insulted by Saint-Megrin, beckons to his henchman and says, as the curtain falls, *"Qu'on me cherche les memes hommes qui ont assassine Dugast!"*]

[2: There are limits to the validity of this rule, as applied to minor incidents.

For example, it may sometimes be a point of art to lead the audience to expect the appearance of one person, when in fact another is about to enter. But it is exceedingly dangerous to baffle the carefully fostered anticipation of an important scene. See Chapters XVII and XXI.]

BOOK III THE MIDDLE

CHAPTER XI
TENSION AND ITS SUSPENSION

In the days of the five-act dogma, each act was supposed to have its special and pre-ordained function. Freytag assigns to the second act, as a rule, the ***Steigerung*** or heightening--the working-up, one might call it--of the interest. But the second act, in modern plays, has often to do all the work of the three middle acts under the older dispensation; wherefore the theory of their special functions has more of a historical than of a practical interest. For our present purposes, we may treat the interior section of a play as a unit, whether it consist of one, two, or three acts.

The first act may be regarded as the porch or vestibule through which we pass into the main fabric--solemn or joyous, fantastic or austere--of the actual drama. Sometimes, indeed, the vestibule is reduced to a mere threshold which can be crossed in two strides; but normally the first act, or at any rate the greater part of it, is of an introductory character. Let us conceive, then, that we have passed the vestibule, and are now to study the principles on which the body of the structure is reared.

In the first place, is the architectural metaphor a just one? Is there, or ought there to be, any analogy between a drama and a finely-proportioned building? The question has already been touched on in the opening paragraphs of Chapter VIII; but we may now look into it a little more closely.

What is the characteristic of a fine piece of architecture? Manifestly an organic relation, a carefully-planned interdependence, between all its parts. A great building is a complete and rounded whole, just like a living organism. It is informed by an inner law of harmony and proportion, and cannot be run up at haphazard, with no definite and pre-determined design. Can we say the same of a great play?

I think we can. Even in those plays which present a picture rather than an action, we ought to recognize a principle of selection, proportion, composition, which, if not absolutely organic, is at any rate the reverse of haphazard. We may not always be able to define the principle, to put it clearly in words; but if we feel that the author has been guided by no principle, that he has proceeded on mere hand-to-mouth caprice, that there is no "inner law of harmony and proportion" in his work, then we instinctively relegate it to a low place in our esteem. Hauptmann's **Weavers** certainly cannot be called a piece of dramatic architecture, like **Rosmersholm** or *Iris*; but that does not mean that it is a mere rambling series of tableaux. It is not easy to define the principle of unity in that brilliant comedy **The Madras House**; but we nevertheless feel that a principle of unity exists; or, if we do not, so much the worse for the play and its author.

There is, indeed, a large class of plays, often popular, and sometimes meritorious, in relation to which the architectural metaphor entirely breaks down. They are what may be called "running fire" plays. We have all seen children setting a number of wooden blocks on end, at equal intervals, and then tilting over the first so that it falls against the second, which in turn falls against the third, and so on, till the whole row, with a rapid clack-clack-clack, lies flat upon the table. This is called a "running fire"; and this is the structural principle of a good many plays. We feel that the playwright is, so to speak, inventing as he goes along--that the action, like the child's fantastic serpentine of blocks, might at any moment take a turn in any possible direction without falsifying its antecedents or our expectations. No part of it is necessarily involved in any other part. If the play were found too long or too short, an act might be cut out or written in without necessitating any considerable readjustments in the other acts. The play is really a series of episodes,

"Which might, odd bobs, sir! in judicious hands,   Extend from here to Mesopotamy."

The episodes may grow out of each other plausibly enough, but by no pre-ordained necessity, and with no far-reaching interdependence. We live, in such

Play-Making

plays, from moment to moment, foreseeing nothing, desiring nothing; and though this frame of mind may be mildly agreeable, it involves none of that complexity of sensation with which we contemplate a great piece of architecture, or follow the development of a finely-constructed drama. To this order belong many cape-and-sword plays and detective dramas--plays like ***The Adventure of Lady Ursula***, ***The Red Robe***, the Musketeer romances that were at one time so popular, and most plays of the ***Sherlock Holmes*** and ***Raffles*** type. But pieces of a more ambitious order have been known to follow the same formula--some of the works, for instance, of Mr. Charles McEvoy, to say nothing of Mr. Bernard Shaw.

We may take it, I think, that the architectural analogy holds good of every play which can properly be said to be "constructed." Construction means dramatic architecture, or in other words, a careful pre-arrangement of proportions and interdependencies. But to carry beyond this point the analogy between the two arts would be fantastic and unhelpful. The one exists in space, the other in time. The one seeks to beget in the spectator a state of placid, though it may be of aspiring, contemplation; the other, a state of more or less acute tension. The resemblances between music and architecture are, as is well known, much more extensive and illuminating. It might not be wholly fanciful to call music a sort of middle term between the two other arts.

A great part of the secret of dramatic architecture lies in the one word "tension." To engender, maintain, suspend, heighten and resolve a state of tension--that is the main object of the dramatist's craft.

What do we mean by tension? Clearly a stretching out, a stretching forward, of the mind. That is the characteristic mental attitude of the theatrical audience. If the mind is not stretching forward, the body will soon weary of its immobility and constraint. Attention may be called the momentary correlative of tension. When we are intent on what is to come, we are attentive to what is there and then happening. The term tension is sometimes applied, not to the mental state of the audience, but to the relation of the characters on the stage. "A scene of high tension" is primarily one in which the actors undergo a great emotional strain. But this is, after all, only a means towards heightening of the mental tension of the audience. In such a scene the mind stretches forward, no longer to something vague and distant, but to something instant and imminent.

In discussing what Freytag calls the *erregende Moment,* we might have defined it as the starting-point of the tension. A reasonable audience will, if necessary, endure a certain amount of exposition, a certain positing of character and circumstance, before the tension sets in; but when it once has set in, the playwright must on no account suffer it to relax until he deliberately resolves it just before the fall of the curtain. There are, of course, minor rhythms of tension and resolution, like the harmonic vibrations of a violin-string. That is implied when we say that a play consists of a great crisis worked out through a series of minor crises. But the main tension, once initiated, must never be relaxed. If it is, the play is over, though the author may have omitted to note the fact. Not infrequently, he begins a new play under the impression that he is finishing the old one. That is what Shakespeare did in *The Merchant of Venice.* The fifth act is an independent afterpiece, though its independence is slightly disguised by the fact that the *erregende Moment* of the new play follows close upon the end of the old one, with no interact between. A very exacting technical criticism might accuse Ibsen of verging towards the same fault in *An Enemy of the People.* There the tension is practically resolved with Dr. Stockmann's ostracism at the end of the fourth act. At that point, if it did not know that there was another act to come, an audience might go home in perfect content. The fifth act is a sort of epilogue or sequel, built out of the materials of the preceding drama, but not forming an integral part of it. With a brief exposition to set forth the antecedent circumstances, it would be quite possible to present the fifth act as an independent comedietta.

But here a point of great importance calls for our notice. Though the tension, once started, must never be relaxed: though it ought, on the contrary, to be heightened or tightened (as you choose to put it) from act to act; yet there are times when it may without disadvantage, or even with marked advantage, be temporarily suspended. In other words, the stretching-forward, without in any way slackening, may fall into the background of our consciousness, while other matters, the relevance of which may not be instantly apparent, are suffered to occupy the foreground. We know all too well, in everyday experience, that tension is not really relaxed by a temporary distraction. The dread of a coming ordeal in the witness-box or on the operating-table may be forcibly crushed down like a child's jack-in-the-box; but we are always conscious of the effort to compress it, and we know that it will spring up again the moment that effort ceases. Sir Arthur Pinero's play, *The Profligate*, was written at a time when it was the fashion to give each act a subtitle; and one of its acts is headed "The Sword of Damocles." That is, indeed, the inevitable symbol of dramatic tension: we see a sword of Damocles (even though it be only a farcical blade of painted lathe) impending over someone's head: and when once we are confident that it will fall at the fated moment, we do not mind having our attention momentarily diverted to other matters. A rather flagrant example of suspended attention is afforded by Hamlet's advice to the Players. We know that Hamlet has hung a sword of Damocles over the King's head in the shape of the mimic murder-scene; and, while it is preparing, we are quite willing to have our attention switched off to certain abstract questions of dramatic criticism. The scene might have been employed to heighten the tension. Instead of giving the Players (in true princely fashion) a lesson in the general principles of their art, Hamlet might have specially "coached" them in the "business" of the scene to be enacted, and thus doubly impressed on the audience his resolve to "tent" the King "to the quick." I am far from suggesting that this would have been desirable; but it would obviously have been possible.[1] Shakespeare, as the experience of three centuries has shown, did right in judging that the audience was already sufficiently intent on the coming ordeal, and would welcome an interlude of aesthetic theory.

There are times, moreover, when it is not only permissible to suspend the tension, but when, by so doing, a great artist can produce a peculiar and admirable effect. A sudden interruption, on the very brink of a crisis, may, as it were, whet the appetite of the audience for what is to come. We see in the Porter scene in Macbeth a suspension of this nature; but Shakespeare used it sparingly, unless, indeed, we are to consider as a deliberate point of art the retardation of movement commonly observable in the fourth acts of his tragedies. Ibsen, on the other hand, deliberately employed this device on three conspicuous occasions. The entrance of Dr. Rank in the last act of ***A Doll's House*** is a wholly unnecessary interruption to the development of the crisis between Nora and Helmer. The scene might be entirely omitted without leaving a perceptible hiatus in the action; yet who does not feel that this brief respite lends gathered impetus to the main action when it is resumed? The other instances are offered by the two apparitions of Ulric Brendel in ***Rosmersholm.*** The first occurs when Rosmer is on the very verge of his momentous confession to Kroll, the second when Rosmer and Rebecca are on the very verge of their last great resolve; and in each case we feel a distinct value (apart from the inherent quality of the Brendel scenes) in the very fact that the tension has been momentarily suspended. Such a *rallentando* effect is like the apparent pause in the rush of a river before it thunders over a precipice.

The possibility of suspending tension is of wider import than may at first sight appear. But for it, our dramas would have to be all bone and muscle, like the figures in an anatomical textbook. As it is, we are able, without relaxing tension, to shift it to various planes of consciousness, and thus find leisure to reproduce the surface aspects of life, with some of its accidents and irrelevances. For example, when the playwright has, at the end of his first act, succeeded in carrying onward the spectator's interest, and giving him something definite to look forward to, it does not at all follow that the expected scene, situation, revelation, or what not, should come at the beginning of the second act. In some cases it must do so; when, as in **The Idyll** above cited, the spectator has been carefully induced to expect some imminent conjuncture which cannot be postponed. But this can scarcely be called a typical case. More commonly, when an author has enlisted the curiosity of his audience of some definite point, he will be in no great hurry to satisfy and dissipate it. He may devote the early part of the second act to working-up the same line of interest to a higher pitch; or he may hold it in suspense while he prepares some further development of the action. The closeness with which a line of interest, once started, ought to be followed up, must depend in some measure on the nature and tone of the play. If it be a serious play, in which character and action are very closely intertwined, any pause or break in the conjoint development is to be avoided. If, on the other hand, it is a play of light and graceful dialogue, in which the action is a pretext for setting the characters in motion rather than the chief means towards their manifestation, then the playwright can afford to relax the rate of his progress, and even to wander a little from the straight line of advance. In such a play, even the old institution of the "underplot" is not inadmissible; though the underplot ought scarcely to be a "plot," but only some very slight thread of interest, involving no strain on the attention.[2] It may almost be called an established practice, on the English stage, to let the dalliance of a pair of boy-and-girl lovers relieve the main interest of a more or less serious comedy; and there is no particular harm in such a convention, if it be not out of keeping with the general character of the play. In some plays the substance--the character-action, if one may so call it--is the main, and indeed the only, thing. In others the substance, though never unimportant, is in some degree subordinate to the embroideries; and it is for the playwright to judge how far this subordination may safely be carried.

One principle, however, may be emphasized as almost universally valid, and that is that the end of an act should never leave the action just where it stood at the beginning. An audience has an instinctive sense of, and desire for, progress. It does not like to realize that things have been merely marking time. Even if it has been thoroughly entertained, from moment to moment, during the progress of an act, it does not like to feel at the end that nothing has really happened. The fall of the curtain gives time for reflection, and for the ordering of impressions which, while the action was afoot, were more or less vague and confused. It is therefore of great importance that each act should, to put it briefly, bear looking back upon--that it should appear to stand in due proportion to the general design of the play, and should not be felt to have been empty, or irrelevant, or disappointing. This is, indeed, a plain corollary from the principle of tension. Suspended it may be, sometimes with positive advantage; but it must not be suspended too long; and suspension for a whole act is equivalent to relaxation.

To sum up: when once a play has begun to move, its movement ought to proceed continuously, and with gathering momentum; or, if it stands still for a space, the stoppage ought to be deliberate and purposeful. It is fatal when the author thinks it is moving, while in fact it is only revolving on its own axis.

* * * * *

Notes:
[1: This method of heightening the tension would have been somewhat analogous to that employed by Oscar Wilde in Lady Windermere's instructions to her butler, cited on p. 115.]

[2: Dryden (Of Dramatic Poesy, p. 56, ed. Arnold, 1903) says: "Our plays, besides the main design, have underplots or by-concernments, of less considerable persons and intrigues, which are carried on with the motion of the main plot; as they say the orb of the fixed stars, and those of the planets, though they have motions of their own, are whirled about by the motion of the *primum mobile*, in which they are contained." This is an admirable description of the ideal underplot, as conceived by our forefathers; but we find that two lines of tension jar with and weaken each other.]

CHAPTER XII
PREPARATION: THE FINGER-POST

We shall find, on looking into it, that most of the technical maxims that have any validity may be traced back, directly or indirectly, to the great principle of tension. The art of construction is summed up, first, in giving the mind of an audience something to which to stretch forward, and, secondly, in not letting it feel that it has stretched forward in vain. "You will find it infinitely pleasing," says Dryden,[1] "to be led in a labyrinth of design, where you see some of your way before you, yet discern not the end till you arrive at it." Or, he might have added, "if you foresee the end, but not the means by which it is to be reached." In drama, as in all art, the "how" is often more important than the "what."

No technical maxim is more frequently cited than the remark of the younger Dumas: "The art of the theatre is the art of preparations." This is true in a larger sense than he intended; but at the same time there are limits to its truth, which we must not fail to observe.

Dumas, as we know, was an inveterate preacher, using the stage as a pulpit for the promulgation of moral and social ideas which were, in their day, considered very advanced and daring. The primary meaning of his maxim, then, was that a startling idea, or a scene wherein such an idea was implied, ought not to be sprung upon an audience wholly unprepared to accept it. For instance, in ***Monsieur Alphonse,*** a husband, on discovering that his wife has had an intrigue before their marriage, and that a little girl whom she wishes to adopt is really her daughter, instantly raises her from the ground where she lies grovelling at his feet, and says: "Creature de Dieu, toi qui as failli et te repens, releve toi, je te pardonne." This evangelical attitude on the part of Admiral de Montaiglin was in itself very surprising, and perhaps not wholly admirable, to the Parisian public of 1873; but Dumas had so "prepared" the *coup de theatre* that it passed with very slight difficulty on the first night, and with none at all at subsequent performances and revivals. How had he "prepared" it? Why, by playing, in a score of subtle ways, upon the sympathies and antipathies of the audience. For instance, as Sarcey points out, he had made M. de Montaiglin a sailor, "accustomed, during his distant voyages, to long reveries in view of the boundless ocean, whence he had acquired a mystical habit of mind.... Dumas certainly would never have placed this pardon in the mouth of a stockbroker." So far so good; but "preparation," in the sense of the word, is a device of rhetoric or of propaganda rather than of dramatic craftsmanship. It is a method of astutely undermining or outflanking prejudice. Desiring to enforce a general principle, you invent a case which is specially favourable to your argument, and insinuate it into the acceptance of the audience by every possible subtlety of adjustment. You trust, it would seem, that people who have applauded an act of pardon in an extreme case will be so much the readier to exercise that high prerogative in the less carefully "prepared" cases which present themselves in real life. This may or may not be a sound principle of persuasion; as we are not here considering the drama as an art of persuasion, we have not to decide between this and the opposite, or Shawesque, principle of shocking and startling an audience by the utmost violence of paradox. There is something to be said for both methods--for conversion by pill-and-jelly and for conversion by nitroglycerine.

Reverting, now, to the domain of pure craftsmanship, can it be said that "the art of the theatre is the art of preparation"? Yes, it is very largely the art of delicate and unobtrusive preparation, of helping an audience to divine whither it is going, while leaving it to wonder how it is to get there. On the other hand, it is also the art of avoiding laborious, artificial and obvious preparations which lead to little or nothing. A due proportion must always be observed between the preparation and the result.

To illustrate the meaning of preparation, as the word is here employed, I may perhaps be allowed to reprint a passage from a review of Mr. Israel Zangwill's play ***Children of the Ghetto***.[2]

"... To those who have not read the novel, it must seem as though the mere illustrations of Jewish life entirely overlaid and overwhelmed the action. It is not so in reality. One who knows the story beforehand can often see that it is progressing even in scenes which seem purely episodic and unconnected either with each other or with the general scheme. But Mr. Zangwill has omitted to provide finger-posts, if I may so express it, to show those who do not know the story beforehand whither he is leading them. He has neglected the great art of forecasting, of keeping anticipation on the alert, which is half the secret of dramatic construction. To forecast, without discounting, your effects--that is all the Law and the Prophets. In the first act of ***Children of the Ghetto***, for instance, we see the marriage in jest of Hannah to Sam Levine, followed by the instant divorce with all its curious ceremonies. This is amusing so far as it goes; but when the divorce is completed, the whole thing seems to be over and done with. We have seen some people, in whom as yet we take no particular interest, enmeshed in a difficulty arising from a strange and primitive formalism in the interpretation of law; and we have seen the meshes cut to the satisfaction of all parties, and the incident to all appearance closed. There is no finger-post to direct our anticipation on the way it should go; and those who have not read the book cannot possibly guess that this mock marriage, instantly and ceremoniously dissolved, can have any ulterior effect upon the fortunes of any one concerned. Thus, the whole scene, however curious in itself, seems motiveless and resultless. How the requisite finger-post was to be provided I cannot tell. That is not my business; but a skilful dramatist would have made it his. Then, in the second act, amid illustrations of social life in the Ghetto, we have the meeting of Hannah with David Brandon, a prettily-written scene of love-at-first-sight. But, so far as any one can see, there is every prospect that the course of true love will run absolutely smooth. Again we lack a finger-post to direct our interest forward; nor do we see anything that seems to bring this act into vital relation with its predecessor. Those who have read the book know that David Brandon is a 'Cohen,' a priest, a descendant of Aaron, and that a priest may not marry a divorced woman. Knowing this, we have a sense of irony, of impending disaster, which renders the love-scene of the second act dramatic. But to those, and they must always be a majority in any given audience, who do not know this, the scene has no more dramatic quality than lies in its actual substance, which, although pretty enough, is entirely commonplace. Not till the middle of the third act (out of four) is the obstacle revealed, and we see that the mighty maze was not without a plan. Here, then, the drama begins, after two acts and a half of preparation, during which we were vouchsafed no inkling of what was preparing. It is capital drama when we come to it, really human, really tragic. The arbitrary prohibitions of the Mosaic law have no religious or moral force either for David or for Hannah. They feel it to be their right, almost their duty, to cast off their shackles. In any community, save that of strict Judaism, they are perfectly free to marry. But in thus flouting the letter of the law, Hannah well knows that she will break her father's heart. Even as she struggles to shake them off, the traditions of her race take firmer hold on her; and in the highly dramatic last act (a not unskilful adaptation to the stage of the crucial scene of the book) she bows her neck beneath the yoke, and renounces love that the Law may be fulfilled."

To state the matter in other terms, we are conscious of no tension in the earlier acts of this play, because we have not been permitted to see the sword of Damocles hanging over the heads of Hannah and David Brandon. For lack of preparation, of pointing-forward, we feel none of that god-like superiority to the people of the mimic world which we have recognized as the characteristic privilege of the spectator. We know no more than they do of the implications of their acts, and the network of embarrassments in which they are involving themselves. Indeed, we know less than they do: for Hannah, as a well brought-up Jewess, is no doubt vaguely aware of the disabilities attaching to a divorced woman. A gentile audience, on the other hand, cannot possibly foresee how--

"Some consequence yet hanging in the stars Shall bitterly begin his fearful date With this night's revels."

and, lacking that foreknowledge, it misses the specifically dramatic effect of the scenes. The author invites it to play at blind-man's-buff with the characters, instead of unsealing its eyes and enabling it to watch the game from its Olympian coign of vantage.

Let the dramatist, then, never neglect to place the requisite finger-posts on the road he would have us follow. It is not, of course, necessary that we should be conscious of all the implications of any given scene or incident, but we must know enough of them not only to create the requisite tension, but to direct it towards the right quarter of the compass. Retrospective elucidations are valueless and sometimes irritating. It is in nowise to the author's interest that we should say, "Ah, if we had only known this, or foreseen that, in time, the effect of such-and-such a scene would have been entirely different!" We have no use for finger-posts that point backwards.[3]

In the works of Sir Arthur Pinero I recall two cases in which the lack of a finger-post impairs the desired effect: slightly, in the one instance, in the other, very considerably. The third act of that delightful comedy *The Princess and the Butterfly* contains no sufficient indication of Fay Zuliani's jealousy of the friendship between Sir George Lamorant and the Princess Pannonia. We are rather at a loss to account for the coldness of her attitude to the Princess, and her perverse naughtiness in going off to the Opera Ball. This renders the end of the act practically ineffective. We so little foresee what is to come of Fay's midnight escapade, that we take no particular interest in it, and are rather disconcerted by the care with which it is led up to, and the prominence assigned to it. This, however, is a trifling fault. Far different is the case in the last act of *The Benefit of the Doubt*, which goes near to ruining what is otherwise a very fine play. The defect, indeed, is not purely technical: on looking into it we find that the author is not in fact working towards an ending which can be called either inevitable or conspicuously desirable. His failure to point forward is no doubt partly due to his having nothing very satisfactory to point forward to. But it is only in retrospect that this becomes apparent. What we feel while the act is in progress is simply the lack of any finger-post to afford us an inkling of the end towards which we are proceeding. Through scene after scene we appear to be making no progress, but going round and round in a depressing circle. The tension, in a word, is fatally relaxed. It may perhaps be suggested as a maxim that when an author finds a difficulty in placing the requisite finger-posts, as he nears the end of his play, he will do well to suspect that the end he has in view is defective, and to try if he cannot amend it.

In the ancient, and in the modern romantic, drama, oracles, portents, prophecies, horoscopes and such-like intromissions of the supernatural afforded a very convenient aid to the placing of the requisite finger-posts--"foreshadowing without forestalling." It has often been said that *Macbeth* approaches the nearest of all Shakespeare's tragedies to the antique model: and in nothing is the resemblance clearer than in the employment of the Witches to point their skinny fingers into the fated future. In **Romeo and Juliet**, inward foreboding takes the place of outward prophecy. I have quoted above Romeo's prevision of "Some consequence yet hanging in the stars"; and beside it may be placed Juliet's--

"I have no joy of this contract to-night; It is too rash, too unadvised, too sudden, Too like the lightning which doth cease to be Ere one can say it lightens."

In **Othello,** on the other hand, the most modern of all his plays, Shakespeare had recourse neither to outward boding, nor to inward foreboding, but planted a plain finger-post in the soil of human nature, when he made Brabantio say--

"Look to her, Moor, if thou hast eyes to see: She has deceived her father, and may thee."

Mr. Stephen Phillips, in the first act of **Paolo and Francesca,** outdoes all his predecessors, ancient or modern, in his daring use of sibylline prophecy. He makes Giovanni's blind foster-mother, Angela, foretell the tragedy in almost every detail, save that, in her vision, she cannot see the face of Francesca's lover. Mr. Phillips, I take it, is here reinforcing ancient tradition by a reference to modern "psychical research." He trusts to our conceiving such clairvoyance to be not wholly impossible, and giving it what may be called provisional credence. Whether the device be artistic or not we need not here consider. I merely point to it as a conspicuous example of the use of the finger-post.[4]

It need scarcely be said that a misleading finger-post is carefully to be avoided, except in the rare cases where it may be advisable to beget a momentary misapprehension on the part of the audience, which shall be almost instantly corrected in some pleasant or otherwise effective fashion.[5] It is naturally difficult to think of striking instances of the misleading finger-posts; for plays which contain such a blunder are not apt to survive, even in the memory. A small example occurs in a clever play named *A Modern Aspasia* by Mr. Hamilton Fyfe. Edward Meredith has two households: a London house over which his lawful wife, Muriel, presides; and a country cottage where dwells his mistress, Margaret, with her two children. One day Muriel's automobile breaks down near Margaret's cottage, and, while the tyre is being repaired, Margaret gives her visitor tea, neither of them knowing the other. Throughout the scene we are naturally wondering whether a revelation is to occur; and when, towards the close, Muriel goes to Margaret's room, "to put her hat straight," we have no longer any doubt on the subject. It is practically inevitable that she should find in the room her husband's photograph, or some object which she should instantly recognize as his, and should return to the stage in full possession of the secret. This is so probable that nothing but a miracle can prevent it: we mentally give the author credit for bringing about his revelation in a very simple and natural way; and we are proportionately disappointed when we find that the miracle has occurred, and that Muriel returns to the sitting-room no wiser than she left it. Very possibly the general economy of the play demanded that the revelation should not take place at this juncture. That question does not here concern us. The point is that, having determined to reserve the revelation for his next act, the author ought not, by sending Muriel into Margaret's bedroom, to have awakened in us a confident anticipation of its occurring there and then. A romantic play by Mr. J. B. Fagan, entitled *Under Which King?* offers another small instance of the same nature. The date is 1746; certain despatches of vast importance have to be carried by a Hanoverian officer from Moidart to Fort William. The Jacobites arrange to drug the officer; and, to make assurance doubly sure, in case the drug should fail to act, they post a Highland marksman in a narrow glen to pick him off as he passes. The drug does act; but his lady-love, to save his military honour, assumes male attire and rides off with the despatches. We hear her horse's hoofs go clattering down the road; and then, as the curtain falls, we hear a shot ring out into the night. This shot is a misleading finger-post. Nothing comes of it: we find in the next act that the marksman has missed! But marksmen, under such circumstances, have no business to miss. It is a breach of the dramatic proprieties. We feel that the author has been trifling with us in inflicting on us this purely mechanical and momentary "scare." The case would be different if the young lady knew that the marksman was lying in ambush, and determined to run the gantlet. In that case the incident would be a trait of character; but, unless my memory deceives me, that is not the case. On the stage, every bullet should have its billet--not necessarily in the person aimed at, but in the emotions or anticipations of the audience. This bullet may, indeed, give us a momentary thrill of alarm; but it is dearly bought at the expense of subsequent disillusionment.

We have now to consider the subject of over-preparation, too obtrusive preparation, mountainous preparation leading only to a mouse-like effect. This is the characteristic error of the so-called "well-made play," the play of elaborate and ingenious intrigue. The trouble with the well-made play is that it is almost always, and of necessity, ill-made. Very rarely does the playwright succeed in weaving a web which is at once intricate, consistent, and clear. In nineteen cases out of twenty there are glaring flaws that have to be overlooked; or else the pattern is so involved that the mind's eye cannot follow it, and becomes bewildered and fatigued. A classical example of both faults may be found in Congreve's so-called comedy **The Double-Dealer**. This is, in fact, a powerful drama, somewhat in the Sardou manner; but Congreve had none of Sardou's deftness in manipulating an intrigue. Maskwell is not only a double-dealer, but a triple--or quadruple-dealer; so that the brain soon grows dizzy in the vortex of his villainies. The play, it may be noted, was a failure.

There is a quite legitimate pleasure to be found, no doubt, in a complex intrigue which is also perspicuous. Plays such as Alexandre Dumas's **Mademoiselle de Belle-Isle**, or the pseudo-historical dramas of Scribe-Adrienne Lecouvreur, Bertrand et Raton, Un Verre d'Eau, Les Trois Maupin, etc.--are amusing toys, like those social or military tableaux, the figures of which you can set in motion by dropping a penny in the slot. But the trick of this sort of "preparation" has long been found out, and even unsophisticated audiences are scarcely to be thrilled by it. We may accept it as a sound principle, based on common sense and justified by experience, that an audience should never be tempted to exclaim, "What a marvellously clever fellow is this playwright! How infinitely cleverer than the dramatist who constructs the tragi-comedy of life."

This is what we inevitably exclaim as we watch Victorien Sardou, in whom French ingenuity culminated and caricatured itself, laying the foundations of one of his labyrinthine intrigues. The absurdities of "preparation" in this sense could scarcely be better satirized than in the following page from Francisque Sarcey's criticism of **Nos Intimes** (known in English as **Peril**)--a page which is intended, not as satire, but as eulogy--

> At the sixth performance, I met, during the first interact, a man of infinite taste who ... complained of the lengthiness of this first act: "What a lot of details," he said, "which serve no purpose, and had better have been omitted! What is the use of that long story about the cactus with a flower that is unique in all the world? Why trouble us with that dahlia-root, which M. Caussade's neighbour has thrown over the garden wall? Was it necessary to inflict on us all that talk about

the fox that plays havoc in the garden? What have we to do with that mischievous beast? And that Tolozan, with his endless digressions! What do we care about his ideas on love, on metempsychosis, on friendship, etc.? All this stuff only retards the action."

"On the contrary," I replied, "all this is just what is going to interest you. You are impatient of these details, because you are looking out for the scenes of passion which have been promised you. But reflect that, without these preparations, the scenes of passion would not touch you. That cactus-flower will play its part, you may be sure; that dahlia-root is not there for nothing; that fox to which you object, and of which you will hear more talk during two more acts, will bring about the solution of one of the most entertaining situations in all drama."

M. Sarcey does not tell us what his interlocutor replied; but he might have said, like the hero of *Le Reveillon*: "Are you sure there is no mistake? Are you defending Sardou, or attacking him?"

For another example of ultra-complex preparation let me turn to a play by Mr. Sydney Grundy, entitled *The Degenerates*. Mr. Grundy, though an adept of the Scribe school, has done so much strong and original work that I apologize for exhuming a play in which he almost burlesqued his own method; but for that very reason it is difficult to find a more convincing or more deterrent example of misdirected ingenuity. The details of the plot need not be recited. It is sufficient to say that the curtain has not been raised ten minutes before our attention has been drawn to the fact that a certain Lady Saumarez has her monogram on everything she wears, even to her gloves: whence we at once foresee that she is destined to get into a compromising situation, to escape from it, but to leave a glove behind her. In due time the compromising situation arrives, and we find that it not only requires a room with three doors,[6] but that a locksmith has to be specially called in to provide two of these doors with peculiar locks, so that, when once shut, they cannot be opened from inside except with a key! What interest can we take in a situation turning on such contrivances? Sane technic laughs at locksmiths. And after all this preparation, the situation proves to be a familiar trick of theatrical thimble-rigging: you lift the thimble, and instead of Pea A, behold Pea B!--instead of Lady Saumarez it is Mrs. Trevelyan who is concealed in Isidore de Lorano's bedroom. Sir William Saumarez must be an exceedingly simple-minded person to accept the substitution, and exceedingly unfamiliar with the French drama of the 'seventies and 'eighties. If he had his wits about him he would say: "I know this dodge: it comes from Sardou. Lady Saumarez has just slipped out by that door, up R., and if I look about I shall certainly find her fan, or her glove, or her handkerchief somewhere on the premises." The author may object that such criticism would end in paralysing the playwright, and that, if men always profited by the lessons of the stage, the world would long ago have become so wise that there would be no more room in it for drama, which lives on human folly. "You will tell me next," he may say, "that I must not make groundless jealousy the theme of a play, because every one who has seen Othello would at once detect the machinations of an Iago!" The retort is logically specious, but it mistakes the point. It would certainly be rash to put any limit to human gullibility, or to deny that Sir William Saumarez, in the given situation, might conceivably be hoodwinked. The question is not one of psychology but of theatrical expediency: and the point is that when a situation is at once highly improbable in real life and exceedingly familiar on the stage, we cannot help mentally caricaturing it as it proceeds, and are thus prevented from lending it the provisional credence on which interest and emotion depend.

An instructive contrast to **The Degenerates** may be found in a nearly contemporary play, **Mrs. Dane's Defence**, by Mr. Henry Arthur Jones. The first three acts of this play may be cited as an excellent example of dexterous preparation and development. Our interest in the sequence of events is aroused, sustained, and worked up to a high tension with consummate skill. There is no feverish overcrowding of incident, as is so often the case in the great French story-plays--Adrienne Lecouvreur, for example, or **Fedora**. The action moves onwards, unhasting, unresting, and the finger-posts are placed just where they are wanted.

The observance of a due proportion between preparation and result is a matter of great moment. Even when the result achieved is in itself very remarkable, it may be dearly purchased by a too long and too elaborate process of preparation. A famous play which is justly chargeable with this fault is **The Gay Lord Quex**. The third act is certainly one of the most breathlessly absorbing scenes in modern drama; but by what long, and serpentine, and gritty paths do we not approach it! The elaborate series of trifling incidents by means of which Sophy Fullgarney is first brought from New Bond Street to Fauncey Court, and then substituted for the

Duchess's maid, is at no point actually improbable; and yet we feel that a vast effort has been made to attain an end which, owing to the very length of the sequence of chances, at last assumes an air of improbability. There is little doubt that the substructure of the great scene might have been very much simpler. I imagine that Sir Arthur Pinero was betrayed into complexity and over-elaboration by his desire to use, as a background for his action, a study of that "curious phase of modern life," the manicurist's parlour. To those who find this study interesting, the disproportion between preliminaries and result may be less apparent. It certainly did not interfere with the success of the play in its novelty; but it may very probably curtail its lease of life. What should we know of *The School for Scandal* to-day, if it consisted of nothing but the Screen Scene and two laborious acts of preparation?

A too obvious preparation is very apt to defeat its end by begetting a perversely quizzical frame of mind in the audience. The desired effect is discounted, like a conjuring trick in which the mechanism is too transparent. Let me recall a trivial but instructive instance of this error. The occasion was the first performance of ***Pillars of Society*** at the Gaiety Theatre, London--the first Ibsen performance ever given in England. At the end of the third act, Krap, Consul Bernick's clerk, knocks at the door of his master's office and says, "It is blowing up to a stiff gale. Is the ***Indian Girl*** to sail in spite of it?" Whereupon Bernick, though he knows that the ***Indian Girl*** is hopelessly unseaworthy, replies, "The ***Indian Girl*** is to sail in spite of it." It had occurred to someone that the effect of this incident would be heightened if Krap, before knocking at the Consul's door, were to consult the barometer, and show by his demeanour that it was falling rapidly. A barometer had accordingly been hung, up stage, near the veranda entrance; and, as the scenic apparatus of a Gaiety matinee was in those days always of the scantiest, it was practically the one decoration of a room otherwise bare almost to indecency. It had stared the audience full in the face through three long acts; and when, at the end of the third, Krap went up to it and tapped it, a sigh of relief ran through the house, as much as to say, "At last! so ***that*** was what it was for!"--to the no small detriment of the situation. Here the fault lay in the obtrusiveness of the preparation. Had the barometer passed practically unnoticed among the other details of a well-furnished hall, it would at any rate have been innocent, and perhaps helpful. As it was, it seemed to challenge the curiosity of the audience, saying, "I am evidently here with some intention; guess, now, what the intention can be!" The producer had failed in the art which conceals art.

Another little trait from a play of those far-past days illustrates the same point. It was a drawing-room drama of the Scribe school. Near the beginning of an act, some one spilt a bottle of red ink, and mopped it up with his (or her) handkerchief, leaving the handkerchief on the escritoire. The act proceeded from scene to scene, and the handkerchief remained unnoticed; but every one in the audience who knew the rules of the game, kept his eye on the escritoire, and was certain that that ink had not been spilt for nothing. In due course a situation of great intensity was reached, wherein the villain produced a pistol and fired at the heroine, who fainted. As a matter of fact he had missed her; but her quick-witted friend seized the gory handkerchief, and, waving it in the air, persuaded the villain that the shot had taken deadly effect, and that he must flee for his life. Even in those days, such an unblushing piece of trickery was found more comic than impressive. It was a case of preparation "giving itself away."

A somewhat later play, ***The Mummy and the Humming Bird***, by Mr. Isaac Henderson, contains a good example of over-elaborate preparation. The Earl of Lumley, lost in his chemical studies with a more than Newtonian absorption, suffers his young wife to form a sentimental friendship with a scoundrel of an Italian novelist, Signor D'Orelli. Remaining at home one evening, when Lady Lumley and a party of friends, including D'Orelli, have gone off to dine at a restaurant, the Earl chances to look out of the window, and observes an organ-grinder making doleful music in the snow. His heart is touched, and he invites the music-monger to join him in his study and share his informal dinner. The conversation between them is carried on by means of signs, for the organ-grinder knows no English, and the Earl is painfully and improbably ignorant of Italian. He does not even know that Roma means Rome, and Londra, London. This ignorance, however, is part of the author's ingenuity. It leads to the establishment of a sort of object-speech, by aid of which the Earl learns that his guest has come to England to prosecute a vendetta against the man who ruined his happy Sicilian home. I need scarcely say that this villain is none other than D'Orelli; and when at last he and the Countess elope to Paris, the object-speech enables Giuseppe to convey to the Earl, by aid of a brandy-bottle, a siphon, a broken plate, and half-a-crown, not only the place of their destination, but the very hotel to which they are going. This is a fair example of that ingenuity for ingenuity's sake which was once thought the very essence of the playwright's craft, but has long ago lost all attraction for intelligent audiences.

We may take it as a rule that any scene which requires an obviously purposeful scenic arrangement is thereby discounted. It may be strong enough to live down the disadvantage; but a disadvantage it is none the less. In a play of Mr. Carton's, *The Home Secretary*, a paper of great importance was known to be contained in an official despatch-box. When the curtain rose on the last act, it revealed this despatch-box on a table right opposite a French window, while at the other side of the room a high-backed arm-chair discreetly averted its face. Every one could see at a glance that the romantic Anarchist was going to sneak in at the window and attempt to abstract the despatch-box, while the heroine was to lie perdue in the high-backed chair; and when, at the fated moment, all this punctually occurred, one could scarcely repress an "Ah!" of sarcastic satisfaction. Similarly, in an able play named Mr. and Mrs. Daventry, Mr. Frank Harris had conceived a situation which required that the scene should be specially built for eavesdropping.[7] As soon as the curtain rose, and revealed a screen drawn halfway down the stage, with a sofa ensconced behind it, we knew what to expect. Of course Mrs. Daventry was to lie on the sofa and overhear a duologue between her husband and his mistress: the only puzzle was to understand why the guilty pair should neglect the precaution of looking behind the screen. As a matter of fact, Mrs. Daventry, before she lay down, switched off the lights, and Daventry and Lady Langham, finding the room dark, assumed it to be empty. With astounding foolhardiness, considering that the house was full of guests, and this a much frequented public room, Daventry proceeded to lock the door, and continue his conversation with Lady Langham in the firelight. Thus, when the lady's husband came knocking at the door, Mrs. Daventry was able to rescue the guilty pair from an apparently hopeless predicament, by calmly switching on the lights and opening the door to Sir John Langham. The situation was undoubtedly a "strong" one; but the tendency of modern technic is to hold "strength" too dearly purchased at such reckless expense of preparation.

There are, then, very clear limits to the validity of the Dumas maxim that "The art of the theatre is the art of preparations." Certain it is that over-preparation is the most fatal of errors. The clumsiest thing a dramatist can possibly do is to lay a long and elaborate train for the ignition of a squib. We take pleasure in an event which has been "prepared" in the sense that we have been led to desire it, and have wondered how it was to be brought about. But we scoff at an occurrence which nothing but our knowledge of the tricks of the stage could possibly lead us to expect, yet which, knowing these tricks, we have foreseen from afar, and resented in advance.

* * * * *

Notes:

[1: *Of Dramatic Poesy,* ed. Arnold, 1903, p. 60.]

[2: *The World*, December 20, 1899.]

[3: At the end of the first act of ***Lady Inger of Ostraat***, Ibsen evidently intends to produce a startling effect through the sudden appearance of Olaf Skaktavl in Lady Inger's hall. But as he has totally omitted to tell us who the strange man is, the incident has no meaning for us. In 1855 Ibsen had all his technical lessons yet to learn.]

[4: The fact that Mr. Phillips should have deemed such a foreshadowing necessary shows how instinctively a dramatist feels that the logic of his art requires him to assume that his audience is ignorant of his fable. In reality, very few members of the first-night audience, or of any other, can have depended on old Angela's vaticination for the requisite foresight of events. But this does not prove Angela to be artistically superfluous.]

[5: See pp. 118, 240.]

[6: There is no special harm in this: the question of exits and entrances and their mechanism is discussed in Chapter XXIII.]

[7: This might be said of the scene of the second act of ***The Benefit of the Doubt***; but here the actual stage-topography is natural enough. The author, however, is rather over-anxious to emphasize the acoustic relations of the two rooms.]

CHAPTER XIII
THE OBLIGATORY SCENE

I do not know whether it was Francisque Sarcey who invented the phrase *scene a faire*; but it certainly owes its currency to that valiant champion of the theatrical theatre, if I may so express it. Note that in this term I intend no disrespect. My conception of the theatrical theatre may not be exactly the same as M. Sarcey's; but at all events I share his abhorrence of the untheatrical theatre.

What is the *scene a faire*? Sarcey has used the phrase so often, and in so many contexts, that it is impossible to tie him down to any strict definition. Instead of trying to do so, I will give a typical example of the way in which he usually employs the term.

In *Les Fourchambault*, by Emile Augier, the first act introduces us to the household of a merchant, of Havre, who has married a wealthy, but extravagant woman, and has a son and daughter who are being gradually corrupted by their mother's worldliness. We learn that Fourchambault, senior, has, in his youth, betrayed a young woman who was a governess in his family. He wanted to marry her, but his relations maligned her character, and he cast her off; nor does he know what has become of her and her child. In the second act we pass to the house of an energetic and successful young shipowner named Bernard, who lives alone with his mother. Bernard, as we divine, is secretly devoted to a young lady named Marie Letellier, a guest in the Fourchambault house, to whom young Leopold Fourchambault is paying undesirable attentions. One day Bernard casually mentions to his mother that the house of Fourchambault is on the verge of bankruptcy; nothing less than a quarter of a million francs will enable it to tide over the crisis. Mme. Bernard, to her son's astonishment, begs him to lend the tottering firm the sum required. He objects that, unless the business is better managed, the loan will only postpone the inevitable disaster. "Well, then, my son," she replied, "you must go into partnership with M. Fourchambault." "I! with that imbecile!" he exclaims. "My son," she says gravely, and emphatically, "you must--it is your duty--I demand it of you!" "Ah!" cries Bernard. "I understand--he is my father!"

After ecstatically lauding this situation and the scenes which have led up to it, M. Sarcey continues--

When the curtain falls upon the words "He is my father," I at once see two ***scenes a faire***, and I know that they will be ***faites***: the scene between the son and the father whom he is to save, the scene between Bernard and his half-brother Leopold, who are in love with the same woman, the one dishonourably and the other secretly and nobly. What will they say to each other? I have no idea. But it is precisely this ***expectation mingled with uncertainly*** that is one of the charms of the theatre. I say to myself, "Ah, they will have an encounter! What will come of it?" And that this is the state of mind of the whole audience is proved by the fact that when the two characters of the ***scenes a faire*** stand face to face, a thrill of anticipation runs round the whole theatre.

This, then, is the obligatory scene as Sarcey generally understands it--a scene which, for one reason or another, an audience expects and ardently desires. I have italicized the phrase "expectation mingled with uncertainty" because it expresses in other terms the idea which I have sought to convey in the formula "foreshadowing without forestalling." But before we can judge of the merits of M. Sarcey's theory, we must look into it a little more closely. I shall try, then, to state it in my own words, in what I believe to be its most rational and defensible form.

An obligatory scene is one which the audience (more or less clearly and consciously) foresees and desires, and the absence of which it may with reason resent. On a rough analysis, it will appear, I think, that there are five ways in which a scene may become, in this sense, obligatory:

(1) It may be necessitated by the inherent logic of the theme.

(2) It may be demanded by the manifest exigencies of specifically dramatic effect.

(3) The author himself may have rendered it obligatory by seeming unmistakably to lead up to it.

(4) It may be required in order to justify some modification of character or alteration of will, too important to be taken for granted.

(5) It may be imposed by history or legend.

These five classes of obligatory scenes may be docketed, respectively, as the Logical, the Dramatic, the Structural, the Psychological, and the Historic. M. Sarcey generally employed the term in one of the first three senses, without clearly distinguishing between them. It is, indeed, not always easy to determine whether the compulsion (assuming it to exist at all) lies in the very essence of the theme or situation, or only in the author's manipulation of it.

Was Sarcey right in assuming such a compulsion to be a constant and dominant factor in the playwright's craft? I think we shall see reason to believe him right in holding that it frequently arises, but wrong if he went the length of maintaining that there can be no good play without a definite **scene a faire**--as eighteenth-century landscape painters are said to have held that no one could be a master of his art till he knew where to place "the brown tree." I remember no passage in which Sarcey explicitly lays down so hard and fast a rule, but several in which he seems to take it for granted.[1]

It may be asked whether--and if so, why--the theory of the obligatory scene holds good for the dramatist and not for the novelist? Perhaps it has more application to the novel than is commonly supposed; but in so far as it applies peculiarly to the drama, the reason is pretty clear. It lies in the strict concentration imposed on the dramatist, and the high mental tension which is, or ought to be, characteristic of the theatrical audience. The leisurely and comparatively passive novel-reader may never miss a scene which an audience, with its instincts of logic and of economy keenly alert, may feel to be inevitable. The dramatist is bound to extract from his material the last particle of that particular order of effect which the stage, and the stage alone, can give us. If he fails to do so, we feel that there has been no adequate justification for setting in motion all the complex mechanism of the theatre. His play is like a badly-designed engine in which a large part of the potential energy is dissipated to no purpose. The novelist, with a far wider range of effects at his command, and employing no special mechanism to bring them home to us, is much more free to select and to reject. He is exempt from the law of rigid economy to which the dramatist must submit. Far from being bound to do things in the most dramatic way, he often does wisely in rejecting that course, as unsuited to his medium. Fundamentally, no doubt, the same principle applies to both arts, but with a wholly different stringency in the case of the drama. "Advisable" in the novelist's vocabulary is translated by "imperative" in the dramatist's. The one is playing a long-drawn game, in which the loss of a trick or two need not prove fatal; the other has staked his all on a single rubber.

* * * * *

Obligatory scenes of the first type--those necessitated by the inherent logic of the theme--can naturally arise only in plays to which a definite theme can be assigned. If we say that woman's claim to possess a soul of her own, even in marriage, is the theme of *A Doll's House*, then evidently the last great balancing of accounts between Nora and Helmer is an obligatory scene. It would have been quite possible for Ibsen to have completed the play without any such scene: he might, for instance, have let Nora fulfil her intention of drowning herself; but in that case his play would have been merely a tragic anecdote with the point omitted. We should have felt vague intimations of a general idea hovering in the air, but it would have remained undefined and undeveloped. As we review, however, the series of Ibsen's plays, and notice how difficult it is to point to any individual scene and say, "This was clearly the *scene à faire*," we feel that, though the phrase may express a useful idea in a conveniently brief form, there is no possibility of making the presence or absence of a *scene à faire* a general test of dramatic merit. In ***The Wild Duck***, who would not say that, theoretically, the scene in which Gregers opens Hialmar's eyes to the true history of his marriage was obligatory in the highest degree? Yet Ibsen, as a matter of fact, does not present it to us: he sends the two men off for "a long walk" together: and who does not feel that this is a stroke of consummate art? In ***Rosmersholm***, as we know, he has been accused of neglecting, not merely the scene, but the play, *a faire*; but who will now maintain that accusation? In ***John Gabriel Borhman***, if we define the theme as the clash of two devouring egoisms, Ibsen has, in the third act, given us the obligatory scene; but he has done it, unfortunately, with an enfeebled hand; whereas the first and second acts, though largely expository, and even (in the Foldal scene) episodic, rank with his greatest achievements.

For abundant examples of scenes rendered obligatory by the logic of the theme, we have only to turn to the works of those remorseless dialecticians, MM. Hervieu and Brieux. In such a play as **La Course du Flambeau**, there is scarcely a scene that may not be called an obligatory deduction from the thesis duly enunciated, with no small parade of erudition, in the first ten minutes of the play. It is that, in handing on the ***vital lampada***, as Plato and "le bon poete Lucrece" express it, the love of the parent for the child becomes a devouring mania, to which everything else is sacrificed, while the love of the child for the parent is a tame and essentially selfish emotion, absolutely powerless when it comes into competition with the passions which are concerned with the transmission of the vital flame. This theorem having been stated, what is the first obligatory scene? Evidently one in which a mother shall refuse a second marriage, with a man whom she loves, because it would injure the prospects and wound the feelings of her adored daughter. Then, when the adored daughter herself marries, the mother must make every possible sacrifice for her, and the daughter must accept them all with indifference, as mere matters of course. But what is the final, triumphant proof of the theorem? Why, of course, the mother must kill her mother to save the daughter's life! And this ultra-obligatory scene M. Hervieu duly serves up to us. Marie-Jeanne (the daughter) is ordered to the Engadine; Sabine (the mother) is warned that Madame Fontenais (the grandmother) must not go to that altitude on pain of death; but, by a series of violently artificial devices, things are so arranged that Marie-Jeanne cannot go unless Madame Fontenais goes too; and Sabine, rather than endanger her daughter's recovery, does not hesitate to let her mother set forth, unwittingly, to her doom. In the last scene of all, Marie-Jeanne light-heartedly prepares to leave her mother and go off with her husband to the ends of the earth; Sabine learns that the man she loved and rejected for Marie-Jeanne's sake is for ever lost to her; and, to complete the demonstration, Madame Fontenais falls dead at her feet. These scenes are unmistakably ***scenes a faire***, dictated by the logic of the theme; but they belong to a conception of art in which the free rhythms of life are ruthlessly sacrificed to the needs of a demonstration. Obligatory scenes of this order are mere diagrams drawn with ruler and compass--the obligatory illustrations of an extravagantly over-systematic lecture.

M. Brieux in some of his plays (not in all) is no less logic-ridden than M. Hervieu. Take, for instance, ***Les Trois Filles de M. Dupont***: every character is a term in a syllogism, every scene is dictated by an imperious craving for symmetry. The main theorem may be stated in some such terms as these: "The French marriage system is immoral and abominable; yet the married woman is, on the whole, less pitiable than her unmarried sisters." In order to prove this thesis in due form, we begin at the beginning, and show how the marriage of Antonin Mairaut and Julie Dupont is brought about by the dishonest cupidity of the parents on both sides. The Duponts flatter themselves that they have cheated the Mairauts, the Mairauts that they have swindled the Duponts; while Antonin deliberately simulates artistic tastes to deceive Julie, and Julie as deliberately makes a show of business capacity in order to take in Antonin. Every scene between father and daughter is balanced by a corresponding scene between mother and son. Every touch of hypocrisy on the one side is scrupulously set off against a trait of dishonesty on the other. Julie's passion for children is emphasized, Antonin's aversion from them is underlined. But lest he should be accused of seeing everything in black, M. Brieux will not make the parents altogether detestable. Still holding the balance true, he lets M. Mairaut on the one side, and Madame Dupont on the other, develop amiable impulses, and protest, at a given moment, against the infamies committed and countenanced by their respective spouses. And in the second and third acts, the edifice of deception symmetrically built up in the first act is no less symmetrically demolished. The parents expose and denounce each other's villainies; Julie and Antonin, in a great scene of conjugal recrimination, lay bare the hypocrisies of allurement that have brought them together. Julie then determines to escape from the loathsome prison-house of her marriage; and this brings us to the second part of the theorem. The title shows that Julie has two sisters; but hitherto they have remained in the background. Why do they exist at all? Why has Providence blessed M. Dupont with "three fair daughters and no more"? Because Providence foresaw exactly the number M. Brieux would require for his demonstration. Are there not three courses open to a penniless woman in our social system--marriage, wage-earning industry, and wage-earning profligacy? Well, M. Dupont must have one daughter to represent each of these contingencies. Julie has illustrated the miseries of marriage; Caroline and Angele shall illustrate respectively the still greater miseries of unmarried virtue and unmarried vice. When Julie declares her intention of breaking away from the house of bondage, her sisters rise up symmetrically, one on either hand, and implore her rather to bear the ills she has than to fly to others that she knows not of. "Symmetry of symmetries, all is symmetry" in the poetics of M. Brieux. But life does not fall into such obvious patterns. The obligatory scene which is imposed upon us, not by the logic of life, but by the logic of demonstration, is not a *scene a faire*, but a *scene a fuir*.

Mr. Bernard Shaw, in some sense the Brieux of the English theatre, is not a man to be dominated by logic, or by anything else under the sun. He has, however, given us one or two excellent examples of the obligatory scene in the true and really artistic sense of the term. The scene of Candida's choice between Eugene and Morell crowns the edifice of ***Candida*** as nothing else could. Given the characters and their respective attitudes towards life, this sententious thrashing-out of the situation was inevitable. So, too, in ***Mrs. Warren's Profession***, the great scene of the second act between Vivie and her mother is a superb example of a scene imposed by the logic of the theme. On the other hand, in Mr. Henry Arthur Jones's finely conceived, though unequal, play, ***Michael and his Lost Angel***, we miss what was surely an obligatory scene. The play is in fact a contest between the paganism of Audrie Lesden and the ascetic, sacerdotal idealism of Michael Feversham. In the second act, paganism snatches a momentary victory; and we confidently expect, in the third act, a set and strenuous effort on Audrie's part to break down in theory the ascetic ideal which has collapsed in practice. It is probable enough that she might not succeed in dragging her lover forth from what she regards as the prison-house of a superstition; but the logic of the theme absolutely demands that she should make the attempt. Mr. Jones has preferred to go astray after some comparatively irrelevant and commonplace matter, and has thus left his play incomplete. So, too, in ***The Triumph of the Philistines***, Mr. Jones makes the mistake of expecting us to take a tender interest in a pair of lovers who have had never a love-scene to set our interest agoing. They are introduced to each other in the first act, and we shrewdly suspect (for in the theatre we are all inveterate match-makers) that they are going to fall in love; but we have not the smallest positive evidence of the fact before we find, in the second act, that misunderstandings have arisen, and the lady declines to look at the gentleman. The actress who played the part at the St. James's Theatre was blamed for failing to enlist our sympathies in this romance; but what actress can make much of a love part which, up to the very last moment, is all suspicion and jealousy? Fancy **Romeo and Juliet** with the love-scenes omitted, "by special request!"

*   *   *   *   *

In a second class, according to our analysis, we place the obligatory scene which is imposed by "the manifest exigencies of specifically dramatic effect." Here it must of course be noted that the conception of "specifically dramatic effect" varies in some degree, from age to age, from generation to generation, and even, one may almost say, from theatre to theatre. Scenes of violence and slaughter were banished from the Greek theatre, mainly, no doubt, because rapid movement was rendered difficult by the hieratic trappings of the actors, and was altogether foreign to the spirit of tragedy; but it can scarcely be doubted that the tragic poets were the less inclined to rebel against this convention, because they extracted "specifically dramatic effects" of a very high order out of their "messenger-scenes." Even in the modern theatre we are thrilled by the description of Hippolytus dragged at his own chariot wheel, or Creusa and Creon devoured by Medea's veil of fire.[2] On the Elizabethan stage, the murder of Agamemnon would no doubt have been "subjected to our faithful eyes" like the blinding of Gloucester or the suffocation of Edward II; but who shall say that there is less "specifically dramatic effect" in Aeschylus's method of mirroring the scene in the clairvoyant ecstasy of Cassandra? I am much inclined to think that the dramatic effect of highly emotional narrative is underrated in the modern theatre.

Again, at one class of theatre, the author of a sporting play--is bound to exhibit a horse-race on the stage, or he is held to have shirked his obligatory scene. At another class of theatre, we shall have a scene, perhaps, in a box in the Grand Stand, where some Lady Gay Spanker shall breathlessly depict, from start to finish, the race which is visible to her, but invisible to the audience. At a third class of the theatre, the "specifically dramatic effect" to be extracted from a horse-race is found in a scene in a Black-Country slum, where a group of working-men and women are feverishly awaiting the evening paper which shall bring them the result of the St. Leger, involving for some of them opulence--to the extent, perhaps, of a L5 note--and for others ruin.[3]

The difficulty of deciding that any one form of scene is predestined by the laws of dramatic effect is illustrated in Tolstoy's grisly drama, *The Power of Darkness*. The scene in which Nikita kills Akoulina's child was felt to be too horrible for representation; whereupon the author wrote an alternative scene between Mitritch and Anna, which passes simultaneously with the murder scene, in an adjoining room. The two scenes fulfil exactly the same function in the economy of the play; it can be acted with either of them, it might be acted with both; and it is impossible to say which produces the intenser or more "specifically dramatic effect."

The fact remains, however, that there is almost always a dramatic and undramatic, a more dramatic and a less dramatic, way of doing a thing; and an author who allows us to foresee and expect a dramatic way of attaining a given end, and then chooses an undramatic or less dramatic way, is guilty of having missed the obligatory scene. For a general discussion of what we mean by the terms "dramatic" and "undramatic" the reader may refer back to Chapter III. Here I need only give one or two particular illustrations.

It will be remembered that one of the *scenes a faire* which M. Sarcey foresaw in *Les Fourchambault* was the encounter between the two brothers; the illegitimate Bernard and the legitimate Leopold. It would have been quite possible, and quite natural, to let the action of the play work itself out without any such encounter; or to let the encounter take place behind the scenes; but this would have been a patent ignoring of dramatic possibilities, and M. Sarcey would have had ample reason to pour the vials of his wrath on Augier's head. He was right, however, in his confidence that Augier would not fail to "make" the scene. And how did he "make" it? The one thing inevitable about it was that the truth should be revealed to Leopold; but there were a dozen different ways in which that might have been effected. Perhaps, in real life, Bernard would have said something to this effect: "Young man, you are making questionable advances to a lady in whom I am interested. I beg that you will cease to persecute her; and if you ask by what right I do so, I reply that I am in fact your elder brother, that I have saved our father from ruin, that I am henceforth the predominant partner in his business, and that, if you do not behave yourself, I shall see that your allowance is withdrawn, and that you have no longer the means to lead an idle and dissolute life." This would have been an ungracious but not unnatural way of going about the business. Had Augier chosen it, we should have had no right to complain on the score of probability; but it would have been evident to the least imaginative that he had left the specifically dramatic opportunities of the scene entirely undeveloped. Let us now see what he actually did. Marie Letellier, compromised by Leopold's conduct, has left the Fourchambault house and taken refuge with Mme. Bernard. Bernard loves her devotedly, but does not dream that she can see anything in his uncouth personality, and imagines that she loves Leopold. Accordingly, he determines that Leopold shall marry her, and tells him so. Leopold scoffs at the idea; Bernard insists; and little by little the conflict rises to a tone of personal altercation. At last Leopold says something slighting of Mile. Letellier, and Bernard--who, be it noted, has begun with no intention of revealing the kinship between them--loses his self-control and cries, "Ah, there speaks the blood of the man who slandered a woman in order to prevent his son from keeping his word to her. I recognize in you your grandfather, who was a miserable calumniator." "Repeat that word!" says Leopold. Bernard does so, and the other strikes him across the face with his glove. For a perceptible interval Bernard struggles with his rage in silence, and then: "It is well for you," he cries, "that you are my brother!"

We need not follow the scene in the sentimental turning which it then takes, whereby it comes about, of course, that Bernard, not Leopold, marries Mile. Letellier. The point is that Augier has justified Sarcey's confidence by making the scene thoroughly and specifically dramatic; in other words, by charging it with emotion, and working up the tension to a very high pitch. And Sarcey was no doubt right in holding that this was what the whole audience instinctively expected, and that they would have been more or less consciously disappointed had the author baulked their expectation.

An instructive example of the failure to "make" a dramatically obligatory scene may be found in ***Agatha*** by Mrs. Humphry Ward and Mr. Louis Parker. Agatha is believed to be the child of Sir Richard and Lady Fancourt; but at a given point she learns that a gentleman whom she has known all her life as "Cousin Ralph" is in reality her father. She has a middle-aged suitor, Colonel Ford, whom she is very willing to marry; but at the end of the second act she refuses him, because she shrinks from the idea, on the one hand, of concealing the truth from him, on the other hand, of revealing her mother's trespass. This is not, in itself, a very strong situation, for we feel the barrier between the lovers to be unreal. Colonel Ford is a man of sense. The secret of Agatha's parentage can make no real difference to him. Nothing material--no point of law or of honour--depends on it. He will learn the truth, and all will come right between them. The only point on which our interest can centre is the question how he is to learn the truth; and here the authors go very far astray. There are two, and only two, really dramatic ways in which Colonel Ford can be enlightened. Lady Fancourt must realize that Agatha is wrecking her life to keep her mother's secret, and must either herself reveal it to Colonel Ford, or must encourage and enjoin Agatha to do so. Now, the authors choose neither of these ways: the secret slips out, through a chance misunderstanding in a conversation between Sir Richard Fancourt and the Colonel. This is a typical instance of an error of construction; and why?--because it leaves to chance what should be an act of will. Drama means a thing done, not merely a thing that happens; and the playwright who lets accident effect what might naturally and probably be a result of volition, or, in other words, of character, sins against the fundamental law of his craft. In the case before us, Lady Fancourt and Agatha--the two characters on whom our interest is centred--are deprived of all share in one of the crucial moments of the action. Whether the actual disclosure was made by the mother or by the daughter, there ought to have been a great scene between the two, in which the mother should have insisted that, by one or other, the truth must be told. It would have been a painful, a delicate, a difficult scene, but it was the obligatory scene of the play; and had we been allowed clearly to foresee it at the end of the second act, our interest would have been decisively carried forward. The scene, too, might have given the play a moral relevance which in fact it lacks. The readjustment of Agatha's scheme of things, so as to make room for her mother's history, might have been made explicit and partly intellectual, instead of implicit, inarticulate and wholly emotional.

This case, then, clearly falls under our second heading. We cannot say that it is the logic of the theme which demands the scene, for no thesis or abstract idea is enunciated. Nor can we say that the course of events is unnatural or improbable; our complaint is that, without being at all less natural, they might have been highly dramatic, and that in fact they are not so.

In a very different type of play, we find another example of the ignoring of a dramatically obligatory scene. The author of that charming fantasy, ***The Passing of the Third Floor Back***, was long ago guilty of a play named ***The Rise of Dick Halward***, chiefly memorable for having elicited from Mr. Bernard Shaw one of the most brilliant pages in English dramatic criticism. The hero of this play, after an adventurous youth in Mexico, has gone to the bar, but gets no briefs, and is therefore unable to marry a lady who announces that no suitor need apply who has less than L5000 a year. One fine day Dick receives from Mexico the will of an old comrade, which purports to leave to him, absolutely, half a million dollars, gold; but the will is accompanied by a letter, in which the old comrade states that the property is really left to him only in trust for the testator's long-lost son, whom Dick is enjoined to search out and endow with a capital which, at 5 per cent, represents accurately the desiderated L5000 a year. As a matter of fact (but this is not to our present purpose), the long-lost son is actually, at that moment, sharing Dick's chambers in the Temple. Dick, however, does not know this, and cannot resist the temptation to destroy the old miner's letter, and grab the property. We know, of course, that retribution is bound to descend upon him; but does not dramatic effect imperatively require that, for a brief space at any rate, he should be seen--with whatever qualms of conscience his nature might dictate--enjoying his ill-gotten wealth? Mr. Jerome, however, baulks us of this just expectation. In the very first scene of the second act we find that the game is up. The deceased miner wrote his letter to Dick seated in the doorway of a hut; a chance photographer took a snap-shot at him; and on returning to England, the chance photographer has nothing more pressing to do than to chance upon the one man who knows the long-lost son, and to show him the photograph of the dying miner, whom he at once recognizes. By aid of a microscope, the letter he is writing can be deciphered, and thus Dick's fraud is brought home to him. Now one would suppose that an author who had invented this monstrous and staggering concatenation of chances, must hope to justify it by some highly dramatic situation, in the obvious and commonplace sense of the word. It is not difficult, indeed, to foresee such a situation, in which Dick Halward should be confronted, as if by magic, with the very words of the letter he has so carefully destroyed. I am far from saying that this scene would, in fact, have justified its amazing antecedents; but it would have shown a realization on the author's part that he must at any rate attempt some effect proportionate to the strain he had placed upon our credulity. Mr. Jerome showed no such realization. He made the man who handed Dick the copy of the letter explain beforehand how it had been obtained; so that Dick, though doubtless surprised and disgusted, was not in the least thunderstruck, and manifested no emotion. Here, then, Mr. Jerome evidently missed a scene rendered obligatory by the law of the maximum of specifically dramatic effect.

* * * * *

The third, or structural, class of obligatory scenes may be more briefly dealt with, seeing that we have already, in the last chapter, discussed the principle involved. In this class we have placed, by definition, scenes which the author himself has rendered obligatory by seeming unmistakably to lead up to them--or, in other words, scenes indicated, or seeming to be indicated, by deliberately-planted finger-posts. It may appear as though the case of Dick Halward, which we have just been examining, in reality came under this heading. But it cannot actually be said that Mr. Jerome either did, or seemed to, point by finger-posts towards the obligatory scene. He rather appears to have been blankly unconscious of its possibility.

We have noted in the foregoing chapter the unwisdom of planting misleading finger-posts; here we have only to deal with the particular case in which they seem to point to a definite and crucial scene. An example given by M. Sarcey himself will, I think, make the matter quite clear.

M. Jules Lemaitre's play, **Revoltée**, tells the story of a would-be intellectual, ill-conditioned young woman, married to a plain and ungainly professor of mathematics, whom she despises. We know that she is in danger of yielding to the fascinations of a seductive man-about-town; and having shown us this danger, the author proceeds to emphasize the manly and sterling character of the husband. He has the gentleness that goes with strength; but where his affections or his honour is concerned, he is not a man to be trifled with. This having been several times impressed upon us, we naturally expect that the wife is to be rescued by some striking manifestation of the husband's masterful virility. But no such matter! Rescued she is, indeed; but it is by the intervention of her half-brother, who fights a duel on her behalf, and is brought back wounded to restore peace to the mathematician's household: that man of science having been quite passive throughout, save for some ineffectual remonstrances. It happens that in this case we know just where the author went astray. Helene (the wife) is the unacknowledged daughter of a great lady, Mme. de Voves; and the subject of the play, as the author first conceived it, was the relation between the mother, the illegitimate daughter, and the legitimate son; the daughter's husband taking only a subordinate place. But Lemaitre chose as a model for the husband a man whom he had known and admired; and he allowed himself to depict in vivid colours his strong and sympathetic character, without noticing that he was thereby upsetting the economy of his play, and giving his audience reason to anticipate a line of development quite different from that which he had in mind. Inadvertently, in fact, he planted, not one, but two or three, misleading finger-posts.

* * * * *

We come now to the fourth, or psychological, class of obligatory scenes--those which are "required in order to justify some modification of character or alteration of will, too important to be taken for granted."

An obvious example of an obligatory scene of this class may be found in the third act of **Othello**. The poet is bound to show us the process by which Iago instils his poison into Othello's mind. He has backed himself, so to speak, to make this process credible to us; and, by a masterpiece of dexterity and daring, he wins his wager. Had he omitted this scene--had he shown us Othello at one moment full of serene confidence, and at his next appearance already convinced of Desdemona's guilt--he would have omitted the pivot and turning--point of the whole structure. It may seem fantastic to conceive that any dramatist could blunder so grossly; but there are not a few plays in which we observe a scarcely less glaring hiatus.

A case in point may be found in Lord Tennyson's **Becket**. I am not one of those who hold Tennyson merely contemptible as a dramatist. I believe that, had he taken to playwriting nearly half-a-century earlier, and studied the root principles of craftsmanship, instead of blindly accepting the Elizabethan conventions, he might have done work as fine in the mass as are the best moments of **Queen Mary** and **Harold**. As a whole, **Becket** is one of his weakest productions; but the Prologue and the first act would have formed an excellent first and third act for a play of wholly different sequel, had he interposed, in a second act, the obligatory scene required to elucidate Becket's character. The historic and psychological problem of Thomas Becket is his startling transformation from an easy-going, luxurious, worldly statesman into a gaunt ecclesiastic, fanatically fighting for the rights of his see, of his order, and of Rome. In any drama which professes to deal (as this does) with his whole career, the intellectual interest cannot but centre in an analysis of the forces that brought about this seeming new-birth of his soul. It would have been open to the poet, no doubt, to take up his history at a later point, when he was already the full-fledged clerical and ultramontane. But this Tennyson does not do. He is at pains to present to us the magnificent Chancellor, the bosom friend of the King, and mild reprover of his vices; and then, without the smallest transition, hey presto! he is the intransigent priest, bitterly combating the Constitutions of Clarendon. It is true that in the Prologue the poet places one or two finger-posts--small, conventional foreshadowings of coming trouble. For instance, the game of chess between King and Chancellor ends with a victory for Becket, who says--

"You see my bishop
Hath brought your king to a standstill. You are beaten."

The symbolical game of chess is a well-worn dramatic device. Becket, moreover, seems to feel some vague disquietude as to what may happen if he accepts the archbishopric; but there is nothing to show that he is conscious of any bias towards the intransigent clericalism of the later act. The character-problem, in fact, is not only not solved, but is ignored. The obligatory scene is skipped over, in the interval between the Prologue and the first act.

One of the finest plays of our time--Sir Arthur Pinero's **Iris**--lacks, in my judgment, an obligatory scene. The character of Iris is admirably true, so far as it goes; but it is incomplete. The author seems to have evaded the crucial point of his play--the scene of her installation in Maldonado's flat. To perfect his psychological study, he was bound to bridge the chasm between the Iris of the third act and the Iris of the fourth. He builds two ends of the bridge, in the incident of the cheque-book at the close of the one act, and in the state of hebetude in which we find her at the opening of the other; but there remains a great gap at which the imagination boggles. The author has tried to throw a retrospective footway across it in Iris's confession to Trenwith in the fifth act; but I do not find that it quite meets the case. It would no doubt have been very difficult to keep the action within reasonable limits had a new act taken the place of the existing fourth; but Sir Arthur Pinero would probably have produced a completer work of art had he faced this difficulty, and contrived to compress into a single last act something like the matter of the existing fourth and fifth. It may be that he deliberately preferred that Iris should give in narrative the history of her decline; but I do not consider this a case in support of that slight plea for impassioned narrative which I ventured to put forth a few pages back. Her confession to Trenwith would have been far more dramatic and moving had it been about one-fourth part as long and one-fourth part as articulate.

*　*　*　*　*

Of the scene imposed by history or legend it is unnecessary to say very much. We saw in Chapter IX that the theatre is not the place for expounding the results of original research, which cast a new light on historic character. It is not the place for whitewashing Richard III, or representing him as a man of erect and graceful figure. It is not the place for proving that Guy Fawkes was an earnest Presbyterian, that Nell Gwynn was a lady of the strictest morals, or that George Washington was incapable of telling the truth. The playwright who deals with Henry VIII is bound to present him, in the schoolboy's phrase, as "a great widower." William the Silent must not be a chatterbox, Torquemada a humanitarian, Ivan the Terrible a conscientious opponent of capital punishment. And legend has its fixed points no less than history. In the theatre, indeed, there is little distinction between them: history is legend, and legend history. A dramatist may, if he pleases (though it is a difficult task), break wholly unfamiliar ground in the past; but where a historic legend exists he must respect it at his peril.

From all this it is a simple deduction that where legend (historic or otherwise) associates a particular character with a particular scene that is by any means presentable on the stage, that scene becomes obligatory in a drama of which he is the leading figure. The fact that Shakespeare could write a play about King John, and say nothing about Runnymede and Magna Charta, shows that that incident in constitutional history had not yet passed into popular legend. When Sir Herbert Tree revived the play, he repaired the poet's omission by means of an inserted tableau. Even Shakespeare had not the hardihood to let Caesar fall without saying, "The Ides of March are come" and "Et tu, Brute!" Nero is bound to fiddle while Rome burns, or the audience will know the reason why.[4] Historic criticism will not hear of the "Thou hast conquered, Galilean!" which legend attributes to Julian the Apostate; yet Ibsen not only makes him say it, but may almost be said to find in the phrase the keynote of his world-historic drama. Tristram and Iseult must drink a love-philtre or they are not Tristram and Iseult. It would be the extreme of paradox to write a Paolo-and-Francesca play and omit the scene of "Quel giorno piu non vi leggemmo avante."

The cases are not very frequent, however, in which an individual incident is thus imposed by history or legend. The practical point to be noted is rather that, when an author introduces a strongly-marked historical character, he must be prepared to give him at least one good opportunity of acting up to the character which legend--the best of evidence in the theatre--assigns to him. When such a personage is presented to us, it ought to be at his highest potency. We do not want to see--

"From Marlborough's eyes the tears of dotage flow,   And Swift expire, a driveller and a show."

If you deal with Napoleon, for instance, it is perfectly clear that he must dominate the stage. As soon as you bring in the name, the idea, of Napoleon Bonaparte, men have eyes and ears for nothing else; and they demand to see him, in a general way, acting up to their general conception of him. That was what Messrs. Lloyd Osbourne and Austin Strong forgot in their otherwise clever play, *The Exile*. It is useless to prove, historically, that at a given moment he was passive, supine, unconscious, while people around him were eagerly plotting his escape and restoration. That may have been so; but it is not what an audience wants to see. It wants to see Napoleon Napoleonizing. For anomalies and uncharacteristic episodes in Napoleon's career we must go to books; the playhouse is not the place for them.

It is true that a dramatist like Mr. Bernard Shaw may, at his own risk and peril, set forth to give us a new reading of Caesar or of Napoleon, which may or may not be dramatically acceptable.[5] But this is not what Messrs. Osbourne and Strong tried to do. Their Napoleon was the Napoleon of tradition--only he failed to act "in a concatenation according."

There are a few figures in history--and Napoleon is one of them--which so thrill the imagination that their mere name can dominate the stage, better, perhaps, than their bodily presence. In *L'Aiglon*, by M. Rostand, Napoleon is in fact the hero, though he lies dead in his far-off island, under the Southern Cross. Another such figure is Abraham Lincoln. In James Herne's sadly underrated play, **Griffith Davenport**, we were always conscious of "Mr. Lincoln" in the background; and the act in which Governor Morton of Indiana brought the President's instructions to Davenport might fairly be called an obligatory scene, inasmuch as it gave us the requisite sense of personal nearness to the master-spirit, without involving any risk of belittlement through imperfections of representation. There is a popular melo-drama, passing in Palestine under the Romans, throughout the course of which we constantly feel the influence of a strange new prophet, unseen but wonder-working, who, if I remember rightly, is personally presented to us only in a final tableau, wherein he appears riding into Jerusalem amid the hosannas of the multitude. The execution of **Ben Hur** is crude and commonplace, but the conception is by no means inartistic. Historical figures of the highest rank may perhaps be best adumbrated in this fashion, with or without one personal appearance, so brief that there shall be no danger of anti-climax.

The last paragraph reminds us that the accomplished playwright shows his accomplishment quite as much in his recognition and avoidance of the **scene a ne pas faire** as in his divination of the obligatory scene. There is always the chance that no one may miss a scene demanded by logic or psychology; but an audience knows too well when it has been bored or distressed by a superfluous, or inconsequent, or wantonly painful scene.

Some twenty years ago, in criticizing a play named **Le Maitre d'Armes**, M. Sarcey took the authors gravely to task, in the name of "Aristotle and common sense," for following the modern and reprehensible tendency to present "slices of life" rather than constructed and developed dramas. Especially he reproached them with deliberately omitting the *scene à faire*. A young lady is seduced, he says, and, for the sake of her child, implores her betrayer to keep his promise of marriage. He renews the promise, without the slightest intention of fulfilling it, and goes on board his yacht in order to make his escape. She discovers his purpose and follows him on board the yacht. "What is the scene," asks M. Sarcey--here I translate literally--"which you expect, you, the public? It is the scene between the abandoned fair one and her seducer. The author may make it in a hundred ways, but make it he must!" Instead of which, the critic proceeds, we are fobbed off with a storm-scene, a rescue, and other sensational incidents, and hear no word of what passes between the villain and his victim. Here, I think, M. Sarcey is mistaken in his application of his pet principle. Words cannot express our unconcern as to what passes between the heroine and the villain on board the yacht--nay, more, our gratitude for being spared that painful and threadbare scene of recrimination. The plot demands, observe, that the villain shall not relent. We know quite well that he cannot, for if he did the play would fall to pieces. Why, then, should we expect or demand a sordid squabble which can lead to nothing? We--and by "we" I mean the public which relishes such plays--cannot possibly have any keen appetite for copious re-hashes of such very cold mutton as the appeals of the penitent heroine to the recalcitrant villain. And the moral seems to be that in this class of play--the drama, if one may call it so, of foregone character--the *scene à faire* is precisely the scene to be omitted.

In plays of a more ambitious class, skill is often shown by the indication, in place of the formal presentment, even of an important scene which the audience may, or might, have expected to witness in full. We have already noted such a case in ***The Wild Duck***: Ibsen knew that what we really required to witness was not the actual process of Gregers's disclosure to Hialmar, but its effects. A small, but quite noticeable, example of a scene thus rightly left to the imagination occurred in Mr. Somerset Maugham's first play, ***A Man of Honour***. In the first act, Jack Halliwell, his wife, and his sister-in-law call upon his friend Basil Kent. The sister-in-law, Hilda Murray, is a rich widow; and she and Kent presently go out on the balcony together and are lost to view. Then it appears, in a scene between the Halliwells, that they fully believe that Kent is in love with Mrs. Murray and is now proposing to her. But when the two re-enter from the balcony, it is evident from their mien that, whatever may have passed between them, they are not affianced lovers; and we presently learn that though Kent is in fact strongly attracted to Mrs. Murray, he considers himself bound in honour to marry a certain Jenny Bush, a Fleet Street barmaid, with whom he has become entangled. Many playwrights would, so to speak, have dotted the i's of the situation by giving us the scene between Kent and Mrs. Murray; but Mr. Maugham has done exactly right in leaving us to divine it. We know all that, at this point, we require to know of the relation between them; to have told us more would have been to anticipate and discount the course of events.

A more striking instance of a scene rightly placed behind the scenes occurs in M. de Curel's terrible drama **Les Fossiles**. I need not go into the singularly unpleasing details of the plot. Suffice it to say that a very peculiar condition of things exists in the family of the Duc de Chantemelle. It has been fully discussed in the second act between the Duke and his daughter Claire, who has been induced to accept it for the sake of the family name. But a person more immediately concerned is Robert de Chantemelle, the only son of the house--will he also accept it quietly? A nurse, who is acquainted with the black secret, misbehaves herself, and is to be packed off. As she is a violent woman, Robert insists on dismissing her himself, and leaves the room to do so. The rest of the family are sure that, in her rage, she will blurt out the whole story; and they wait, in breathless anxiety, for Robert's return. What follows need not be told: the point is that this scene--the scene of tense expectancy as to the result of a crisis which is taking place in another room of the same house--is really far more dramatic than the crisis itself would be. The audience already knows all that the angry virago can say to her master; and of course no discussion of the merits of the case is possible between these two. Therefore M. de Curel is conspicuously right in sparing us the scene of vulgar violence, and giving us the scene of far higher tension in which Robert's father, wife and sister expect his return, their apprehension deepening with every moment that he delays.

We see, then, that there is such a thing as a false ***scene a faire***--a scene which at first sight seems obligatory, but is in fact much better taken for granted. It may be absolutely indispensable that it should be suggested to the mind of the audience, but neither indispensable nor advisable that it should be presented to their eyes. The judicious playwright will often ask himself, "Is it the actual substance of this scene that I require, or only its repercussion?"

* * * * *

Notes:

[1: For example, in his criticism of Becque's La Parisienne (Quarante Ans de Theatre, VI, p. 364), he tells how, at the end of the second act, one of his neighbours said to him, "Eh! bien, vous voila bien attrape! Ou est la *scene a faire*?" "I freely admit," he continues, "that there is no *scene a faire*; if there had been no third act I should not have been greatly astonished. When you make it your business to recite on the stage articles from the *Vie Parisienne*, it makes no difference whether you stop at the end of the second article or at the end of the third." This clearly implies that a play in which there is no *scene a faire* is nothing but a series of newspaper sketches. Becque, one fancies, might have replied that the scene between Clotilde and Monsieur Simpson at the beginning of Act III was precisely the *scene a faire* demanded by the logic of his cynicism.]

[2: I need scarcely direct the reader's attention to Mr. Gilbert Murray's noble renderings of these speeches.]

[3: Such a scene occurs in that very able play, *The Way the Money Goes*, by Lady Bell.]

[4: In Mr. Stephen Phillips's play he does not actually play on the lyre, but he improvises and recites an ode to the conflagration.]

[5: And, after all, Mr. Shaw does not run counter to the legend. He exhibits Caesar and Napoleon "in their well-known attitudes": only, by an odd metempsychosis, the soul of Mr. Shaw has somehow entered into them.]

CHAPTER XIV
THE PERIPETY

In the Greek theatre, as every one knows, the *peripeteia* or reversal of fortune--the turning of the tables, as we might say--was a clearly-defined and recognized portion of the dramatic organism. It was often associated with the *anagnorisis* or recognition. Mr. Gilbert Murray has recently shown cause for believing that both these dramatic "forms" descended from the ritual in which Greek drama took its origin--the ritual celebrating the death and resurrection of the season of "mellow fruitfulness." If this theory be true, the *peripeteia* was at first a change from sorrow to joy--joy in the rebirth of the beneficent powers of nature. And to this day a sudden change from gloom to exhilaration is a popular and effective incident--as when, at the end of a melodrama, the handcuffs are transferred from the wrists of the virtuous naval lieutenant to those of the wicked baronet, and, through the disclosure of a strawberry-mark on his left arm, the lieutenant is recognized as the long-lost heir to a dukedom and L50,000 a year.

But when, as soon happened in Greece, the forms appropriate to a celebration of the death and resurrection of Dionysus came to be blent with the tomb-ritual of a hero, the term *peripeteia* acquired a special association with a sudden decline from prosperity into adversity. In the Middle Ages, this was thought to be the very essence and meaning of tragedy, as we may see from Chaucer's lines:

> "Tragedie is to seyn a certeyn storie,
> As olde bokes maken us memorie,
> Of him that stood in gret prosperitee,
> And is y-fallen out of heigh degree

Into miserie, and endeth wrecchedly."

Aristotle cites a good instance of a peripety--to Anglicize the word--"where, in the ***Lynceus***, the hero is led away to execution, followed by Danaus as executioner; but, as the effect of the antecedents, Danaus is executed and Lynceus escapes." But here, as in so many other contexts, we must turn for the classic example to the ***Oedipus Rex***. Jocasta, hearing from the Corinthian stranger that Polybus, King of Corinth, the reputed father of Oedipus, is dead, sends for her husband to tell him that the oracle which doomed him to parricide is defeated, since Polybus has died a natural death. Oedipus exults in the news and triumphs over the oracles; but, as the scene proceeds, the further revelations made by the same stranger lead Jocasta to recognize in Oedipus her own child, who was exposed on Mount Kithairon; and, in the subsequent scene, the evidence of the old Shepherd brings Oedipus himself to the same crushing realization. No completer case of ***anagnorisis*** and ***peripeteia*** could well be conceived--whatever we may have to say of the means by which it is led up to.[1]

Has the conception of the peripety, as an almost obligatory element in drama, any significance for the modern playwright? Obligatory, of course, it cannot be: it is easy to cite a hundred admirable plays in which it is impossible to discover anything that can reasonably be called a peripety. But this, I think, we may safely say: the dramatist is fortunate who finds in the development of his theme, without unnatural strain or too much preparation, opportunity for a great scene, highly-wrought, arresting, absorbing, wherein one or more of his characters shall experience a marked reversal either of inward soul-state or of outward fortune. The theory of the peripety, in short, practically resolves itself for us into the theory of the "great scene," Plays there are, many and excellent plays, in which some one scene stands out from all the rest, impressing itself with peculiar vividness on the spectator's mind; and, nine times out of ten, this scene will be found to involve a peripety. It can do no harm, then, if the playwright should ask himself: "Can I, without any undue sacrifice, so develop my theme as to entail upon my leading characters, naturally and probably, an experience of this order?"

The peripeties of real life are frequent, though they are apt to be too small in scale, or else too fatally conclusive, to provide material for drama. One of the commonest, perhaps, is that of the man who enters a physician's consulting-room to seek advice in some trifling ailment, and comes out again, half an hour later, doomed either to death or to some calamity worse than death. This situation has been employed, not ineffectively, by Sir Arthur Conan Doyle, in the first act of a romantic drama, *The Fires of Fate*; but it is very difficult to find any dramatic sequel to a peripety involving mere physical disaster.[2] The moral peripety--the sudden dissipation of some illusion, or defeat of some imposture, or crumbling of some castle in the air--is a no less characteristic incident of real life, and much more amenable to the playwright's uses. Certainly there are few things more impressive in drama than to see a man or woman--or a man and woman--come upon the stage, radiant, confident, assured that

"God's in his heaven,
All's right with the world,"

and leave it crushed and desperate, after a gradual and yet swift descent into Avernus. Such a scene is of the very marrow of drama. It is a play within a play; a concentrated, quintessentiated crisis.

In the third act of **Othello** we have a peripety handled with consummate theatrical skill. To me--I confess it with bated breath--the craftsmanship seems greatly superior to the psychology. Othello, when we look into it, succumbs with incredible facility to Iago's poisoned pin-pricks; but no audience dreams of looking into it; and there lies the proof of Shakespeare's technical mastery. In the Trial Scene in **The Merchant of Venice** we have another great peripety. It illustrates the obvious principle that, where the drama consists in a conflict between two persons or parties, the peripety is generally a double one--the sudden collapse of Shylock's case implying an equally sudden restoration of Antonio's fortunes. Perhaps the most striking peripety in Ibsen is Stockmann's fall from jubilant self-confidence to defiant impotence in the third act of **An Enemy of the People**. Thinking that he has the "compact majority" at his back, he assumes the Burgomaster's insignia of office, and lords it over his incensed brother, only to learn, by blow on blow of disillusionment, that "the compact majority" has ratted, that he is to be deprived of his position and income, and that the commonest freedom of speech is to be denied him. In **A Doll's**

House there are two peripeties: Nora's fall from elation to despair in the first scene with Krogstad, and the collapse of Helmer's illusions in the last scene of all.

A good instance of the "great scene" which involves a marked peripety occurs in Sardou's ***Dora***, once famous in England under the title of ***Diplomacy***. The "scene of the three men" shows how Tekli, a Hungarian exile, calls upon his old friend Andre de Maurillac, on the day of Andre's marriage, and congratulates him on having eluded the wiles of a dangerous adventuress, Dora de Rio-Zares, by whom he had once seemed to be attracted. But it is precisely Dora whom Andre has married; and, learning this, Tekli tries to withdraw, or minimize, his imputation. For a moment a duel seems imminent; but Andre's friend, Favrolles, adjures him to keep his head; and the three men proceed to thrash the matter out as calmly as possible, with the result that, in the course of half-an-hour or so, it seems to be proved beyond all doubt that the woman Andre adores, and whom he has just married, is a treacherous spy, who sells to tyrannical foreign governments the lives of political exiles and the honour of the men who fall into her toils. The crushing suspicion is ultimately disproved, by one of the tricks in which Sardou delighted; but that does not here concern us. Artificial as are its causes and its consequences, the "scene of the three men," while it lasts, holds us breathless and absorbed; and Andre's fall from the pinnacle of happiness to the depth of misery, is a typical peripety.

Equally typical and infinitely more tragic is another postnuptial peripety--the scene of the mutual confession of Angel Clare and Tess in Mr. Hardy's great novel. As it stands on the printed page, this scene is a superb piece of drama. Its greatness has been obscured in the English theatre by the general unskilfulness of the dramatic version presented. One magnificent scene does not make a play. In America, on the other hand, the fine acting of Mrs. Fiske secured popularity for a version which was, perhaps, rather better than that which we saw in England.

I have said that dramatic peripeties are not infrequent in real life; and their scene, as is natural, is often laid in the law courts. It is unnecessary to recall the awful "reversal of fortune" that overtook one of the most brilliant of modern dramatists. About the same period, another drama of the English courts ended in a startling and terrible peripety. A young lady was staying as a guest with a half-pay officer and his wife. A valuable pearl belonging to the hostess disappeared; and the hostess accused her guest of having stolen it. The young lady, who had meanwhile married, brought an action for slander against her quondam friend. For several days the case continued, and everything seemed to be going in the plaintiff's favour. Major Blank, the defendant's husband, was ruthlessly cross-examined by Sir Charles Russell, afterwards Lord Chief Justice of England, with a view to showing that he was the real thief. He made a very bad witness, and things looked black against him. The end was nearing, and every one anticipated a verdict in the plaintiff's favour, when there came a sudden change of scene. The stolen pearl had been sold to a firm of jewellers, who had recorded the numbers of the Bank of England notes with which they paid for it. One of these notes was produced in court, and lo! it was endorsed with the name of the plaintiff.[3] In a moment, in the twinkling of an eye, the whole edifice of mendacity and perjury fell to pieces. The thief was arrested and imprisoned; but the peripety for her was less terrible than for her husband, who had married her in chivalrous faith in her innocence.

Would it have been--or may it some day prove to be--possible to transfer this "well-made" drama of real life bodily to the stage? I am inclined to think not. It looks to me very much like one of those "blind alley" themes of which mention has been made. There is matter, indeed, for most painful drama in the relations of the husband and wife, both before and after the trial; but, from the psychological point of view, one can see nothing in the case but a distressing and inexplicable anomaly.[4] At the same time, the bare fact of the sudden and tremendous peripety is irresistibly dramatic; and Mr. Henry Arthur Jones has admitted that it suggested to him the great scene of the unmasking of Felicia Hindemarsh in **Mrs. Dane's Defence.**

It is instructive to note the delicate adjustment which Mr. Jones found necessary in order to adapt the theme to dramatic uses. In the first place, not wishing to plunge into the depths of tragedy, he left the heroine unmarried, though on the point of marriage. In the second place, he made the blot on her past, not a theft followed by an attempt to shift the guilt on to other shoulders, but an error of conduct, due to youth and inexperience, serious in itself, but rendered disastrous by tragic consequences over which she, Felicia, had no control. Thus Mr. Jones raised a real and fairly sufficient obstacle between his lovers, without rendering his heroine entirely unsympathetic, or presenting her in the guise of a bewildering moral anomaly. Thirdly, he transferred the scene of the peripety from a court of justice, with its difficult adjuncts and tedious procedure, to the private study of a great lawyer. At the opening of the scene between Mrs. Dane and Sir Daniel Carteret, she is, no doubt, still anxious and ill-at-ease, but reasonably confident of having averted all danger of exposure. Sir Daniel, too (like Sir Charles Russell in the pearl suit), is practically convinced of her innocence. He merely wants to get the case absolutely clear, for the final confounding of her accusers. At first, all goes smoothly. Mrs. Dane's answers to his questions are pat and plausible. Then she makes a single, almost imperceptible, slip of the tongue: she says, "We had governesses," instead of "I had governesses." Sir Daniel pricks up his ears: "We? You say you were an only child. Who's we?" "My cousin and I," she answers. Sir Daniel thinks it odd that he has not heard of this cousin before; but he continues his interrogatory without serious suspicion. Then it occurs to him to look up, in a topographical dictionary, the little town of Tawhampton, where Mrs. Dane spent her youth. He reads the bald account of it, ending thus, "The living is a Vicarage, net yearly value L376, and has been held since 1875 by"--and he turns round upon her--"by the Rev. Francis Hindemarsh! Hindemarsh?"

Mrs. Dane: He was my uncle.

Sir Daniel: Your uncle?

Mrs. Dane: Sir Daniel, I've done wrong to hide from you that Felicia Hindemarsh was my cousin.

Sir Daniel: Felicia Hindemarsh was your cousin!

Mrs. Dane: Can't you understand why I have hidden it? The whole affair was so terrible.

And so she stumbles on, from one inevitable admission to another, until the damning truth is clear that she herself is Felicia Hindemarsh, the central, though not the most guilty, figure in a horrible scandal.

This scene is worthy of study as an excellent type of what may be called the judicial peripety, the crushing cross-examination, in which it is possible to combine the tension of the detective story with no small psychological subtlety. In Mr. Jones's scene, the psychology is obvious enough; but it is an admirable example of nice adjustment without any obtrusive ingenuity. The whole drama, in short, up to the last act is, in the exact sense of the word, a well-made play--complex yet clear, ingenious yet natural. In the comparative weakness of the last act we have a common characteristic of latter-day drama, which will have to be discussed in due course.

In this case we have a peripety of external fortune. For a clearly-marked moral peripety we may turn to the great scene between Vivie and her mother in the second act of *Mrs. Warren's Profession.* Whatever may be thought of the matter of this scene, its movement is excellent. After a short, sharp opening, which reveals to Mrs. Warren the unfilial dispositions of her daughter, and reduces her to whimpering dismay, the following little passage occurs:

Mrs. Warren: You're very rough with me, Vivie.

Vivie: Nonsense. What about bed? It's past ten.

Mrs. Warren (passionately): What's the use of my going to bed? Do you think I could sleep?

Vivie: Why not? I shall.

Then the mother turns upon the daughter's stony self-righteousness, and pours forth her sordid history in such a way as to throw a searchlight on the conditions which make such histories possible; until, exhausted by her outburst, she says, "Oh, dear! I do believe I am getting sleepy after all," and Vivie replies, "I believe it is I who will not be able to sleep now." Mr. Shaw, we see, is at pains to emphasize his peripety.

Some "great scenes" consist, not of one decisive turning of the tables, but of a whole series of minor vicissitudes of fortune. Such a scene is the third act of *The Gay Lord Quex*, a prolonged and thrilling duel, in which Sophy Fullgarney passes by degrees from impertinent exultation to abject surrender and then springs up again to a mood of reckless defiance. In the "great scene" of *The Thunderbolt*, on the other hand--the scene of Thaddeus's false confession of having destroyed his brother's will--though there is, in fact, a great peripety, it is not that which attracts and absorbs our interest. All the greedy Mortimore family fall from the height of jubilant confidence in their new-found wealth to the depth of disappointment and exasperation. But this is not the aspect of the scene which grips and moves us. Our attention is centred on Thaddeus's struggle to take his wife's misdeed upon himself; and his failure cannot be described as a peripety, seeing that it sinks him only one degree lower in the slough of despair. Like the scene in Mrs. Dane's Defence, this is practically a piece of judicial drama--a hard-fought cross-examination. But as there is no reversal of fortune for the character in whom we are chiefly interested, it scarcely ranks as a scene of peripety.[5]

Before leaving this subject, we may note that a favourite effect of romantic drama is an upward reversal of fortune through the recognition--the *anagnorisis*--of some great personage in disguise. Victor Hugo excelled in the superb gestures appropriate to such a scene: witness the passage in **Hernani**, before the tomb of Charlemagne, where the obscure bandit claims the right to take his place at the head of the princes and nobles whom the newly-elected Emperor has ordered off to execution:

Hernani:

Dieu qui donne le sceptre et qui te le donna
M'a fait duc de Segorbe et duc de Cardona,
Marquis de Monroy, comte Albatera, vicomte
De Gor, seigneur de lieux dont j'ignore le compte.
Je suis Jean d'Aragon, grand maitre d'Avis, ne
Dans l'exil, fils proscrit d'un pere assassine
Par sentence du tien, roi Carlos de Castille.

* * * * *

(Aux autres conjures)
Couvrons nous, grands d'Espagnol
(Tous les Espagnols se couvrent)
Oui, nos tetes, o roi!
Ont le droit de tomber couvertes devant toi!

An effective scene of this type occurs in **Monsieur Beaucaire**, where the supposed hairdresser is on the point of being ejected with contumely from the pump-room at Bath, when the French Ambassador enters, drops on his knee, kisses the young man's hand, and presents him to the astounded company as the Duc d'Orleans, Comte de Valois, and I know not what besides--a personage who immeasurably outshines the noblest of his insulters. Quieter, but not less telling, is the peripety in *The Little Father of the Wilderness*, by Messrs. Lloyd Osbourne and Austin Strong. The Pere Marlotte, who, by his heroism and self-devotion, has added vast territories to the French possessions in America, is summoned to the court of Louis XV, and naturally concludes that the king has heard of his services and wishes to reward them. He finds, on the contrary, that he is wanted merely to decide a foolish bet; and he is treated with the grossest insolence and contempt. Just as he is departing in humiliation, the Governor-General of Canada arrives, with a suite of officers and Indians. The moment they are aware of Pere Marlotte's presence, they all kneel to him and pay him deeper homage than they have paid to the king, who accepts the rebuke and joins in their demonstration. A famous peripety of the romantic order occurs in *H.M.S. Pinafore*, where, on the discovery that Captain Corcoran and Ralph Rackstraw have been changed at birth, Ralph instantly becomes captain of the ship, while the captain declines into an able-bodied seaman. This is one of the instances in which the idealism of art ekes out the imperfections of reality.

* * * * *

Notes:
[1: That great spiritual drama known as the Book of Job opens, after the Prologue in Heaven, with one of the most startling of peripeties.]

[2: The first act of Mr. Gilbert Murray's *Carlyon Sahib* contains an incident of this nature; but it can scarcely be called a peripety, since the victim remains unconscious of his doom.]

[3: For the benefit of American readers, it may be well to state that the person who changes a Bank of England note is often asked to write his or her name on the back of it. It must have been in a moment of sheer aberration that the lady in question wrote her own name.]

[4: M. Bernstein, dishing up a similar theme with a piquant sauce of sensuality, made but a vulgar and trivial piece of work of it.]

[5: One of the most striking peripeties in recent English drama occurs in the third act of The Builder of Bridges, by Mr. Alfred Sutro.]

CHAPTER XV
PROBABILITY, CHANCE, AND COINCIDENCE

Aristotle indulges in an often-quoted paradox to the effect that, in drama, the probable impossible is to be preferred to the improbable possible. With all respect, this seems to be a somewhat cumbrous way of stating the fact that plausibility is of more importance on the stage than what may be called demonstrable probability. There is no time, in the rush of a dramatic action, for a mathematical calculation of the chances for and against a given event, or for experimental proof that such and such a thing can or cannot be done. If a thing seem plausible, an audience will accept it without cavil; if it, seem incredible on the face of it, no evidence of its credibility will be of much avail. This is merely a corollary from the fundamental principle that the stage is the realm of appearances; not of realities, where paste jewels are at least as effective as real ones, and a painted forest is far more sylvan than a few wilted and drooping saplings, insecurely planted upon the boards.

That is why an improbable or otherwise inacceptable incident cannot be validly defended on the plea that it actually happened: that it is on record in history or in the newspapers. In the first place, the dramatist can never put it on the stage as it happened. The bare fact may be historical, but it is not the bare fact that matters. The dramatist cannot restore it to its place in that intricate plexus of cause and effect, which is the essence and meaning of reality. He can only give his interpretation of the fact; and one knows not how to calculate the chances that his interpretation may be a false one. But even if this difficulty could be overcome; if the dramatist could prove that he had reproduced the event with photographic and cinematographic accuracy, his position would not thereby be improved. He would still have failed in his peculiar task, which is precisely that of interpretation. Not truth, but verisimilitude, is his aim; for the stage is the realm of appearances, in which intrusive realities become unreal. There are, as I have said, incalculable chances to one that the playwright's version of a given event will not coincide with that of the Recording Angel: but it may be true and convincing in relation to human nature in general, in which case it will belong to the sphere of great art; or, on a lower level, it may be agreeable and entertaining without being conspicuously false to human nature, in which case it will do no harm, since it makes no pretence to historic truth. It may be objected that the sixteenth-century public, and even, in the next century, the great Duke of Marlborough, got their knowledge of English history from Shakespeare, and the other writers of chronicle-plays. Well, I leave it to historians to determine whether this very defective and, in great measure, false vision of the past was better or worse than none. The danger at any rate, if danger there was, is now past and done with. Even our generals no longer go to the theatre or to the First Folio for their history. The dramatist may, with an easy conscience, interpret historic fact in the light of his general insight into human nature, so long as he does not so falsify the recorded event that common knowledge cries out against him.[1]

Plausibility, then, not abstract or concrete probability, and still less literal faithfulness to recorded fact, is what the dramatist is bound to aim at. To understand this as a belittling of his art is to misunderstand the nature of art in general. The plausibility of bad art is doubtless contemptible and may be harmful. But to say that good art must be plausible is only to say that not every sort of truth, or every aspect of truth, is equally suitable for artistic representation--or, in more general terms, that the artist, without prejudice to his allegiance to nature, must respect the conditions of the medium in which he works.

Our standards of plausibility, however, are far from being invariable. To each separate form of art, a different standard is applicable. In what may roughly be called realistic art, the terms plausible and probable are very nearly interchangeable. Where the dramatist appeals to the sanction of our own experience and knowledge, he must not introduce matter against which our experience and knowledge cry out. A very small inaccuracy in a picture which is otherwise photographic will often have a very disturbing effect. In plays of society in particular, the criticism "No one does such things," is held by a large class of playgoers to be conclusive and destructive. One has known people despise a play because Lady So-and-so's manner of speaking to her servants was not what they (the cavillers) were accustomed to. On the other hand, one has heard a whole production highly applauded because the buttons on a particular uniform were absolutely right. This merely means that when an effort after literal accuracy is apparent, the attention of the audience seizes on the most trifling details and is apt to magnify their importance. Niceties of language in especial are keenly, and often unjustly, criticized. If a particular expression does not happen to be current in the critic's own circle, he concludes that nobody uses it, and that the author is a pedant or a vulgarian. In view of this inevitable tendency, the prudent dramatist will try to keep out of his dialogue expressions that are peculiar to his own circle, and to use only what may be called everybody's English, or the language undoubtedly current throughout the whole class to which his personage belongs.

It may be here pointed out that there are three different planes on which plausibility may or may not, be achieved. There is first the purely external plane, which concerns the producer almost as much as the playwright. On this plane we look for plausibility of costume, of manners, of dialect, of general environment. Then we have plausibility of what may be called uncharacteristic event--of such events as are independent of the will of the characters, and are not conditioned by their psychology. On this plane we have to deal with chance and accident, coincidence, and all "circumstances over which we have no control." For instance, the playwright who makes the "Marseillaise" become popular throughout Paris within half-an-hour of its having left the composer's desk, is guilty of a breach of plausibility on this plane. So, too, if I were to make my hero enter Parliament for the first time, and rise in a single session to be Prime Minister of England--there would be no absolute impossibility in the feat, but it would be a rather gross improbability of the second order. On the third plane we come to psychological plausibility, the plausibility of events dependent mainly or entirely on character. For example--to cite a much disputed instance--is it plausible that Nora, in ***A Doll's House***, should suddenly develop the mastery of dialectics with which she crushes Helmer in the final scene, and should desert her husband and children, slamming the door behind her?

It need scarcely be said that plausibility on the third plane is vastly the most important. A very austere criticism might even call it the one thing worth consideration. But, as a matter of fact, when we speak of plausibility, it is almost always the second plane--the plane of uncharacteristic circumstance--that we have in mind. To plausibility of the third order we give a more imposing name--we call it truth. We say that Nora's action is true--or untrue--to nature. We speak of the truth with which the madness of Lear, the malignity of Iago, the race hatred of Shylock, is portrayed. Truth, in fact, is the term which we use in cases where the tests to be applied are those of introspection, intuition, or knowledge sub-consciously garnered from spiritual experience. Where the tests are external, and matters of common knowledge or tangible evidence, we speak of plausibility.

It would be a mistake, however, to imagine that because plausibility of the third degree, or truth, is the noblest attribute of drama, it is therefore the one thing needful. In some forms of drama it is greatly impaired, or absolutely nullified, if plausibility of the second degree, its necessary preliminary, be not carefully secured. In the case above imagined, for instance, of the young politician who should become Prime Minister immediately on entering Parliament: it would matter nothing with what profundity of knowledge or subtlety of skill the character was drawn: we should none the less decline to believe in him. Some dramatists, as a matter of fact, find it much easier to attain truth of character than plausibility of incident. Every one who is in the habit of reading manuscript plays, must have come across the would-be playwright who has a good deal of general ability and a considerable power of characterization, but seems to be congenitally deficient in the sense of external reality, so that the one thing he (or she) can by no means do is to invent or conduct an action that shall be in the least like any sequence of events in real life. It is naturally difficult to give examples, for the plays composed under this curious limitation are apt to remain in manuscript, or to be produced for one performance, and forgotten. There is, however, one recent play of this order which holds a certain place in dramatic literature. I do not know that Mr. Granville Barker was well-advised in printing *The Marrying of Anne Leete* along with such immeasurably maturer and saner productions as *The Voysey Inheritance* and *Waste*; but by doing so he has served my present purpose in providing me with a perfect example of a play as to which we cannot tell whether it possesses plausibility of the third degree, so absolutely does it lack that plausibility of the second degree which is its indispensable condition precedent.

Francisque Sarcey was fond of insisting that an audience would generally accept without cavil any postulates in reason which an author chose to impose upon it, with regard to events supposed to have occurred before the rise of the curtain; always provided that the consequences deduced from them within the limits of the play were logical, plausible, and entertaining. The public will swallow a camel, he would maintain, in the past, though they will strain at a gnat in the present. A classical example of this principle is (once more) the **Oedipus Rex**, in which several of the initial postulates are wildly improbable: for instance, that Oedipus should never have inquired into the circumstances of the death of Laius, and that, having been warned by an oracle that he was doomed to marry his mother, he should not have been careful, before marrying any woman, to ascertain that she was younger than himself. There is at least so much justification for Sarcey's favourite principle, that we are less apt to scrutinize things merely narrated to us than events which take place before our eyes. It is simply a special instance of the well-worn

"Segnius irritant animos demissa per aurem   Quam quae sunt oculis subjecta fidelibus."

But the principle is of very limited artistic validity. No one would nowadays think of justifying a gross improbability in the antecedents of a play by Ibsen or Sir Arthur Pinero, by Mr. Galsworthy or Mr. Granville Barker, on the plea that it occurred outside the frame of the picture. Such a plea might, indeed, secure a mitigation of sentence, but never a verdict of acquittal. Sarcey, on the other hand, brought up in the school of the "well-made" play, would rather have held it a feather in the playwright's cap that he should have known just where, and just how, he might safely outrage probability [2]. The inference is that we now take the dramatist's art more seriously than did the generation of the Second Empire in France.

This brings us, however, to an important fact, which must by no means be overlooked. There is a large class of plays--or rather, there are several classes of plays, some of them not at all to be despised--the charm of which resides, not in probability, but in ingenious and delightful improbability. I am, of course, not thinking of sheer fantasies, like **A Midsummer Night's Dream**, or **Peter Pan**, or **The Blue Bird**. They may, indeed, possess plausibility of the third order, but plausibility of the second order has no application to them. Its writs do not run on their extra-mundane plane. The plays which appeal to us in virtue of their pleasant departures from probability are romances, farces, a certain order of light comedies and semi-comic melodramas--in short, the thousand and one plays in which the author, without altogether despising and abjuring truth, makes it on principle subsidiary to delightfulness. Plays of the **Prisoner of Zenda** type would come under this head: so would Sir Arthur Pinero's farces, **The Magistrate**, **The Schoolmistress**, **Dandy Dick**; so would Mr. Carton's light comedies, **Lord and Lady Algy**, **Wheels within Wheels**, **Lady Huntworth's Experiment**; so would most of Mr. Barrie's comedies; so would Mr. Arnold Bennett's play, **The Honeymoon**. In a previous chapter I have sketched the opening act of Mr. Carton's **Wheels within Wheels**, which is a typical example of this style of work. Its charm lies in a subtle, all-pervading improbability, an infusion of fantasy so delicate that, while at no point can one say, "This is impossible," the total effect is far more entertaining than that of any probable sequence of events in real life. The whole atmosphere of such a play should be impregnated with humour, without reaching that gross supersaturation which we find in the lower order of farce-plays of the type of **Charlie's Aunt** or **Niobe**.

* * * * *

Plausibility of development, as distinct from plausibility of theme or of character, depends very largely on the judicious handling of chance, and the exclusion, or very sparing employment, of coincidence. This is a matter of importance, into which we shall find it worth while to look somewhat closely.

It is not always clearly recognized that chance and coincidence are by no means the same thing. Coincidence is a special and complex form of chance, which ought by no means to be confounded with the everyday variety. We need not here analyse chance, or discuss the philosophic value of the term. It is enough that we all know what we mean by it in common parlance. It may be well, however, to look into the etymology of the two words we are considering. They both come ultimately, from the Latin "cadere," to fall. Chance is a falling-out, like that of a die from the dice-box; and coincidence signifies one falling-out on the top of another, the concurrent happening of two or more chances which resemble or somehow fit into each other. If you rattle six dice in a box and throw them, and they turn up at haphazard--say, two aces, a deuce, two fours, and a six--there is nothing remarkable in this falling out. But if they all turn up sixes, you at once suspect that the dice are cogged; and if that be not so--if there be no sufficient cause behind the phenomenon--you say that this identical falling-out of six separate possibilities was a remarkable coincidence. Now, applying the illustration to drama, I should say that the playwright is perfectly justified in letting chance play its probable and even inevitable part in the affairs of his characters; but that, the moment we suspect him of cogging the dice, we feel that he is taking an unfair advantage of us, and our imagination either cries, "I won't play!" or continues the game under protest.

Some critics have considered it a flaw in Shakespeare's art that the catastrophe of **Romeo and Juliet** should depend upon a series of chances, and especially on the miscarriage of the Friar's letter to Romeo. This is not, I think, a valid criticism. We may, if we are so minded, pick to pieces the course of action which brought these chances into play. The device of the potion--even if such a drug were known to the pharmacopoeia--is certainly a very clumsy method of escape from the position in which Juliet is placed by her father's obstinacy. But when once we have accepted that integral part of the legend, the intervention of chance in the catastrophe is entirely natural and probable. Observe that there is no coincidence in the matter, no interlinking or dovetailing of chances. The catastrophe results from the hot-headed impetuosity of all the characters, which so hurries events that there is no time for the elimination of the results of chance. Letters do constantly go astray, even under our highly-organized system of conveyance; but their delay or disappearance seldom leads to tragic results, because most of us have learnt to take things calmly and wait for the next post. Yet if we could survey the world at large, it is highly probable that every day or every hour we should somewhere or other find some Romeo on the verge of committing suicide because of a chance misunderstanding with regard to his Juliet; and in a certain percentage of cases the explanatory letter or telegram would doubtless arrive too late.

We all remember how, in Mr. Hardy's **Tess**, the main trouble arises from the fact that the letter pushed under Angel Clare's door slips also under the carpet of his room, and so is never discovered. This is an entirely probable chance; and the sternest criticism would hardly call it a flaw in the structure of the fable. But take another case: Madame X has had a child, of whom she has lost sight for more than twenty years, during which she has lived abroad. She returns to France, and immediately on landing at Bordeaux she kills a man who accompanies her. The court assigns her defence to a young advocate, and this young advocate happens to be her son. We have here a piling of chance upon chance, in which the long arm of coincidence[3] is very apparent. The coincidence would have been less startling had she returned to the place where she left her son and where she believed him to be. But no! she left him in Paris, and it is only by a series of pure chances that he happens to be in Bordeaux, where she happens to land, and happens to shoot a man. For the sake of a certain order of emotional effect, a certain order of audience is willing to accept this piling up of chances; but it relegates the play to a low and childish plane of art. The ***Oedipus Rex***, indeed--which meets us at every turn--is founded on an absolutely astounding series of coincidences; but here the conception of fate comes in, and we vaguely figure to ourselves some malignant power deliberately pulling the strings which guide its puppets into such abhorrent tangles. On the modern view that "character is destiny," the conception of supernatural wire-pulling is excluded. It is true that amazing coincidences do occur in life; but when they are invented to serve an artist's purposes, we feel that he is simplifying his task altogether beyond reason, and substituting for normal and probable development an irrelevant plunge into the merely marvellous.

Of the abuse of coincidence, I have already given a specimen in speaking of ***The Rise of Dick Halward*** (Chapter XII). One or two more examples may not be out of place. I need not dwell on the significance of the fact that most of them occur in forgotten plays.

In ***The Man of Forty***, by Mr. Walter Frith, we find the following conjuncture of circumstances: Mr. Lewis Dunster has a long-lost wife and a long-lost brother. He has been for years in South Africa; they have meanwhile lived in London, but they do not know each other, and have held no communication. Lewis, returning from Africa, arrives in London. He does not know where to find either wife or brother, and has not the slightest wish to look for them; yet in the first house he goes to, the home of a lady whose acquaintance he chanced to make on the voyage, he encounters both his wife and his brother! Not quite so startling is the coincidence on which ***Mrs. Willoughby's Kiss***, by Mr. Frank Stayton, is founded. An upper and lower flat in West Kensington are inhabited, respectively, by Mrs.

Brandram and Mrs. Willoughby, whose husbands have both been many years absent in India. By pure chance the two husbands come home in the same ship; the two wives go to Plymouth to meet them, and by pure chance, for they are totally unacquainted with each other, they go to the same hotel; whence it happens that Mrs. Willoughby, meeting Mr. Brandram in a half-lighted room, takes him for her husband, flies to his arms and kisses him. More elaborate than either of these is the tangle of coincidences in Mr. Stuart Ogilvie's play, ***The White Knight***--

Giulietta, the ward of David Pennycuick, goes to study singing at Milan. Mr. Harry Rook, Pennycuick's most intimate friend, meets her by chance in Milan, and she becomes his mistress, neither having the least idea that the other knows Pennycuick. Then Viscount Hintlesham, like Pennycuick, a dupe of Rook's, meets her by chance at Monte Carlo and falls in love with her. He does not know that she knows Rook or Pennycuick, and she does not know that he knows them. Arriving in England, she finds in the manager, the promoter, and the chairman of the Electric White Lead Company her guardian, her seducer, and her lover. When she comes to see her guardian, the first person she meets is her seducer, and she learns that her lover has just left the house. Up to that moment, I repeat, she did not know that any one of these men knew any other; yet she does not even say, "How small the world is!"[4] Surely some such observation was obligatory under the circumstances.

Let us turn now to a more memorable piece of work; that interesting play of Sir Arthur Pinero's transition period, ***The Profligate***. Here the great situation of the third act is brought about by a chain of coincidences which would be utterly unthinkable in the author's maturer work. Leslie Brudenell, the heroine, is the ward of Mr. Cheal, a solicitor. She is to be married to Dunstan Renshaw; and, as she has no home, the bridal party meets at Mr. Cheal's office before proceeding to the registrar's. No sooner have they departed than Janet Preece, who has been betrayed and deserted by Dunstan Renshaw (under an assumed name) comes to the office to state her piteous case. This is not in itself a pure coincidence; for Janet happened to come to London in the same train with Leslie Brudenell and her brother Wilfrid; and Wilfrid, seeing in her a damsel in distress, recommended her to lay her troubles before a respectable solicitor, giving her Mr. Cheal's address. So far, then, the coincidence is not startling. It is natural enough that Renshaw's mistress and his betrothed should live in the same country town; and it is not improbable that they should come to

London by the same train, and that Wilfrid Brudenell should give the bewildered and weeping young woman a commonplace piece of advice. The concatenation of circumstances is remarkable rather than improbable. But when, in the next act, not a month later, Janet Preece, by pure chance, drops in at the Florentine villa where Renshaw and Leslie are spending their honeymoon, we feel that the long arm of coincidence is stretched to its uttermost, and that even the thrilling situation which follows is very dearly bought. It would not have been difficult to attenuate the coincidence. What has actually happened is this: Janet has (we know not how) become a sort of maid-companion to a Mrs. Stonehay, whose daughter was a school-friend of Leslie's; the Stonehays have come to Florence, knowing nothing of Leslie's presence there; and they happen to visit the villa in order to see a fresco which it contains. If, now, we had been told that Janet's engagement by the Stonehays had resulted from her visit to Mr. Cheal, and that the Stonehays had come to Florence knowing Leslie to be there, and eager to find her, several links would have been struck off the chain of coincidence; or, to put it more exactly, a fairly coherent sequence of events would have been substituted for a series of incoherent chances. The same result might no doubt have been achieved in many other and neater ways. I merely indicate, by way of illustration, a quite obvious method of reducing the element of coincidence in the case.

The coincidence in ***The Second Mrs. Tanqueray***, by which Ellean meets and falls in love with one of Paula's ex-lovers, has been very severely criticized. It is certainly not one of the strong points of the play; but, unlike the series of chances we have just been examining, it places no excessive strain on our credulity. Such coincidences do occur in real life; we have all of us seen or heard of them; the worst we can say of this one is that it is neither positively good nor positively bad--a piece of indifferent craftsmanship. On the other hand, if we turn to ***Letty***, the chance which, in the third act, leads Letchmere's party and Mandeville's party to choose the same restaurant, seems to me entirely justified. It is not really a coincidence at all, but one of those everyday happenings which are not only admissible in drama, but positively desirable, as part of the ordinary surface-texture of life. Entirely to eliminate chance from our representation of life would be a very unreasonable austerity. Strictly speaking, indeed, it is impossible; for even when we have worked out an unbroken chain of rational and commensurate causes and effects, it remains a chance, and an unlikely chance, that chance should not have interfered with it.

All the plays touched upon in the last four paragraphs are in intention realistic. They aim, that is to say, at a literal and sober representation of life. In the other class of plays, which seek their effect, not in plodding probability, but in delightful improbability, the long arm of coincidence has its legitimate functions. Yet even here it is not quite unfettered. One of the most agreeable coincidences in fiction, I take it, is the simultaneous arrival in Bagdad, from different quarters of the globe, of three one-eyed calenders, all blind of the right eye, and all, in reality, the sons of kings. But it is to be noted that this coincidence is not a crucial occurrence in a story, but only a part of the story-teller's framework or mechanism--a device for introducing fresh series of adventures. This illustrates the Sarceyan principle above referred to, which Professor Brander Matthews has re-stated in what seems to me an entirely acceptable form--namely, that improbabilities which may be admitted on the outskirts of an action, must be rigidly excluded when the issue is joined and we are in the thick of things. Coincidences, in fact, become the more improbable in the direct ratio of their importance. We have all, in our own experience, met with amazing coincidences; but how few of us have ever gained or lost, been made happy or unhappy, by a coincidence, as distinct from a chance! It is not precisely probable that three brothers, who have separated in early life, and have not heard of one another for twenty years, should find themselves seated side by side at an Italian *table-d'hote*; yet such coincidences have occurred, and are creditable enough so long as nothing particular comes of them. But if a dramatist were to make these three brothers meet in Messina on the eve of the earthquake, in order that they might all be killed, and thus enable his hero (their cousin) to succeed to a peerage and marry the heroine, we should say that his use of coincidence was not strictly artistic. A coincidence, in short, which coincides with a crisis is thereby raised to the nth power, and is wholly inacceptable in serious art. Mr. Bernard Shaw has based the action of **You Never Can Tell** on the amazing coincidence that Mrs. Clandon and her children, coming to England after eighteen years' absence, should by pure chance run straight into the arms, or rather into the teeth, of the husband and father whom the mother, at any rate, only wishes to avoid. This is no bad starting-point for an extravaganza; but even Mr. Shaw, though a despiser of niceties of craftsmanship, introduces no coincidences into serious plays such as **Candida** or *The Doctor's Dilemma*.

* * * * *

Notes:

[1: The malignant caricature of Cromwell in W.G. Wills' **Charles** I did not, indeed, prevent the acceptance of the play by the mid-Victorian public; but it will certainly shorten the life of the one play which might have secured for its author a lasting place in dramatic literature. It is unimaginable that future generations should accept a representation of Cromwell as

"A mouthing patriot, with an itching palm, In one hand menace, in the other greed."]

[2: It is only fair to say that Sarcey drew a distinction between antecedent ***events*** and what he calls "postulates of character." He did not maintain that an audience ought to accept a psychological impossibility, merely because it was placed outside the frame of the picture. See **Quarante Ans de Theatre**, vii, p. 395.]

[3: This phrase, which occurs in Mr. Haddon Chambers's romantic melodrama, **Captain Swift**, was greeted with a burst of laughter by the first-night audience; but little did we then think that Mr. Chambers was enriching the English language. It is not, on examination, a particularly luminous phrase: "the three or four arms of coincidence" would really be more to the point. But it is not always the most accurate expression that is fittest to survive.]

[4: The abuse of coincidence is a legacy to modern drama from the Latin comedy, which, again, was founded on the Greek New Comedy. It is worth noting that in the days of Menander the world really was much smaller than it is to-day, when "thalassic" has grown into "oceanic" civilization. Travellers in those days followed a few main routes; half a dozen great seaports were rendezvous for all the world; the slave-trade was active, and kidnappings and abductions with the corresponding meetings and recognitions were no doubt frequent. Thus such a plot as that of the **Menaechmi** was by no means the sheer impossibility which Shakespeare made it by attaching indistinguishable Dromios to his indistinguishable Antipholuses. To reduplicate a coincidence is in fact to multiply it by a figure far beyond my mathematics. It may be noted, too, that the practice of exposing children, on which the ***Oedipus***, and many plays of Menander, are founded, was common in historic Greece, and that the hapless children were generally provided with identification-tokens ***gnorismata*.]**

CHAPTER XVI
LOGIC

The term logic is often very vaguely used in relation to drama. French writers especially, who regard logic as one of the peculiar faculties of their national genius, are apt to insist upon it in and out of season. But, as we have already seen, logic is a gift which may easily be misapplied. It too often leads such writers as M. Brieux and M. Hervieu to sacrifice the undulant and diverse rhythms of life to a stiff and symmetrical formalism. The conception of a play as the exhaustive demonstration of a thesis has never taken a strong hold on the Anglo-Saxon mind; and, though some of M. Brieux's plays are much more than mere dramatic arguments, we need not, in the main, envy the French their logician-dramatists.

But, though the presence of logic should never be forced upon the spectator's attention, still less should he be disturbed and baffled by its conspicuous absence. If the playwright announces a theme at all: if he lets it be seen that some general idea underlies his work: he is bound to present and develop that idea in a logical fashion, not to shift his ground, whether inadvertently or insidiously, and not to wander off into irrelevant side-issues. He must face his problem squarely. If he sets forth to prove anything at all, he must prove that thing and not some totally different thing. He must beware of the red-herring across the trail.

For a clear example of defective logic, I turn to a French play--Sardou's ***Spiritisme***. Both from internal and from external evidence, it is certain that M. Sardou was a believer in spiritualism--in the existence of disembodied intelligences, and their power of communicating with the living. Yet he had not the courage to assign to them an essential part in his drama. The spirits hover round the outskirts of the action, but do not really or effectually intervene in it. The hero's ***belief*** in them, indeed, helps to bring about the conclusion; but the apparition which so potently works upon him is an admitted imposture, a pious fraud. Earlier in the play, two or three trivial and unnecessary miracles are introduced--just enough to hint at the author's faith without decisively affirming it. For instance: towards the close of Act I Madame d'Aubenas has gone off, nominally to take the night train for Poitiers, in reality to pay a visit to her lover, M. de Stoudza. When she has gone, her husband and his guests arrange a seance and evoke a spirit. No sooner have preliminaries been settled than the spirit spells out the word "O-u-v-r-e-z." They open the window, and behold! the sky is red with a glare which proves to proceed from the burning of the train in which Madame d'Aubenas is supposed to have started. The incident is effective enough, and a little creepy; but its effect is quite incommensurate with the strain upon our powers of belief. The thing is supposed to be a miracle, of that there can be no doubt; but it has not the smallest influence on the course of the play, except to bring on the hurry-scurry and alarm a few minutes earlier than might otherwise have been the case. Now, if the spirit, instead of merely announcing the accident, had informed M. d'Aubenas that his wife was not in it--if, for example, it had rapped out "Gilberte chez Stoudza"--it would have been an honest ghost (though indiscreet), and we should not have felt that our credulity had been taxed to no purpose. As it is, the logical deduction from M. Sardou's fable is that, though spirit communications are genuine enough, they are never of the slightest use; but we can scarcely suppose that that was what he intended to convey.

It may be said, and perhaps with truth, that what Sardou lacked in this instance was not logic, but courage: he felt that an audience would accept episodic miracles, but would reject supernatural interference at a determining crisis in the play. In that case he would have done better to let the theme alone: for the manifest failure of logic leaves the play neither good drama nor good argument. This is a totally different matter from Ibsen's treatment of the supernatural in such plays as ***The Lady from the Sea***, ***The Master Builder*** and ***Little Eyolf***. Ibsen, like Hawthorne, suggests without affirming the action of occult powers. He shows us nothing that is not capable of a perfectly natural explanation; but he leaves us to imagine, if we are so disposed, that there may be influences at work that are not yet formally recognized in physics and psychology. In this there is nothing illogical. The poet is merely appealing to a mood, familiar to all of us, in which we wonder whether there may not be more things in heaven and earth than are crystallized in our scientific formulas.

It is a grave defect of logic to state, or hint at, a problem, and then illustrate it in such terms of character that it is solved in advance. In *The Liars*, by Mr. Henry Arthur Jones, there is an evident suggestion of the problem whether a man is ever justified in rescuing a woman, by means of the Divorce Court, from marital bondage which her soul abhors. The sententious Sir Christopher Deering argues the matter at great length: but all the time we are hungering for him to say the one thing demanded by the logic of the situation: to wit: "Whatever the abstract rights and wrongs of the case, this man would be an imbecile to elope with this woman, who is an empty-headed, empty-hearted creature, incapable either of the passion or of the loathing which alone could lend any semblance of reason to a breach of social law." Similarly, in *The Profligate*, Sir Arthur Pinero no doubt intended us to reflect upon the question whether, in entering upon marriage, a woman has a right to assume in her husband the same purity of antecedent conduct which he demands of her. That is an arguable question, and it has been argued often enough; but in this play it does not really arise, for the husband presented to us is no ordinary loose-liver, but (it would seem--for the case is not clearly stated) a particularly base and heartless seducer, whom it is evidently a misfortune for any woman to have married. The authors of these two plays have committed an identical error of logic: namely, that of suggesting a broad issue, and then stating such a set of circumstances that the issue does not really arise. In other words, they have from the outset begged the question. The plays, it may be said, were both successful in their day. Yes; but had they been logical their day might have lasted a century. A somewhat similar defect of logic constitutes a fatal blemish in *The Ideal Husband*, by Oscar Wilde. Intentionally or otherwise, the question suggested is whether a single flaw of conduct (the betrayal to financiers of a state secret) ought to blast a political career. Here, again, is an arguable point, on the assumption that the statesman is penitent and determined never to repeat his misdeed; but when we find that this particular statesman is prepared to go on betraying his country indefinitely, in order to save his own skin, the question falls to the ground--the answer is too obvious.

It happened some years ago that two plays satirizing "yellow journalism" were produced almost simultaneously in London--The Earth by Mr. James B. Fagan, and *What the Public Wants* by Mr. Arnold Bennett. In point of intellectual grasp, or power of characterization, there could be no comparison between the two writers; yet I hold that, from the point of view of dramatic composition, *The Earth* was the better play of the two, simply because it dealt logically with the theme announced, instead of wandering away into all sorts of irrelevances. Mr. Bennett, to begin with, could not resist making his Napoleon of the Press a native of the "Five Towns," and exhibiting him at large in provincial middle-class surroundings. All this is sheer irrelevance; for the type of journalism in question is not characteristically an outcome of any phase of provincial life. Mr. Bennett may allege that Sir Charles Worgan had to be born somewhere, and might as well be born in Bursley as anywhere else. I reply that, for the purposes of the play, he need not have been born anywhere. His birthplace and the surroundings of his boyhood have nothing to do with what may be called his journalistic psychology, which is, or ought to be, the theme of the play. Then, again, Mr. Bennett shows him dabbling in theatrical management and falling in love--irrelevances both. As a manager, no doubt, he insists on doing "what the public wants" (it is nothing worse than a revival of *The Merchant of Venice*) and thus offers another illustration of the results of obeying that principle. But all this is beside the real issue. The true gravamen of the charge against a Napoleon of the Press is not that he gives the public what it wants, but that he can make the public want what *he* wants, think what *he* thinks, believe what *he* wants them to believe, and do what *he* wants them to do. By dint of assertion, innuendo, and iteration in a hundred papers, he can create an apparent public opinion, or public emotion, which may be directed towards the most dangerous ends. This point Mr. Bennett entirely missed. What he gave us was in reality a comedy of middle-class life with a number of incidental allusions to "yellow" journalism and kindred topics. Mr. Fagan, working in broader outlines, and, it must be owned, in cruder colours, never strayed from the logical line of development, and took us much nearer the heart of his subject.

A somewhat different, and very common, fault of logic was exemplified in Mr. Clyde Fitch's last play, *The City*. His theme, as announced in his title and indicated in his exposition, was the influence of New York upon a family which migrates thither from a provincial town. But the action is not really shaped by the influence of "the city." It might have taken practically the same course if the family had remained at home. The author had failed to establish a logical connection between his theme and the incidents supposed to illustrate it.[1]

Fantastic plays, which assume an order of things more or less exempt from the limitations of physical reality, ought, nevertheless, to be logically faithful to their own assumptions. Some fantasies, indeed, which sinned against this principle, have had no small success. In ***Pygmalion and Galatea***, for example, there is a conspicuous lack of logic. The following passage from a criticism of thirty years ago puts my point so clearly that I am tempted to copy it:

As we have no scientific record of a statue coming to life, the probable moral and intellectual condition of a being so created is left to the widest conjecture. The playwright may assume for it any stage of development he pleases, and his audience will readily grant his assumption. But if his work is to have any claim to artistic value, he must not assume all sorts of different stages of development at every second word his creation utters. He must not make her a child in one speech, a woman of the world in the next, and an idiot in the next again. Of course, it would be an extremely difficult task clearly to define in all its bearings and details the particular intellectual condition assumed at the outset, and then gradually to indicate the natural growth of a fuller consciousness. Difficult it would be, but by no means impossible; nay, it would be this very problem which would tempt the true dramatist to adopt such a theme. Mr. Gilbert has not essayed the task. He regulates Galatea's state of consciousness by the fluctuating exigencies of dialogue whose humour is levelled straight at the heads of the old Haymarket pit.

To indicate the nature of the inconsistencies which abound in every scene, I may say that, in the first act, Galatea does not know that she is a woman, but understands the word "beauty," knows (though Pygmalion is the only living creature she has ever seen) the meaning of agreement and difference of taste, and is alive to the distinction between an original and a copy. In the second act she has got the length of knowing the enormity of taking life, and appreciating the fine distinction between taking it of one's own motive, and taking it for money. Yet the next moment, when Leucippe enters with a fawn he has killed, it appears that she does not realize the difference between man and the brute creation. Thus we are for ever shifting from one plane of convention to another. There is no fixed starting-point for our imagination, no logical development of a clearly-stated initial condition.

The play, it is true, enjoyed some five-and-twenty years of life; but it certainly cannot claim an enduring place either in literature or on the stage. It is still open to the philosophic dramatist to write a logical **Pygmalion and Galatea**.

* * * * *

Note:
[1: I am here writing from memory, having been unable to obtain a copy of **The City**; but my memory is pretty clear.]

CHAPTER XVII
KEEPING A SECRET

It has been often and authoritatively laid down that a dramatist must on no account keep a secret from his audience. Like most authoritative maxims, this one seems to require a good deal of qualification. Let us look into the matter a little more closely.

So far as I can see, the strongest reason against keeping a secret is that, try as you may, you cannot do it. This point has already been discussed in Chapter IX, where we saw that from only one audience can a secret be really hidden, a considerable percentage of any subsequent audience being certain to know all about it in advance. The more striking and successful is the first-night effect of surprise, the more certainly and rapidly will the report of it circulate through all strata of the theatrical public. But for this fact, one could quite well conceive a fascinating melodrama constructed, like a detective story, with a view to keeping the audience in the dark as long as possible. A pistol shot might ring out just before the rise of the curtain: a man (or woman) might be discovered in an otherwise empty room, weltering in his (or her) gore: and the remainder of the play might consist in the tracking down of the murderer, who would, of course, prove to be the very last person to be suspected. Such a play might make a great first-night success; but the more the author relied upon the mystery for his effect, the more fatally would that effect be discounted at each successive repetition.

One author of distinction, M. Hervieu, has actually made the experiment of presenting an enigma--he calls the play ***L'Enigme***--and reserving the solution to the very end. We know from the outset that one of two sisters-in-law is unfaithful to her husband, and the question is--which? The whole ingenuity of the author is centred on keeping the secret, and the spectator who does not know it in advance is all the time in the attitude of a detective questing for clues. He is challenged to guess which of the ladies is the frail one; and he is far too intent on this game to think or care about the emotional process of the play. I myself (I remember) guessed right, mainly because the name Giselle seemed to me more suggestive of flightiness than the staid and sober Leonore, wherefore I suspected that M. Hervieu, in order to throw dust in our eyes, had given it to the virtuous lady. But whether we guess right or wrong, this clue-hunting is an intellectual sport, not an artistic enjoyment. If there is any aesthetic quality in the play, it can only come home to us when we know the secret. And the same dilemma will present itself to any playwright who seeks to imitate M. Hervieu.

The actual keeping of a secret, then--the appeal to the primary curiosity of actual ignorance--may be ruled out as practically impossible, and, when possible, unworthy of serious art. But there is also, as we have seen, the secondary curiosity of the audience which, though more or less cognizant of the essential facts, instinctively assumes ignorance, and judges the development of a play from that point of view. We all realize that a dramatist has no right to trust to our previous knowledge, acquired from outside sources. We know that a play, like every other work of art, ought to be self-sufficient, and even if, at any given moment, we have, as a matter of fact, knowledge which supplements what the playwright has told us, we feel that he ought not to have taken for granted our possession of any such external and fortuitous information. To put it briefly, the dramatist must formally **assume** ignorance in his audience, though he must not practically **rely upon** it. Therefore it becomes a point of real importance to determine how long a secret may be kept from an audience, assumed to have no outside knowledge, and at what point it ought to be revealed.

When **Lady Windermere's Fan** was first produced, no hint was given in the first act of the fact that Mrs. Erlynne was Lady Windermere's mother; so that Lord Windermere's insistence on inviting her to his wife's birthday reception remained wholly unexplained. But after a few nights the author made Lord Windermere exclaim, just as the curtain fell, "My God! What shall I do? I dare not tell her who this woman really is. The shame would kill her." It was, of course, said that this change had been made in deference to newspaper criticism; and Oscar Wilde, in a characteristic letter to the *St. James's Gazette*, promptly repelled this calumny. At a first-night supper-party, he said--

> "All of my friends without exception were of the opinion that the psychological interest of the second act would be greatly increased by the disclosure of the actual relationship existing between Lady Windermere and Mrs. Erlynne--an opinion, I may add, that had previously been strongly held and urged by Mr. Alexander.... I determined, consequently, to make a change in the precise moment of revelation."

It is impossible to say whether Wilde seriously believed that "psychology" entered into the matter at all, or whether he was laughing in his sleeve in putting forward this solemn plea. The truth is, I think, that this example cannot be cited either for or against the keeping of a secret, the essential fact being that the secret was such a bad and inacceptable one--inacceptable, I mean, as an explanation of Lord Windermere's conduct--that it was probably wise to make a clean breast of it as soon as possible, and get it over. It may be said with perfect confidence that it is useless to keep a secret which, when revealed, is certain to disappoint the audience, and to make it feel that it has been trifled with. That is an elementary dictate of prudence. But if the reason for Lord Windermere's conduct had been adequate, ingenious, such as to give us, when revealed, a little shock of pleasant surprise, the author need certainly have been in no hurry to disclose it. It is not improbable (though my memory is not clear on the point) that part of the strong interest we undoubtedly felt on the first night arose from the hope that Lord Windermere's seemingly unaccountable conduct might be satisfactorily accounted for. As this hope was futile, there was no reason, at subsequent performances, to keep up the pretence of preserving a secret which was probably known, as a matter of fact, to most of the audience, and which was worthless when revealed.

In the second act of *The Devil's Disciple*, by Mr. Bernard Shaw, we have an instance of wholly inartistic secrecy, which would certainly be condemned in the work of any author who was not accepted in advance as a law unto himself. Richard Dudgeon has been arrested by the British soldiers, who mistake him for the Reverend Anthony Anderson. When Anderson comes home, it takes a very long time for his silly wife, Judith, to acquaint him with a situation that might have been explained in three words; and when, at last, he does understand it, he calls for a horse and his boots, and rushes off in mad haste, as though his one desire were to escape from the British and leave Dudgeon to his fate. In reality his purpose is to bring up a body of Continental troops to the rescue of Dudgeon; and this also he might (and certainly would) have conveyed in three words. But Mr. Shaw was so bent on letting Judith continue to conduct herself idiotically, that he made her sensible husband act no less idiotically, in order to throw dust in her eyes, and (incidentally) in the eyes of the audience. In the work of any other man, we should call this not only an injudicious, but a purposeless and foolish, keeping of a secret. Mr. Shaw may say that in order to develop the character of Judith as he had conceived it, he was forced to make her misunderstand her husband's motives. A development of character obtained by such artificial means cannot be of much worth; but even granting this plea, one cannot but point out that it would have been easy to keep Judith in the dark as to Anderson's purpose, without keeping the audience also in the dark, and making him behave like a fool. All that was required was to get Judith off the stage for a few moments, just before the true state of matters burst upon Anthony. It would then have been perfectly natural and probable that, not foreseeing her misunderstanding, he should hurry off without waiting to explain matters to her. But that he should deliberately leave her in her delusion, and even use phrases carefully calculated to deceive both her and the audience,[1] would be, in a writer who professed to place reason above caprice, a rather gross fault of art.

Mr. Henry Arthur Jones's light comedy, **Whitewashing Julia**, proves that it is possible, without incurring disaster, to keep a secret throughout a play, and never reveal it at all. More accurately, what Mr. Jones does is to pretend that there is some explanation of Mrs. Julia Wren's relations with the Duke of Savona, other than the simple explanation that she was his mistress, and to keep us waiting for this "whitewashing" disclosure, when in fact he has nothing of the sort up his sleeve, and the plain truth is precisely what the gossips of Shanctonbury surmise. Julia does not even explain or justify her conduct from her own point of view. She gives out that "an explanation will be forthcoming at the right moment"; but the right moment never arrives. All we are told is that she, Julia, considers that there was never anything degrading in her conduct; and this we are asked to accept as sufficient. It was a daring policy to dangle before our eyes an explanation, which always receded as we advanced towards it, and proved in the end to be wholly unexplanatory. The success of the play, however, was sufficient to show that, in light comedy, at any rate, a secret may with impunity be kept, even to the point of tantalization.[2]

Let us now look at a couple of cases in which the keeping of a secret seems pretty clearly wrong, inasmuch as it diminishes tension, and deprives the audience of that superior knowledge in which lies the irony of drama. In a play named ***Her Advocate***, by Mr. Walter Frith (founded on one of Grenville Murray's ***French Pictures in English Chalk***), a K.C. has fallen madly in love with a woman whose defence he has undertaken. He believes passionately in her innocence, and, never doubting that she loves him in return, he is determined to secure for her a triumphant acquittal. Just at the crucial moment, however, he learns that she loves another man; and, overwhelmed by this disillusion, he has still to face the ordeal and plead her cause. The conjuncture would be still more dramatic if the revelation of this love were to put a different complexion on the murder, and, by introducing a new motive, shake the advocate's faith in his client's innocence. But that is another matter; the question here to be considered is whether the author did right in reserving the revelation to the last possible moment. In my opinion he would have done better to have given us an earlier inkling of the true state of affairs. To keep the secret, in this case, was to place the audience as well as the advocate on a false trail, and to deprive it of the sense of superiority it would have felt in seeing him marching confidently towards a happiness which it knew to be illusory.

The second case is that of ***La Douloureuse***, by M. Maurice Donnay. Through two acts out of the four an important secret is so carefully kept that there seems to be no obstacle between the lovers with whom (from the author's point of view) we are supposed to sympathize. The first act is devoted to an elaborate painting of a somewhat revolting phase of parvenu society in Paris. Towards the end of the act we learn that the sculptor, Philippe Lauberthie, is the lover of Helene Ardan, a married woman; and at the very end her husband, Ardan, commits suicide. This act, therefore, is devoted, not, as the orthodox formula goes, to raising an obstacle between the lovers, but rather to destroying one. In the second act there still seems to be no obstacle of any sort. Helene's year of widowhood is nearly over; she and

Philippe are presently to be married; all is harmony, adoration, and security. In the last scene of the act, a cloud no bigger than a man's hand appears on the horizon. We find that Gotte des Trembles, Helene's bosom friend, is also in love with Philippe, and is determined to let him know it. But Philippe resists her blandishments with melancholy austerity, and when the curtain falls on the second act, things seem to be perfectly safe and in order. Helene a widow, and Philippe austere--what harm can Gotte possibly do?

The fact is, M. Donnay is carefully keeping a secret from us. Philippe is not Helene's first lover; her son, Georges, is not the child of her late husband; and Gotte, and Gotte alone, knows the truth. Had we also been initiated from the outset (and nothing would have been easier or more natural--three words exchanged between Gotte and Helene would have done it) we should have been at no loss to foresee the impending drama, and the sense of irony would have tripled the interest of the intervening scenes. The effect of M. Donnay's third act is not a whit more forcible because it comes upon us unprepared. We learn at the beginning that Philippe's austerity has not after all been proof against Gotte's seductions; but it has now returned upon him embittered by remorse, and he treats Gotte with sternness approaching to contumely. She takes her revenge by revealing Helene's secret; he tells Helene that he knows it; and she, putting two and two together, divines how it has come to his knowledge. This long scene of mutual reproach and remorseful misery is, in reality, the whole drama, and might have been cited in Chapter XIV as a fine example of a peripety. Helene enters Philippe's studio happy and serene, she leaves it broken-hearted; but the effect of the scene is not a whit greater because, in the two previous acts, we have been studiously deprived of the information that would have led us vaguely to anticipate it.

To sum up this question of secrecy: the current maxim, "Never keep a secret from your audience," would appear to be an over-simplification of a somewhat difficult question of craftsmanship. We may agree that it is often dangerous and sometimes manifestly foolish to keep a secret; but, on the other hand, there is certainly no reason why the playwright should blurt out all his secrets at the first possible opportunity. The true art lies in knowing just how long to keep silent, and just the right time to speak. In the first act of **Letty**, Sir Arthur Pinero gains a memorable effect by keeping a secret, not very long, indeed, but long enough and carefully enough to show that he knew very clearly what he was doing. We are introduced to Nevill Letchmere's bachelor apartments. Animated scenes occur between Letchmere and his brother-in-law, Letchmere and his sister, Letchmere and Letty, Marion and Hilda Gunning. It is evident that Letty dreams of marriage with Letchmere; and for aught that we see or hear, there is no just cause or impediment to the contrary. It is only, at the end of the very admirable scene between Letchmere and Mandeville that the following little passage occurs:

MANDEVILLE: ... At all events I *am* qualified to tell her I'm fairly gone on her--honourably gone on her--if I choose to do it.

LETCHMERE: Qualified?

MANDEVILLE: Which is more than you are, Mr. Letchmere. I *am* a single man; you ain't, bear in mind.

LETCHMERE: (imperturbably): Very true.

This one little touch is a masterpiece of craftsmanship. It would have been the most natural thing in the world for either the sister or the brother-in-law, concerned about their own matrimonial difficulties, to let fall some passing allusion to Letchmere's separation from his wife; but the author carefully avoided this, carefully allowed us to make our first acquaintance with Letty in ignorance of the irony of her position, and then allowed the truth to slip out just in time to let us feel the whole force of that irony during the last scene of the act and the greater part of the second act. A finer instance of the delicate grading of tension it would be difficult to cite.

One thing is certain; namely, that if a secret is to be kept at all, it must be worth the keeping; if a riddle is propounded, its answer must be pleasing and ingenious, or the audience will resent having been led to cudgel its brains for nothing. This is simply a part of the larger principle, before insisted on, that when a reasonable expectation is aroused, it can be baffled only at the author's peril. If the crux of a scene or of a whole play lie in the solution of some material difficulty or moral problem, it must on no account be solved by a mere trick or evasion. The dramatist is very ill-advised who sets forth with pomp and circumstance to perform some intellectual or technical feat, and then merely skirts round it or runs away from it. A fair proportion should always be observed between effort and effect, between promise and performance.

"But if the audience happens to misread the playwright's design, and form exaggerated and irrational expectations?" That merely means that the playwright does not know his business, or, at any rate, does not know his audience. It is his business to play upon the collective mind of his audience as upon a keyboard--to arouse just the right order and measure of anticipation, and fulfil it, or outdo it, in just the right way at just the right time. The skill of the dramatist, as distinct from his genius or inspiration, lies in the correctness of his insight into the mind of his audience.

* * * * *

Notes:
[1: For instance: "If you can get a word with him by pretending that you are his wife, tell him to hold his tongue until morning; *that will give me all the start I need*."]

[2: In *The Idyll*, by Herr Egge, of which some account is given in Chapter X, the author certainly does right in not allowing the audience for a moment to share the hero's doubts as to the heroine's past. It would have been very easy for him to have kept the secret; but he takes the earliest opportunity of assuring us that her relations with Ringve were quite innocent.]

BOOK IV THE END

CHAPTER XVIII
CLIMAX AND ANTICLIMAX

If it were as easy to write a good last act as a good first act, we should be able to reckon three masterpieces for every one that we can name at present. The reason why the last act should offer special difficulties is not far to seek. We have agreed to regard a play as essentially a crisis in the lives of one or more persons; and we all know that crises are much more apt to have a definite beginning than a definite end. We can almost always put our finger upon the moment--not, indeed, when the crisis began--but when we clearly realized its presence or its imminence. A chance meeting, the receipt of a letter or a telegram, a particular turn given to a certain conversation, even the mere emergence into consciousness of a previously latent feeling or thought, may mark quite definitely the moment of germination, so to speak, of a given crisis; and it is comparatively easy to dramatize such a moment. But how few crises come to a definite or dramatic conclusion! Nine times out of ten they end in some petty compromise, or do not end at all, but simply subside, like the waves of the sea when the storm has blown itself out. It is the playwright's chief difficulty to find a crisis with an ending which satisfies at once his artistic conscience and the requirements of dramatic effect.

And the difficulty becomes greater the nearer we approach to reality. In the days when tragedy and comedy were cast in fixed, conventional moulds, the playwright's task was much simpler. It was thoroughly understood that a tragedy ended with one or more deaths, a comedy with one or more marriages; so that the question of a strong or a weak ending did not arise. The end might be strongly or weakly led up to, but, in itself, it was fore-ordained. Now that these moulds are broken, and both marriage and death may be said to have lost their prestige as the be-all and end-all of drama, the playwright's range of choice is unlimited, and the difficulty of choosing has become infinitely greater. Our comedies are much more apt to begin than to end with marriage, and death has come to be regarded as a rather cheap and conventional expedient for cutting the knots of life.

From the fact that "the difficulty becomes greater the nearer we approach to reality," it further follows that the higher the form of drama, the more probable is it that the demands of truth and the requirements of dramatic effect may be found to clash. In melodrama, the curtain falls of its own accord, so to speak, when the handcuffs are transferred from the hero's wrists to the villain's. In an adventure-play, whether farcical or romantic, when the adventure is over the play is done. The author's task is merely to keep the interest of the adventure afoot until he is ready to drop his curtain. This is a point of craftsmanship in which playwrights often fail; but it is a point of craftsmanship only. In plays of a higher order, on the other hand, the difficulty is often inherent in the theme, and not to be overcome by any feat of craftsmanship. If the dramatist were to eschew all crises that could not be made to resolve themselves with specifically dramatic crispness and decisiveness, he would very seriously limit the domain of his art. Many excellent themes would be distorted and ruined by having an emphatic ending forced upon them. It is surely much better that they should be brought to their natural unemphatic ending, than that they should be either falsified or ignored.

I suggest, then, that the modern tendency to take lightly Aristotle's demand that the drama should have a "beginning, a middle, ***and an end***," arises from the nature of things, and implies, not necessarily, nor even probably, a decline in craftsmanship, but a new intimacy of relation to life, and a new sincerity of artistic conscience. I suggest that the "weak last act," of which critics so often complain, is a natural development from which authors ought not, on occasion, to shrink, and of which critics ought, on occasion, to recognize the necessity. To elevate it into a system is absurd. There is certainly no more reason for deliberately avoiding an emphatic ending than for mechanically forcing one. But authors and critics alike should learn to distinguish the themes which do, from the themes which do not, call for a definite, trenchant solution, and should handle them, and judge them, in accordance with their inherent quality.

Let us, however, define our terms, and be sure that we know what we are talking about. By an "unemphatic ending" I am far from meaning a makeshift ending, an ending carelessly and conventionally huddled up. Nor do I mean an indecisive ending, where the curtain falls, as the saying goes, on a note of interrogation. An unemphatic ending, as I understand it, is a deliberate anticlimax, an idyllic, or elegiac, or philosophic last act, following upon a penultimate act of very much higher tension. The disposition to condemn such an ending off-hand is what I am here pleading against. It is sometimes assumed that the playwright ought always to make his action conclude within five minutes of its culmination; but for such a hard-and-fast rule I can find no sufficient reason. The consequences of a great emotional or spiritual crisis cannot always be worked out, or even foreshadowed, within so brief a space of time. If, after such a crisis, we are unwilling to keep our seats for another half-hour, in order to learn "what came of it all," the author has evidently failed to awaken in us any real interest in his characters.

A good instance of the unemphatic ending is the last act of Sir Arthur Pinero's ***Letty***. This "epilogue"--so the author calls it--has been denounced as a concession to popular sentimentality, and an unpardonable anticlimax. An anticlimax it is, beyond all doubt; but it does not follow that it is an artistic blemish. Nothing would have been easier than not to write it--to make the play end with Letty's awakening from her dream, and her flight from Letchmere's rooms. But the author has set forth, not merely to interest us in an adventure, but to draw a character; and it was essential to our full appreciation of Letty's character that we should know what, after all, she made of her life. When Iris, most hapless of women, went out into the dark, there was nothing more that we needed to know of her. We could guess the sequel only too easily. But the case of Letty was wholly different. Her exit was an act of will, triumphing over a form of temptation peculiarly alluring to her temperament. There was in her character precisely that grit which Iris lacked; and we wanted to know what it would do for her. This was not a case for an indecisive ending, a note of interrogation. The author felt no doubt as to Letty's destiny, and he wanted to leave his audience in no doubt. From Iris's fate we were only too willing to avert our eyes; but it would have been a sensible discomfort to us to be left in the dark about Letty's.

This, then, I regard as a typical instance of justified anticlimax. Another is the idyllic last act of ***The Princess and the Butterfly***, in which, moreover, despite its comparatively subdued tone, the tension is maintained to the end. A very different matter is the third act of ***The Benefit of the Doubt***, already alluded to. This is a pronounced case of the makeshift ending, inspired (to all appearance) simply by the fact that the play must end somehow, and that no better idea happens to present itself. Admirable as are the other acts, one is almost inclined to agree with Dumas that an author ought not to embark upon a theme unless he foresees a better way out of it than this. It should be noted, too, that ***The Benefit of the Doubt*** is a three-act play, and that, in a play laid out on this scale, a whole act of anticlimax is necessarily disproportionate. It is one thing to relax the tension in the last act out of four or five; quite another thing in the last act out of three. In other words, the culminating point of a four-or five-act play may be placed in the penultimate act; in a three-act play, it should come, at earliest, in the penultimate scene.[1]

In the works of Mr. Henry Arthur Jones we find several instances of the unemphatic last act--some clearly justified, others much less so. Among the former I unhesitatingly reckon the fourth act of ***Mrs. Dane's Defence***. It would not have been difficult, but surely most inartistic, to huddle up the action in five minutes after Mrs. Dane's tragic collapse under Sir Daniel Carteret's cross-examination. She might have taken poison and died in picturesque contortions on the sofa; or Lionel might have defied all counsels of prudence and gone off with her in spite of her past; or she might have placed Lionel's hand in Janet's, saying: "The game is up. Bless you, my children. I am going into the nearest nunnery." As a matter of fact, Mr. Jones brought his action to its natural close in a quiet, sufficiently adroit, last act; and I do not see that criticism has any just complaint to make.

In recent French drama, ***La Douloureuse***, already cited, affords an excellent instance of a quiet last act. After the violent and heartrending rupture between the lovers in the third act, we feel that, though this paroxysm of pain is justified by the circumstances, it will not last for ever, and Philippe and Helene will come together again. This is also M. Donnay's view; and he devotes his whole last act, quite simply, to a duologue of reconciliation. It seems to me a fault of proportion, however, that he should shift his locality from Paris to the Riviera, and should place the brief duologue in a romantic woodland scene. An act of anticlimax should be treated, so to speak, as unpretentiously as possible. To invent an elaborate apparatus for it is to emphasize the anticlimax by throwing it into unnecessary relief.

This may be a convenient place for a few words on the modern fashion of eschewing emphasis, not only in last acts, but at every point where the old French dramaturgy demanded it, and especially in act-endings. **Punch** has a pleasant allusion to this tendency in two suggested examination-papers for an "Academy of Dramatists":

A--FOR THE CLASSICAL SIDE ONLY.
1. What is a "curtain"; and how should it be led up to?

B--FOR THE MODERN SIDE ONLY.
1. What is a "curtain"; and how can it be avoided?

Some modern playwrights have fled in a sort of panic from the old "picture-poster situation" to the other extreme of always dropping their curtain when the audience least expects it. This is not a practice to be commended. One has often seen an audience quite unnecessarily chilled by a disconcerting "curtain." There should be moderation even in the shrinking from theatricality.

This shrinking is particularly marked, though I do not say it is carried too far, in the plays of Mr. Galsworthy. Even the most innocent tricks of emphasis are to him snares of the Evil One. He would sooner die than drop his curtain on a particularly effective line. It is his chief ambition that you should never discern any arrangement, any intention, in his work. As a rule, the only reason you can see for his doing thus or thus is his desire that you should see no reason for it. He does not carry this tendency, as some do, to the point of eccentricity; but he certainly goes as far as any one should be advised to follow. A little further, and you incur the danger of becoming affectedly unaffected, artificially inartificial.

I am far from pleading for the conventional tableau at the end of each act, with all the characters petrified, as it were, in penny-plain-twopence-coloured attitudes. But it is certainly desirable that the fall of the curtain should not take an audience entirely by surprise, and even that the spectator should feel the moment to be rightly chosen, though he might be unable to give any reason for his feeling. Moreover--this may seem a super-subtlety, but one has seen it neglected with notably bad effect--a playwright should never let his audience expect the fall of a curtain at a given point, and then balk their expectancy, unless he is sure that he holds in reserve a more than adequate compensation. There is nothing so dangerous as to let a play, or an act, drag on when the audience feels in its heart that it is really over, and that "the rest is silence"--or ought to be. The end of Mr. Granville Barker's fine play, *The Voysey Inheritance*, was injured by the fact that, several minutes before the curtain actually fell, he had given what seemed an obvious "cue for curtain." I do not say that what followed was superfluous; what I do say is that the author ought to have been careful not to let us imagine that the colloquy between Edward and Alice was over when in fact it had still some minutes to run. An even more remarkable play, *The Madras House*, was ruined, on its first night, by a long final anticlimax. Here, however, the fault did not lie in awakening a premature expectation of the close, but in the fact that we somehow were more interested in the other characters of the play than in the pair who held the stage throughout the long concluding scene.

Once more I turn to *La Douloureuse* for an instance of an admirable act-ending of the quiet modern type. The third act--the terrible peripety in the love of Philippe and Helene--has run its agonizing course, and worked itself out. The old dramaturgy would certainly have ended the scene with a bang, so to speak--a swoon or a scream, a tableau of desolation, or, at the very least, a piece of tearful rhetoric. M. Donnay does nothing of the sort. He lets his lovers unpack their hearts with words until they are exhausted, broken, dazed with misery, and have nothing more to say. Then Helene asks: "What o'clock is it?" Philippe looks at his watch: "Nearly seven." "I must be going"--and she dries her eyes, smoothes her hair, pulls herself together, in a word, to face the world again. The mechanical round of life re-asserts its hold upon them. "Help me with my cloak," she says; and he holds her mantle for her, and tucks in the puffed sleeves of her blouse. Then he takes up the lamp and lights her out--and the curtain falls. A model "curtain"!

* * * * *

Note:

[1: The fact that a great poet can ignore such precepts with impunity is proved by the exquisite anticlimax of the third act of D'Annunzio's ***La Gioconda***.]

CHAPTER XIX
CONVERSION

The reader may have noticed, possibly with surprise, that some of the stock terms of dramatic criticism occur but rarely in these pages, or not at all. One of them is *denouement*. According to orthodox theory, I ought to have made the *denouement* the subject of a whole chapter, if not of a whole book. Why have I not done so?

For two reasons. The lesser, but not negligible, reason is that we possess no convenient English word for the unknotting or disentangling of a complication. Denouement itself cannot be plausibly Anglicized, and no native word has as yet, by common consent, been accepted as its equivalent. I sometimes wish we could adopt, and print without italics, the excellent and expressive Greek word "lusis"; but I cannot, on my own responsibility, attempt so daring an innovation. The second and determining reason for not making the *denouement* one of the heads of my argument, is that, the play of intrigue being no longer the dominant dramatic form, the image of disentangling has lost some of its special fitness. It is only in a somewhat strained and conventional sense that the term *nodus*, or knot, can be applied to the sort of crisis with which the modern drama normally deals; and if we do not naturally think of the crisis as a knot, we naturally do not think of its close as an unknotting.

Nevertheless, there are frequent cases in which the end of a play depends on something very like the unravelling of a tangled skein; and still more often, perhaps, is it brought about through the loosening of some knot in the mind of one or more of the characters. This was the characteristic end of the old comedy. The heavy father, or cantankerous guardian, who for four acts and a half had stood between the lovers, suddenly changed his mind, and all was well. Even by our ancestors this was reckoned a rather too simple method of disentanglement. Lisideius, in Dryden's dialogue,[1] in enumerating the points in which the French drama is superior to the English notes that--

> You never see any of their plays end with a conversion, or simple change of will, which is the ordinary way which our poets use to end theirs. It shew little art in the conclusion of a dramatick poem, when they who have hindered the felicity during the four acts, desist from it in the fifth, without some powerful cause to take them off their design.

The remark of Lisideius is suggested by a passage in Corneille, who instances, as an apt and artistic method of bringing about the conversion of a heavy father, that his daughter's lover should earn his gratitude by rescuing him from assassination!

Conversions, closely examined, will be found to fall into two classes: changes in volition, and changes in sentiment. It was the former class that Dryden had in mind; and, with reference to this class, the principle he indicates remains a sound one. A change of resolve should never be due to a mere lapse of time--to the necessity for bringing the curtain down and letting the audience go home. It must always be rendered plausible by some new fact or new motive: some hitherto untried appeal to reason or emotion. This rule, however, is too obvious to require enforcement. It was not quite superfluous so long as the old convention of comedy endured. For a century and a half after Dryden's time, hard-hearted parents were apt to withdraw their opposition to their children's "felicity" for no better reason than that the fifth act was drawing to a close. But this formula is practically obsolete. Changes of will, on the modern stage, are not always adequately motived; but that is because of individual inexpertness, not because of any failure to recognize theoretically the necessity for adequate motivation.

Changes of sentiment are much more important and more difficult to handle. A change of will can always manifest itself in action but it is very difficult to externalize convincingly a mere change of heart. When the conclusion of a play hinges (as it frequently does) on a conversion of this nature, it becomes a matter of the first moment that it should not merely be asserted, but proved. Many a promising play has gone wrong because of the author's neglect, or inability, to comply with this condition.

It has often been observed that of all Ibsen's thoroughly mature works, from *A Doll's House* to *John Gabriel Borkman*, *The Lady from the Sea* is the loosest in texture, the least masterly in construction. The fact that it leaves this impression on the mind is largely due, I think, to a single fault. The conclusion of the play--Ellida's clinging to Wangel and rejection of the Stranger--depends entirely on a change in Wangel's mental attitude, **of which we have no proof whatever beyond his bare assertion**. Ellida, in her overwrought mood, is evidently inclining to yield to the uncanny allurement of the Stranger's claim upon her, when Wangel, realizing that her sanity is threatened, says:

> WANGEL: It shall not come to that. There is no other way of deliverance for you--at least I see none. And therefore--therefore I--cancel our bargain on the spot. Now you can choose your own path, in full--full freedom.
>
> ELLIDA (_Gazes at him awhile, as if speechless_): Is this true--true--what you say? Do you mean it--from your inmost heart?
>
> WANGEL: Yes--from the inmost depths of my tortured heart, I mean it.... Now your own true life can return to its--its right groove again. For now you can choose in freedom; and on your own responsibility, Ellida.
>
> ELLIDA: In freedom--and on my own responsibility? Responsibility? This--this transforms everything.

--and she promptly gives the Stranger his dismissal. Now this is inevitably felt to be a weak conclusion, because it turns entirely on a condition of Wangel's mind of which he gives no positive and convincing evidence. Nothing material is changed by his change of heart. He could not in any case have restrained Ellida by force; or, if the law gave him the abstract right to do so, he certainly never had the slightest intention of exercising it. Psychologically, indeed, the incident is acceptable enough. The saner part of Ellida's will was always on Wangel's side; and a merely verbal undoing of the "bargain" with which she reproached herself might quite naturally suffice to turn the scale decisively in his favour. But what may suffice for Ellida is not enough for the audience. Too much is made to hang upon a verbally announced conversion. The poet ought to have invented some material--or, at the very least, some impressively symbolic--proof of Wangel's change of heart. Had he done so, *The Lady from the Sea* would assuredly have taken a higher rank among his works.

Let me further illustrate my point by comparing a very small thing with a very great. The late Captain Marshall wrote a "farcical romance" named ***The Duke of Killiecrankie***, in which that nobleman, having been again and again rejected by the Lady Henrietta Addison, kidnapped the obdurate fair one, and imprisoned her in a crag-castle in the Highlands. Having kept her for a week in deferential durance, and shown her that he was not the inefficient nincompoop she had taken him for, he threw open the prison gate, and said to her: "Go! I set you free!" The moment she saw the gate unlocked, and realized that she could indeed go when and where she pleased, she also realized that she had not the least wish to go, and flung herself into her captor's arms. Here we have Ibsen's situation transposed into the key of fantasy, and provided with the material "guarantee of good faith" which is lacking in *The Lady from the Sea*. The Duke's change of mind, his will to set the Lady Henrietta free, is visibly demonstrated by the actual opening of the prison gate, so that we believe in it, and believe that she believes in it. The play was a trivial affair, and is deservedly forgotten; but the situation was effective because it obeyed the law that a change of will or of feeling, occurring at a crucial point in a dramatic action, must be certified by some external evidence, on pain of leaving the audience unimpressed.

This is a more important matter than it may at first sight appear. How to bring home to the audience a decisive change of heart is one of the ever-recurring problems of the playwright's craft. In *The Lady from the Sea*, Ibsen failed to solve it: in **Rosmersholm** he solved it by heroic measures. The whole catastrophe is determined by Rosmer's inability to accept without proof Rebecca's declaration that Rosmersholm has "ennobled" her, and that she is no longer the same woman whose relentless egoism drove Beata into the mill-race. Rebecca herself puts it to him: "How can you believe me on my bare word after to-day?" There is only one proof she can give--that of "going the way Beata went." She gives it: and Rosmer, who cannot believe her if she lives, and will not survive her if she dies, goes with her to her end. But the cases are not very frequent, fortunately, in which such drastic methods of proof are appropriate or possible. The dramatist must, as a rule, attain his end by less violent means; and often he fails to attain it at all.

A play by Mr. Haddon Chambers, *The Awakening*, turned on a sudden conversion--the "awakening," in fact, referred to in the title. A professional lady-killer, a noted Don Juan, has been idly making love to a country maiden, whose heart is full of innocent idealisms. She discovers his true character, or, at any rate, his reputation, and is horror-stricken, while practically at the same moment, he "awakens" to the error of his ways, and is seized with a passion for her as single minded and idealistic as hers for him. But how are the heroine and the audience to be assured of the fact? That is just the difficulty; and the author takes no effectual measures to overcome it. The heroine, of course, is ultimately convinced; but the audience remains sceptical, to the detriment of the desired effect. "Sceptical," perhaps, is not quite the right word. The state of mind of a fictitious character is not a subject for actual belief or disbelief. We are bound to accept theoretically what the author tells us; but in this case he has failed to make us intimately feel and know that it is true. [2]

In Mr. Alfred Sutro's play *The Builder of Bridges*, Dorothy Faringay, in her devotion to her forger brother, has conceived the rather disgraceful scheme of making one of his official superiors fall in love with her, in order to induce him to become practically an accomplice in her brother's crime. She succeeds beyond her hopes. Edward Thursfield does fall in love with her, and, at a great sacrifice, replaces the money the brother has stolen. But, in a very powerful peripety-scene in the third act, Thursfield learns that Dorothy has been deliberately beguiling him, while in fact she was engaged to another man. The truth is, however, that she has really come to love Thursfield passionately, and has broken her engagement with the other, for whom she never truly cared. So the author tells us, and so we are willing enough to believe--if he can devise any adequate method of making Thursfield believe it. Mr. Sutro's handling of the difficulty seems to me fairly, but not conspicuously, successful. I cite the case as a typical instance of the problem, apart from the merits or demerits of the solution.

It may be said that the difficulty of bringing home to us the reality of a revulsion of feeling, or a radical change of mental attitude, is only a particular case of the playwright's general problem of convincingly externalizing inward conditions and processes. That is true: but the special importance of a conversion which unties the knot and brings the curtain down seemed to render it worthy of special consideration.

*   *   *   *   *

Notes:
[1: *Of Dramatic Poesy*, ed. Arnold, 1903, p. 51.]
[2: In Mr. Somerset Maugham's **Grace** the heroine undergoes a somewhat analogous change of heart, coming to love the husband whom she has previously despised. But we have no difficulty in accepting her conversion, partly because its reasons are clear and fairly adequate, partly because there is no question of convincing the husband, who has never realized her previous contempt for him.]

CHAPTER XX
BLIND-ALLEY THEMES--AND OTHERS

A blind-alley theme, as its name imports, is one from which there is no exit. It is a problem incapable of solution, or, rather, of which all possible solutions are equally unsatisfactory and undesirable. The playwright cannot too soon make sure that he has not strayed into such a no-thoroughfare. Whether an end be comic or tragic, romantic or ironic, happy or disastrous, it should satisfy something within us--our sense of truth, or of beauty, or of sublimity, or of justice, or of humour, or, at the least or lowest, our cynical sense of the baseness of human nature, and the vanity of human aspirations. But a play which satisfies neither our higher nor our lower instincts, baffles our sympathies, and leaves our desires at fault between equally inacceptable alternatives--such a play, whatever beauties of detail it may possess, is a weariness of the spirit, and an artistic blunder.

There are in literature two conspicuous examples of the blind-alley theme-- two famous plays, wherein two heroines are placed in somewhat similar dilemmas, which merely paralyse our sympathies and inhibit our moral judgment. The first of these is *Measure for Measure*. If ever there was an insoluble problem in casuistry, it is that which Shakespeare has here chosen to present to us. Isabella is forced to choose between what we can only describe as two detestable evils. If she resists Angelo, and lets her brother die, she recoils from an act of self-sacrifice; and, although we may coldly approve, we cannot admire or take pleasure in her action. If, on the other hand, she determines at all costs to save her brother's life, her sacrifice is a thing from which we want only to avert the mind: it belongs to the region of what Aristotle calls to *miaron*, the odious and intolerable. Shakespeare, indeed, confesses the problem insoluble in the fact that he leaves it unsolved--evading it by means of a mediaeval trick. But where, then, was the use of presenting it? What is the artistic profit of letting the imagination play around a problem which merely baffles and repels it? Sardou, indeed, presented the same problem, not as the theme of a whole play, but only of a single act; and he solved it by making Floria Tosca kill Scarpia. This is a solution which, at any rate, satisfies our craving for crude justice, and is melodramatically effective. Shakespeare probably ignored it, partly because it was not in his sources, partly because, for some obscure reason, he supposed himself to be writing a comedy. The result is that, though the play contains some wonderful poetry, and has been from time to time revived, it has never taken any real hold upon popular esteem.

The second glaring instance of a blind-alley theme is that of *Monna Vanna*. We have all of us, I suppose, stumbled, either as actors or onlookers, into painful situations, which not even a miracle of tact could possibly save. As a rule, of course, they are comic, and the agony they cause may find a safety-valve in laughter. But sometimes there occurs some detestable incident, over which it is equally impossible to laugh and to weep. The wisest words, the most graceful acts, are of no avail. One longs only to sink into the earth, or vanish into thin air. Such a situation, on the largest possible scale, is that presented in *Monna Vanna*. It differs from that of *Measure for Measure* in the fact that there can be no doubt as to the moral aspect of the case. It is quite clear that Giovanna ought to sacrifice herself to save, not one puling Claudio, but a whole city full of men, women, and children. What she does is absolutely right; but the conjuncture is none the less a grotesque and detestable one, which ought to be talked about and thought about as little as possible. Every word that is uttered is a failure in tact. Guido, the husband, behaves, in the first act, with a violent egoism, which is certainly lacking in dignity; but will any one tell me what would be a dignified course for him to pursue under the circumstances? The sage old Marco, too--that fifteenth-century Renan--flounders just as painfully as the hot-headed Guido. It is the fatality of the case that "he cannot open his mouth without putting his foot in it"; and a theme which exposes a well-meaning old gentleman to this painful necessity is one by all means to be avoided. The fact that it is a false alarm, and that there is no rational explanation for Prinzivalle's wanton insult to a woman whom he reverently idolizes, in no way makes matters better.

[1] Not the least grotesque thing in the play is Giovanna's expectation that Guido will receive Prinzivalle with open arms because he has--changed his mind. We can feel neither approval nor disapproval, sympathy nor antipathy, in such a deplorable conjunction of circumstances. All we wish is that we had not been called upon to contemplate it.[2] Maeterlinck, like Shakespeare, was simply dallying with the idea of a squalid heroism--so squalid, indeed, that neither he nor his predecessor had the courage to carry it through.

Pray observe that the defect of these two themes is not merely that they are "unpleasant." It is that there is no possible way out of them which is not worse than unpleasant: humiliating, and distressing. Let the playwright, then, before embarking on a theme, make sure that he has some sort of satisfaction to offer us at the end, if it be only the pessimistic pleasure of realizing some part of "the bitter, old and wrinkled truth" about life. The crimes of destiny there is some profit in contemplating; but its stupid vulgarities minister neither to profit nor delight.

*   *   *   *   *

It may not be superfluous to give at this point a little list of subjects which, though not blind-alley themes, are equally to be avoided. Some of them, indeed, are the reverse of blind-alley themes, their drawback lying in the fact that the way out of them is too tediously apparent.

At the head of this list I would place what may be called the "white marriage" theme: not because it is ineffective, but because its effectiveness is very cheap and has been sadly overdone. It occurs in two varieties: either a proud but penniless damsel is married to a wealthy parvenu, or a woman of culture and refinement is married to a "rough diamond." In both cases the action consists of the transformation of a nominal into a real marriage; and it is almost impossible, in these days, to lend any novelty to the process. In the good old **Lady of Lyons** the theme was decked in trappings of romantic absurdity, which somehow harmonized with it. One could hear in it a far-off echo of revolutionary rodomontade. The social aspect of the matter was emphasized, and the satire on middle-class snobbery was cruelly effective. The personal aspect, on the other hand--the unfulfilment of the nominal marriage--was lightly and discreetly handled, according to early-Victorian convention. In later days--from the time of M. George Ohnet's ***Maitre de Forges*** onwards--this is the aspect on which playwrights have preferred to dwell. Usually, the theme shades off into the almost equally hackneyed ***Still Waters Run Deep*** theme; for there is apt to be an aristocratic lover whom the unpolished but formidable husband threatens to shoot or horsewhip, and thereby overcomes the last remnant of repugnance in the breast of his haughty spouse. In ***The Ironmaster*** the lover was called the Duc de Bligny, or, more commonly, the Dook de Bleeny; but he has appeared under many aliases. In the chief American version of the theme, Mr. Vaughn Moody's ***Great Divide***, the lover is dispensed with altogether, being inconsistent, no doubt, with the austere manners of Milford Corners, Mass. In one of the recent French versions, on the other hand--M. Bernstein's ***Samson***--the aristocratic lover is almost as important a character as the virile, masterful, plebeian husband. It appears from this survey--which might be largely extended--that there are several ways of handling the theme; but there is no way of renewing and deconventionalizing it. No doubt it has a long life before it on the plane of popular melodrama, but scarcely, one hopes, on any higher plane.

Another theme which ought to be relegated to the theatrical lumber-room is that of patient, inveterate revenge. This form of vindictiveness is, from a dramatic point of view, an outworn passion. It is too obviously irrational and anti-social to pass muster in modern costume. The actual vendetta may possibly survive in some semi-barbarous regions, and Grangerfords and Shepherdsons (as in Mark Twain's immortal romance) may still be shooting each other at sight. But these things are relics of the past; they do not belong to the normal, typical life of our time. It is useless to say that human nature is the same in all ages. That is one of the facile axioms of psychological incompetence. Far be it from me to deny that malice, hatred, spite, and the spirit of retaliation are, and will be until the millennium, among the most active forces in human nature. But most people are coming to recognize that life is too short for deliberate, elaborate, cold-drawn revenge. They will hit back when they conveniently can; they will cherish for half a lifetime a passive, an obstructive, ill-will; they will even await for years an opportunity of "getting their knife into" an enemy. But they have grown chary of "cutting off their nose to spite their face"; they will very rarely sacrifice their own comfort in life to the mere joy of protracted, elaborate reprisals. Vitriol and the revolver--an outburst of rage, culminating in a "short, sharp shock"--these belong, if you will, to modern life. But long-drawn, unhasting, unresting machination, with no end in view beyond an ultimate unmasking, a turn of the tables--in a word, a strong situation--this, I take it, belongs to a phase of existence more leisurely than ours. There is no room in our crowded century for such large and sustained passions. One could mention plays--but they are happily forgotten--in which retribution was delayed for some thirty or forty years, during which the unconscious object of it enjoyed a happy and prosperous existence. These, no doubt, are extreme instances; but cold-storage revenge, as a whole, ought to be as rare on the stage as it is in real life. The serious playwright will do well to leave it to the melodramatists.

A third theme to be handled with the greatest caution, if at all, is that of heroic self-sacrifice. Not that self-sacrifice, like revenge, is an outworn passion. It still rages in daily life; but no audience of average intelligence will to-day accept it with the uncritical admiration which it used to excite in the sentimental dramas of last century. Even then--even in 1869--Meilhac and Halevy, in their ever-memorable *Froufrou*, showed what disasters often result from it; but it retained its prestige with the average playwright--and with some who were above the average--for many a day after that. I can recall a play, by a living English author, in which a Colonel in the Indian Army pleaded guilty to a damning charge of cowardice rather than allow a lady whom he chivalrously adored to learn that it was her husband who was the real coward and traitor. He knew that the lady detested her husband; he knew that they had no children to suffer by the husband's disgrace; he knew that there was a quite probable way by which he might have cleared his own character without casting any imputation on the other man. But in a sheer frenzy of self-sacrifice he blasted his own career, and thereby inflicted far greater pain upon the woman he loved than if he had told the truth or suffered it to be told. And twenty years afterwards, when the villain was dead, the hero still resolutely refused to clear his own character, lest the villain's widow should learn the truth about her wholly unlamented husband. This was an extravagant and childish case; but the superstition of heroic self-sacrifice still lingers in certain quarters, and cannot be too soon eradicated. I do not mean, of course, that self-sacrifice is never admirable, but only that it can no longer be accepted as a thing inherently noble, apart from its circumstances and its consequences. An excellent play might be written with the express design of placing the ethics of self-sacrifice in their true light. Perhaps the upshot might be the recognition of the simple principle that it is immoral to make a sacrifice which the person supposed to benefit by it has no right to accept.

Another motive against which it is perhaps not quite superfluous to warn the aspiring playwright is the "voix du sang." It is only a few years since this miraculous voice was heard speaking loud and long in His Majesty's Theatre, London, and in a play by a no less modern-minded author than the late Clyde Fitch. It was called *The Last of the Dandies*,[3] and its hero was Count D'Orsay. At a given moment, D'Orsay learned that a young man known as Lord Raoul Ardale was in reality his son. Instantly the man of the world, the squire of dames, went off into a deliquium of tender emotion. For "my bo-o-oy" he would do anything and everything. He would go down to Crockford's and win a pot of money to pay "my boy's" debts--Fortune could not but be kind to a doting parent. In the beautiful simplicity of his soul, he looked forward with eager delight to telling Raoul that the mother he adored was no better than she should be, and that he had no right to his name or title. Not for a moment did he doubt that the young man would share his transports. When the mother opposed his purpose of betraying her secret, he wept with disappointment. "All day," he said, "I have been saying to myself: When that sun sets, I shall hear him say, 'Good-night, Father!'" He postulated in so many words the "voix du sang," trusting that, even if the revelation were not formally made, "Nature would send the boy some impulse" of filial affection. It is hard to believe-- but it is the fact--that, well within the present century, such ingenuous nonsense as this was gravely presented to the public of a leading theatre, by an author of keen intelligence, who, but for an unhappy accident, would now be at the zenith of his career. There are few more foolish conventions than that of the "voix du sang." Perhaps, however, the rising generation of playwrights has more need to be warned against the opposite or Shawesque convention, that kinship utters itself mainly in wrangling and mutual dislike.

Among inherently feeble and greatly overdone expedients may be reckoned the oath or promise of secrecy, exacted for no sufficient reason, and kept in defiance of common sense and common humanity. Lord Windermere's conduct in Oscar Wilde's play is a case in point, though he has not even an oath to excuse his insensate secretiveness. A still clearer instance is afforded by Clyde Fitch's play *The Girl with the Green Eyes*. In other respects a very able play, it is vitiated by the certainty that Austin ought to have, and would have, told the truth ten times over, rather than subject his wife's jealous disposition to the strain he puts upon it.

It would not be difficult to prolong this catalogue of themes and motives that have come down in the world, and are no longer presentable in any society that pretends to intelligence. But it is needless to enter into further details. There is a general rule, of sovereign efficacy, for avoiding such anachronisms: "Go to life for your themes, and not to the theatre." Observe that rule, and you are safe. But it is easier said than done.

* * * * *

Notes:

[1: I have good reason for believing that, in M. Maeterlinck's original scheme, Prinzivalle imposed no such humiliating condition. Giovanna went of her own motive to appeal to his clemency; and her success was so complete that her husband, on her return, could not believe that it had been won by avowable means. This is a really fine conception--what a pity that the poet departed from it!]

[2: Much has been made of the Censor's refusal to license **Monna Vanna**; but I think there is more to be said for his action in this than in many other cases. In those countries where the play has succeeded, I cannot but suspect that the appeal it made was not wholly to the higher instincts of the public.]

[3: I am not sure what was the precise relationship of this play to the same author's **Beau Brummel**. D'Orsay's death scene was certainly a repetition of Brummel's.]

CHAPTER XXI
THE FULL CLOSE

In an earlier chapter, I have tried to show that a certain tolerance for anticlimax, for a fourth or fifth act of calm after the storm of the penultimate act, is consonant with right reason, and is a practically inevitable result of a really intimate relation between drama and life. But it would be a complete misunderstanding of my argument to suppose that I deny the practical, and even the artistic, superiority of those themes in which the tension can be maintained and heightened to the very end.

The fact that tragedy has from of old been recognized as a higher form than comedy is partly due, no doubt, to the tragic poet's traditional right to round off a human destiny in death. "Call no man happy till his life be ended," said Sophocles, quoting from an earlier sage; and it needed no profundity of wisdom to recognize in the "happy ending" of comedy a conventional, ephemeral thing. But when, after all the peripeties of life, the hero "home has gone and ta'en his wages," we feel that, at any rate, we have looked destiny squarely in the face, without evasion or subterfuge. Perhaps the true justification of tragedy as a form of art is that, after this experience, we should feel life to be, not less worth living, but greater and more significant than before.

This is no place, however, for a discussion of the aesthetic basis of tragedy in general.[1] What is here required, from the point of view of craftsmanship, is not so much a glorification of the tragic ending, as a warning against its facile misuse. A very great play may, and often must, end in death; but you cannot make a play great by simply killing off your protagonist. Death is, after all, a very inexpensive means of avoiding anticlimax. Tension, as we saw, is symbolized in the sword of

Damocles; and it can always be maintained, in a mechanical way, by letting your hero play about with a revolver, or placing an overdose of chloral well within your heroine's reach. At the time when the English drama was awaking from the lethargy of the 'seventies, an idea got abroad that a non-sanguinary ending was always and necessarily inartistic, and that a self-respecting playwright must at all hazards kill somebody before dropping his curtain. This was an extravagant reaction against the purely commercial principle that the public would not, on any terms, accept a tragic ending. As a matter of fact, the mortality was not very great; for managers were resolute in the old belief, and few dramatists had the courage or authority to stand up against them. But I have often heard playwrights lamenting their inability to massacre the luckless children of their fancy, who, nine times out of ten, had done nothing to incur such a doom. The real trouble was that death seemed to be the only method of avoiding anticlimax.

It is a very sound rule that, before you determine to write a tragedy, you should make sure that you have a really tragic theme: that you can place your hero at such odds with life that reconciliation, or mere endurance, would be morally base or psychologically improbable. Moreover, you must strike deep into character before you are justified in passing capital sentence on your personages. Death is a disproportionate close for a commonplace and superficially-studied life. It is true that quite commonplace people do die; indeed, they preponderate in the bills of mortality; but death on the stage confers a sort of distinction which ought not to be accorded without due and sufficient cause. To one god in particular we may apply the Horatian maxim, "Nec deus intersit, nisi dignus vindice nodus."

In German aesthetic theory, the conception ***tragische Schuld***--"tragic guilt"--plays a large part. It descends, no doubt, from the Aristotelian maxim that a tragic hero must neither be too good nor too bad; but it also belongs to a moralizing conception, which tacitly or explicitly assumes that the dramatist's aim ought to be "to justify the ways of God to man." In these days we look at drama more objectively, and do not insist on deciding in what degree a man has deserved death, if only we feel that he has necessarily or probably incurred it. But in order that we may be satisfied of this, we must know him intimately and feel with him intensely. We must, in other words, believe that he dies because he cannot live, and not merely to suit the playwright's convenience and help him to an effective "curtain."

As we review the series of Ibsen's modern plays, we cannot but feel that, though he did not shrink from death, he never employed it, except perhaps in his last melancholy effort, as a mere way of escape from a difficulty. In five out of his thirteen modern plays, no one dies at all.[2] One might even say six: for Oswald, in **Ghosts**, may live for years; but I hold it as only fair to count the death of his mind as more than equivalent to bodily death. Solness, on the plane of literal fact, dies by an accident; on the plane of symbolic interpretation, he dies of the over-great demands which Hilda makes upon his "sickly conscience." Little Eyolf's death can also be regarded from a symbolic point of view; but there is no substantial reason to think of it otherwise than as an accident. John Gabriel Borkman dies of heart seizure, resulting from sudden exposure to extreme cold. In the case of Solness and Borkman, death is a quite natural and probable result of the antecedent conditions; and in the case of Eyolf, it is not a way out of the action, but rather the way into it. There remain the three cases of suicide: Rebecca and Rosmer, Hedda Gabler, and Hedvig. I have already, in Chapter XIX, shown how the death of Rebecca was the inevitable outcome of the situation--the one conclusive proof of her "ennoblement"--and how it was almost equally inevitable that Rosmer should accompany her to her end. Hedda Gabler was constitutionally fated to suicide: a woman of low vitality, overmastering egoism, and acute supersensitiveness, placed in a predicament which left her nothing to expect from life but tedium and humiliation. The one case left--that of Hedvig--is the only one in which Ibsen can possibly be accused of wanton bloodshed. Bjoernson, in a very moving passage in his novel, **The Paths of God**, did actually, though indirectly, make that accusation. Certainly, there is no more heart-rending incident in fiction; and certainly it is a thing that only consummate genius can justify. Ibsen happened to possess that genius, and I am not far from agreeing with those who hold **The Wild Duck** to be his greatest work. But for playwrights who are tempted to seek for effects of pathos by similar means, one may without hesitation lay down this maxim: Be sure you are an Ibsen before you kill your Hedvig.

This analysis of Ibsen's practice points to the fact--for such I believe it to be--that what the modern playwright has chiefly to guard against is the temptation to overdo suicide as a means of cutting the dramatic knot. In France and Germany there is another temptation, that of the duel;[3] but in Anglo-Saxon countries it scarcely presents itself. Death, other than self-inflicted, is much less tempting, and less apt to be resorted to in and out of season. The heroine, whether virtuous or erring, who dies of consumption, has gone greatly out of vogue. A broken heart is no longer held to be necessarily fatal. The veriest tyro realizes that death by crude accident is inadmissible as a determining factor in serious drama; and murder is practically (though not absolutely) relegated to the melodramatic domain. The one urgent question, then, is that of the artistic use and abuse of suicide.

The principle is pretty plain, I think, that it ought to be the artist's, as it is the man's, last resort. We know that, in most civilized countries, suicide is greatly on the increase. It cannot be called an infrequent incident in daily life. It is certain, too, that the motives impelling to it are apt to be of a dramatic nature, and therefore suited to the playwright's purposes. But it is, on the other hand, such a crude and unreasoning means of exit from the tangle of existence that a playwright of delicate instincts will certainly employ it only under the strongest compulsion from his artistic conscience.

Sir Arthur Pinero has three suicides on his record, though one of them was, so to speak, nipped in the bud. In *The Profligate*, as presented on the stage, Dunstan Renshaw changed his mind before draining the fatal goblet; and in this case the stage version was surely the right one. The suicide, to which the author still clings in the printed text, practically dates the play as belonging to the above-mentioned period of rebellion against the conventional "happy ending," when the ambitious British dramatist felt that honour required him to kill his man on the smallest provocation.[4] Nearly a quarter of a century has passed since then, and the disproportion between such a play and such a catastrophe is now apparent to everyone. It is not that we judge Renshaw's delinquencies to be over-punished by death--that is not the question. The fact is simply that the characters are not large enough, true enough, living enough--that the play does not probe deep enough into human experience--to make the august intervention of death seem other than an incongruity. The suicide of Paula Tanqueray, though it, too, has been much criticized, is a very different matter. Inevitable it cannot be called: if the play had been written within the past ten years, Sir Arthur would very likely have contrived to do without it. But it is, in itself, probable enough: both the good and the bad in Paula's character might easily make her feel that only the dregs of life remained to her, and they not worth drinking. The worst one can say of it is that it sins against the canon of practical convenience which enjoins on the prudent dramatist strict economy in suicide. The third case, Zoe Blundell's leap to nothingness, in that harsh and ruthless masterpiece, *Mid-Channel*, is as inevitable as anything can well be in human destiny. Zoe has made a miserable and hopeless muddle of her life. In spite of her goodness of heart, she has no interests and no ideals, apart from the personal satisfactions which have now been poisoned at their source. She has intervened disastrously in the destinies of others. She is ill; her nerves are all on edge; and she is, as it were, driven into a corner, from which there is but one easy and rapid exit. Here is a case, if ever there was one, where the end is imposed upon the artist by the whole drift of his action. It may be said that chance plays a large part in the concatenation of events--that, for instance, if Leonard Ferris had not happened to live at the top of a very high building, Zoe would not have encountered the sudden temptation to which she yields. But this, as I have tried to show above, is a baseless complaint. Chance is a constant factor in life, now aiding, now thwarting, the will. To eliminate it altogether would be to produce a most unlifelike world. It is only when the playwright so manipulates and reduplicates chance as to make it seem no longer chance, but purposeful arrangement, that we have the right to protest.

Another instance of indisputably justified suicide may be found in Mr. Galsworthy's *Justice*. The whole theme of the play is nothing but the hounding to his end of a luckless youth, who has got on the wrong side of the law, and finds all the forces of society leagued against him. In Mr. Granville Barker's *Waste*, the artistic justification for Trebell's self-effacement is less clear and compulsive. It is true that the play was suggested by the actual suicide, not of a politician, but of a soldier, who found his career ruined by some pitiful scandal. But the author has made no attempt to reproduce the actual circumstances of that case; and even if he had reproduced the external circumstances, the psychological conditions would clearly have eluded him. Thus the appeal to fact is, as it always must be, barred. In two cases, indeed, much more closely analogous to Trebell's than that which actually suggested it-- two famous cases in which a scandal cut short a brilliant political career--suicide played no part in the catastrophe. These real-life instances are, I repeat, irrelevant. The only question is whether Mr. Barker has made us feel that a man of Trebell's character would certainly not survive the paralysing of his energies; and that question every spectator must answer for himself. I am far from answering it in the negative. I merely suggest that the playwright may one day come across a theme for which there is no conceivable ending but suicide, and may wish that he had let Trebell live, lest people should come to regard him as a spendthrift of self-slaughter.

The suicide which brings to a close Mr. Clyde Fitch's very able play, *The Climbers*, stands on a somewhat different level. Here it is not the protagonist who makes away with himself, nor is his destiny the main theme of the play. Mr. Fitch has painted a broad social picture, in which, if there is any concentration of interest, it is upon Blanche and Warden. Sterling's suicide, then, though it does in fact cut the chief knot of the play, is to be regarded rather as a characteristic and probable incident of a certain phase of life, than as the culmination of a spiritual tragedy. It has not the artistic significance, either good or bad, that it would have if the character and destiny of Sterling were our main concernment.

* * * * *

The happy playwright, one may say, is he whose theme does not force upon him either a sanguinary or a tame last act, but enables him, without troubling the coroner, to sustain and increase the tension up to the very close. Such themes are not too common, but they do occur. Dumas found one in *Denise*, and another in *Francillon*, where the famous "Il en a menti!" comes within two minutes of the fall of the curtain. In *Heimat* (Magda) and in *Johannisfeuer*, Sudermann keeps the tension at its height up to the fall of the curtain. Sir Arthur Pinero's *Iris* is a case in point; so are Mr. Shaw's *Candida* and *The Devil's Disciple*; so is Mr. Galsworthy's *Strife*. Other instances will no doubt occur to the reader; yet he will probably be surprised to find that it is not very easy to recall them.

For this is not, in fact, the typical modern formula. In plays which do not end in death, it will generally be found that the culminating scene occurs in the penultimate act, and that, if anticlimax is avoided, it is not by the maintenance of an unbroken tension, by its skilful renewal and reinforcement in the last act. This is a resource which the playwright will do well to bear in mind. Where he cannot place his "great scene" in his last act, he should always consider whether it be not possible to hold some development in reserve whereby the tension may be screwed up again--if unexpectedly, so much the better. Some of the most successful plays within my recollection have been those in which the last act came upon us as a pleasant surprise. An anticlimax had seemed inevitable; and behold! the author had found a way out of it.

An Enemy of the People may perhaps be placed in this class, though, as before remarked, the last act is almost an independent comedy. Had the play ended with the fourth act, no one would have felt that anything was lacking; so that in his fifth act, Ibsen was not so much grappling with an urgent technical problem, as amusing himself by wringing the last drop of humour out of the given situation. A more strictly apposite example may be found in Sir Arthur Pinero's play, **His House in Order**. Here the action undoubtedly culminates in the great scene between Nina and Hilary Jesson in the third act; yet we await with eager anticipation the discomfiture of the Ridgeley family; and when we realize that it is to be brought about by the disclosure to Filmer of Annabel's secret, the manifest rightness of the proceeding gives us a little shock of pleasure. Mr. Somerset Maugham, again, in the last act of **Grace**, employs an ingenious device to keep the tension at a high pitch. The matter of the act consists mainly of a debate as to whether Grace Insole ought, or ought not, to make a certain painful avowal to her husband. As the negative opinion was to carry the day, Mr. Maugham saw that there was grave danger that the final scene might appear an almost ludicrous anticlimax. To obviate this, he made Grace, at the beginning of the act, write a letter of confession, and address it to Claude; so that all through the discussion we had at the back of our mind the question "Will the letter reach his hands? Will the sword of Damocles fall?" This may seem like a leaf from the book of Sardou; but in reality it was a perfectly natural and justified expedient. It kept the tension alive throughout a scene of ethical discussion, interesting in itself, but pretty clearly destined to lead up to the undramatic alternative--a policy of silence and inaction. Mr. Clyde Fitch, in the last act of **The Truth**, made an elaborate and daring endeavour to relieve the mawkishness of the clearly-foreseen reconciliation between Warder and Becky. He let Becky fall in with her father's mad idea of working upon Warder's compassion by pretending that she had tried to kill herself. Only at the last moment did she abandon the sordid comedy, and so prove herself (as we are asked to suppose) cured for ever of the habit of fibbing. Mr.

Fitch here showed good technical insight marred by over-hasty execution. That Becky should be tempted to employ her old methods, and should overcome the temptation, was entirely right; but the actual deception attempted was so crude and hopeless that there was no plausibility in her consenting to it, and no merit in her desisting from it.

In light comedy and farce it is even more desirable than in serious drama to avoid a tame and perfunctory last act. Very often a seemingly trivial invention will work wonders in keeping the interest afoot. In Mr. Anstey's delightful farce, *The Brass Bottle*, one looked forward rather dolefully to a flat conclusion; but by the simple device of letting the Jinny omit to include Pringle in his "act of oblivion," the author is enabled to make his last scene quite as amusing as any of its predecessors. Mr. Arnold Bennett, in *The Honeymoon*, had the audacity to play a deliberate trick on the audience, in order to evade an anticlimax. Seeing that his third act could not at best be very good, he purposely put the audience on a false scent, made it expect an absolutely commonplace ending (the marriage of Flora to Charles Haslam), and then substituted one which, if not very brilliant, was at least ingenious and unforeseen. Thus, by defeating the expectation of a superlatively bad act, he made a positively insignificant act seem comparatively good. Such feats of craftsmanship are entertaining, but too dangerous to be commended for imitation.

In some modern plays a full close is achieved by the simple expedient of altogether omitting the last act, or last scene, and leaving the end of the play to the imagination. This method is boldly and (I understand) successfully employed by Mr. Edward Sheldon in his powerful play, *The Nigger*. Philip Morrow, the popular Governor of one of the Southern States, has learnt that his grandmother was a quadroon, and that consequently he has in him a much-attenuated strain of African blood. In the Southern States, attenuation matters nothing: if the remotest filament of a man's ancestry runs back to Africa, he is "a nigger all right." Philip has just suppressed a race-riot in the city, and, from the balcony of the State Capitol, is to address the troops who have aided him, and the assembled multitude. Having resolutely parted from the woman he adores, but can no longer marry, he steps out upon the balcony to announce that he is a negro, that he resigns the Governorship, and that henceforth he casts in his lot with his black brethren. The stage-direction runs thus--

The afternoon sun strikes his figure. At his appearance a shout goes up--long, steady, enthusiastic cheering; and, after a moment, the big regimental band begins playing, very slowly, "My Country, 'tis of Thee." ... All the people in the room are smiling and applauding enthusiastically; and--as Phil in vain raises his hand for silence, and the band crashes through the National Anthem, and the roar of voices still rises from below--

THE CURTAIN FALLS.

One does not know whether to praise Mr. Sheldon for having adroitly avoided an anticlimax, or to reproach him with having unblushingly shirked a difficulty. To my sense, the play has somewhat the air of a hexameter line with the spondee cut off.[5] One **does** want to see the peripety through. But if the audience is content to imagine the sequel, Mr. Sheldon's craftsmanship is justified, and there is no more to be said. M. Brieux experienced some difficulty in bringing his early play, **Blanchette**, to a satisfactory close. The third act which he originally wrote was found unendurably cynical; a more agreeable third act was condemned as an anticlimax; and for some time the play was presented with no third act at all. It did not end, but simply left off. No doubt it is better that a play should stop in the middle than that it should drag on tediously and ineffectually. But it would be foolish to make a system of such an expedient. It is, after all, an evasion, not a solution, of the artist's problem.

An incident which occurred during the rehearsals for the first production of *A Doll's House*, at the Novelty Theatre, London, illustrates the difference between the old, and what was then the new, fashion of ending a play. The business manager of the company, a man of ripe theatrical experience, happened to be present one day when Miss Achurch and Mr. Waring were rehearsing the last great scene between Nora and Helmar. At the end of it, he came up to me, in a state of high excitement. "This is a fine play!" he said. "This is sure to be a big thing!" I was greatly pleased. "If this scene, of all others," I thought, "carries a man like Mr. Smith off his feet, it cannot fail to hold the British public." But I was somewhat dashed when, a day or two later, Mr. Smith came up to me again, in much less buoyant spirits. "I made a mistake about that scene," he said. "They tell me it's the end of the *last* act--I thought it was the end of the *first*!"

* * * * *

Notes:

[1: The reader who wishes to pursue the theme may do so to excellent advantage in Professor Bradley's ***Shakespearean Tragedy***.]

[2: It is true that in ***A Doll's House***, Dr. Rank announces his approaching demise: but he does not actually die, nor is his fate an essential part of the action of the play.]

[3: The duel, even in countries whose customs permit of it, is essentially an inartistic end; for it leaves the catastrophe to be decided either by Chance or Providence--two equally inadmissible arbiters in modern drama. Alexandre Dumas *fils*, in his preface to ***Heloise Paranquet***, condemns the duel as a dramatic expedient. "Not to mention," he says, "the fact that it has been much over-done, we are bound to recognize that Providence, in a fit of absence of mind, sometimes suffers the rascal to kill the honest man. Let me recommend my young colleagues," he proceeds, "never to end a piece which pretends to reproduce a phase of real life, by an intervention of chance." The recommendation came rather oddly from the dramatist who, in ***L'Etrangere***, had disposed of his "vibrion," the Duc de Septmonts, by making Clarkson kill him in a duel. Perhaps he did not reckon ***L'Etrangere*** as pretending to reproduce a phase of real life. A duel is, of course, perfectly admissible in a French or German play, simply as part of a picture of manners. Its stupid inconclusiveness may be the very point to be illustrated. It is only when represented as a moral arbitrament that it becomes an anachronism.]

[4: I am glad to see, from Mr. Malcolm Salaman's introduction to the printed play, that, even in those days of our hot youth, my own aesthetic principles were less truculent.]

[5: This image is sometimes suggested by an act-ending which leaves a marked situation obviously unresolved. The curtain should never be dropped at such a point as to leave the characters in a physical or mental attitude which cannot last for more than a moment, and must certainly be followed, then and there, by important developments. In other words, a situation ought not to be cut short at the very height of its tension, but only when it has reached a point of--at any rate momentary--relaxation.]

BOOK V EPILOGUE

CHAPTER XXII
CHARACTER AND PSYCHOLOGY

For the invention and ordering of incident it is possible, if not to lay down rules, at any rate to make plausible recommendations; but the power to observe, to penetrate, and to reproduce character can neither be acquired nor regulated by theoretical recommendations. Indirectly, of course, all the technical discussions of the previous chapters tend, or ought to tend, towards the effective presentment of character; for construction, in drama of any intellectual quality, has no other end. But specific directions for character-drawing would be like rules for becoming six feet high. Either you have it in you, or you have it not.

Under the heading of character, however, two points arise which may be worth a brief discussion: first, ought we always to aim at development in character? second, what do we, or ought we to, mean by "psychology"?

It is a frequent critical complaint that in such-and-such a character there is "no development": that it remains the same throughout a play; or (so the reproach is sometimes worded) that it is not a character but an invariable attitude. A little examination will show us, I think, that, though the critic may in these cases be pointing to a real fault, he does not express himself quite accurately.

What is character? For the practical purposes of the dramatist, it may be defined as a complex of intellectual, emotional, and nervous habits. Some of these habits are innate and temperamental--habits formed, no doubt, by far-off ancestors. [1] But this distinction does not here concern us. Temperamental bias is a habit, like another, only somewhat older, and, therefore, harder to deflect or eradicate. What do we imply, then, when we complain that, in a given character, no development has taken place? We imply that he ought, within the limits of the play, to have altered the mental habits underlying his speech and actions. But is this a reasonable demand? Is it consistent with the usual and desirable time-limits of drama? In the long process of a novel, there may be time for the gradual alteration of habits: in the drama, which normally consists of a single crisis, any real change of character would have to be of a catastrophic nature, in which experience does not encourage us to put much faith. It was, indeed--as Dryden pointed out in a passage quoted above[2]--one of the foibles of our easy-going ancestors to treat character as practically reversible when the time approached for ringing down the curtain. The same convention survives to this day in certain forms of drama. Even Ibsen, in his earlier work, had not shaken it off; witness the sudden ennoblement of Bernick in ***Pillars of Society***. But it can scarcely be that sort of "development" which the critics consider indispensable. What is it, then, that they have in mind?

By "development" of character, I think they mean, not change, but rather unveiling, disclosure. They hold, not unreasonably, that a dramatic crisis ought to disclose latent qualities in the persons chiefly concerned in it, and involve, not, indeed, a change, but, as it were, an exhaustive manifestation of character. The interest of the highest order of drama should consist in the reaction of character to a series of crucial experiences. We should, at the end of a play, know more of the protagonist's character than he himself, or his most intimate friend, could know at the beginning; for the action should have been such as to put it to some novel and searching test. The word "development" might be very aptly used in the photographic sense. A drama ought to bring out character as the photographer's chemicals "bring out" the forms latent in the negative. But this is quite a different thing from development in the sense of growth or radical change. In all modern drama, there is perhaps no character who "develops," in the ordinary sense of the word, so startlingly as Ibsen's Nora; and we cannot but feel that the poet has compressed into a week an evolution which, in fact, would have demanded many months.

The complaint that a character preserves the same attitude throughout means (if it be justified) that it is not a human being at all, but a mere embodiment of two or three characteristics which are fully displayed within the first ten minutes, and then keep on repeating themselves, like a recurrent decimal. Strong theatrical effects can be produced by this method, which is that of the comedy of types, or of "humors." But it is now generally, and rightly, held that a character should be primarily an individual, and only incidentally (if at all) capable of classification under this type or that. It is a little surprising to find Sarcey, so recently as 1889, laying it down that "a character is a master faculty or passion, which absorbs all the rest.... To study and paint a character is, therefore, by placing a man in a certain number of situations, to show how this principal motive force in his nature annihilates or directs all those which, if he had been another man, would probably have come into action." This dogma of the "ruling passion" belongs rather to the eighteenth century than to the close of the nineteenth.

* * * * *

We come now to the second of the questions above propounded, which I will state more definitely in this form: Is "psychology" simply a more pedantic term for "character-drawing"? Or can we establish a distinction between the two ideas? I do not think that, as a matter of fact, any difference is generally and clearly recognized; but I suggest that it is possible to draw a distinction which might, if accepted, prove serviceable both to critics and to playwrights.

Let me illustrate my meaning by an example. In **Bella Donna**, by Messrs. Robert Hichens and James B. Fagan, we have a murder-story of a not uncommon or improbable type. A woman of very shady reputation marries an amiable idealist who is infatuated with her. She naturally finds his idealism incomprehensible and his amiability tedious. His position as heir-presumptive to a peerage is shattered by the birth of an heir-apparent. She becomes passionately enamoured of an Egyptian millionaire; and she sets to work to poison her husband with sugar-of-lead, provided by her oriental lover. How her criminal purpose is thwarted by a wise Jewish physician is nothing to the present purpose. In intent she is a murderess, no less than Lucrezia Borgia or the Marquise de Brinvilliers. And the authors have drawn her character cleverly enough. They have shown her in the first act as a shallow-souled materialist, and in the later acts as a vain, irritable, sensual, unscrupulous creature. But have they given us any insight into her psychology? No, that is just what they have not done. They have assigned to her certain characteristics without which cruel and cold-blooded murder would be inconceivable; but they have afforded us no insight into the moral conditions and, mental processes which make it, not only conceivable, but almost an everyday occurrence. For the average human mind, I suppose, the psychology of crime, and especially of fiendish, hypocritical murder-by-inches, has an undeniable fascination. To most of us it seems an abhorrent miracle; and it would interest us greatly to have it brought more or less within the range of our comprehension, and co-ordinated with other mental phenomena which we can and do understand. But of such illumination we find nothing in **Bella Donna**. It leaves the working of a poisoner's mind as dark to us as ever. So far as that goes, we might just as well have read the report of a murder-trial, wherein the facts are stated with, perhaps, some superficial speculation as to motive, but no attempt is made to penetrate to underlying soul-states. Yet this is surely the highest privilege of art--to take us behind and beneath those surfaces of things which are apparent to the detective and the reporter, the juryman and the judge.

Have we not here, then, the distinction between character-drawing and psychology? Character-drawing is the presentment of human nature in its commonly-recognized, understood, and accepted aspects; psychology is, as it were, the exploration of character, the bringing of hitherto unsurveyed tracts within the circle of our knowledge and comprehension. In other words, character-drawing is synthetic, psychology analytic. This does not mean that the one is necessarily inferior to the other. Some of the greatest masterpieces of creative art have been achieved by the synthesis of known elements. Falstaff, for example--there is no more brilliant or more living character in all fiction; yet it is impossible to say that Shakespeare has here taken us into previously unplumbed depths of human nature, as he has in Hamlet, or in Lear. No doubt it is often very hard to decide whether a given personage is a mere projection of the known or a divination of the unknown. What are we to say, for example, of Cleopatra, or of Shylock, or of Macbeth? Richard II, on the other hand, is as clearly a piece of psychology as the Nurse in **Romeo and Juliet** is a piece of character-drawing. The comedy of types necessarily tends to keep within the limits of the known, and Moliere--in spite of Alceste and Don Juan--is characteristically a character-drawer, as Racine is characteristically a psychologist. Ibsen is a psychologist or he is nothing. Earl Skule and Bishop Nicholas, Hedda Gabler and John Gabriel Borkman are daring explorations of hitherto uncharted regions of the human soul. But Ibsen, too, was a character-drawer when it suited him. One is tempted to say that there is no psychology in Brand--he is a mere incarnation of intransigent idealism--while Peer Gynt is as brilliant a psychological inspiration as Don Quixote. Dr. Stockmann is a vigorously-projected character, Hialmar Ekdal a piece of searching psychology. Finally, my point could scarcely be better illustrated than by a comparison--cruel but instructive --between Rebecca in **Rosmersholm** and the heroine in **Bella Donna**. Each is, in effect, a murderess, though it was a moral, not a mineral, poison that Rebecca employed. But while we know nothing whatever of Mrs. Armine's mental processes, Rebecca's temptations, struggles, sophistries, hesitations, resolves, and revulsions of feeling are all laid bare to us, so that we feel her to be no monster, but a living woman, comprehensible to our intelligence, and, however blameworthy, not wholly beyond the range of our sympathies. There are few greater achievements of psychology.

Among the playwrights of to-day, I should call Mr. Granville Barker above all things a psychologist. It is his instinct to venture into untrodden fields of character, or, at any rate, to probe deeply into phenomena which others have noted but superficially, if at all. Hence the occasional obscurity of his dialogue. Mr. Shaw is not, primarily, either a character-drawer or a psychologist, but a dealer in personified ideas. His leading figures are, as a rule, either his mouthpieces or his butts. When he gives us a piece of real character-drawing, it is generally in some subordinate personage. Mr. Galsworthy, I should say, shows himself a psychologist in **Strife**, a character-drawer in **The Silver Box** and **Justice**. Sir Arthur Pinero, a character-drawer of great versatility, becomes a psychologist in some of his studies of feminine types--in Iris, in Letty, in the luckless heroine of **Mid-Channel**. Mr. Clyde Fitch had, at least, laudable ambitions in the direction of psychology. Becky in **The Truth**, and Jinny in **The Girl with the Green Eyes**, in so far as they are successfully drawn, really do mean a certain advance on our knowledge of feminine human nature. Unfortunately, owing to the author's over-facile and over-hasty method of work, they are now and then a little out of drawing. The most striking piece of psychology known to me in American drama is the Faith Healer in William Vaughn Moody's drama of that name. If the last act of **The Faith Healer** were as good as the rest of it, one might safely call it the finest play ever written, at any rate in the English language, beyond the Atlantic. The psychologists of the modern French stage, I take it, are M. de Curel and M. de Porto-Riche. MM. Brieux and Hervieu are, like Mr. Shaw, too much concerned with ideas to probe very deep into character. In Germany, Hauptmann, and, so far as I understand him, Wedekind, are psychologists, Sudermann, a vigorous character-drawer.

It is pretty clear that, if this distinction were accepted, it would be of use to the critic, inasmuch as we should have two terms for two ideas, instead of one popular term with a rather pedantic synonym. But what would be its practical use to the artist, the craftsman? Simply this, that if the word "psychology" took on for him a clear and definite meaning, it might stimulate at once his imagination and his ambition. Messrs. Hichens and Fagan, for example, might have asked themselves--or each other--"Are we getting beneath the surface of this woman's nature? Are we plucking the heart out of her mystery? Cannot we make the specific processes of a murderess's mind clearer to ourselves and to our audiences?" Whether they would have been capable of rising to the opportunity, I cannot tell; but in the case of other authors one not infrequently feels: "This man could have taken us deeper into this problem if he had only thought of it." I do not for a moment mean that every serious dramatist should always be aiming at psychological exploration. The character-drawer's appeal to common knowledge and instant recognition is often all that is required, or that would be in place. But there are also occasions not a few when the dramatist shows himself unequal to his opportunities if he does not at least attempt to bring hitherto unrecorded or unscrutinized phases of character within the scope of our understanding and our sympathies.

* * * * *

Notes:
[1: If this runs counter to the latest biological orthodoxy, I am sorry. Habits are at any rate transmissible by imitation, if not otherwise.]
[2: Chapter XIX.]

CHAPTER XXIII
DIALOGUE AND DETAILS

The extraordinary progress made by the drama of the English language during the past quarter of a century is in nothing more apparent than in the average quality of modern dialogue. Tolerably well-written dialogue is nowadays the rule rather than the exception. Thirty years ago, the idea that it was possible to combine naturalness with vivacity and vigour had scarcely dawned upon the playwright's mind. He passed and repassed from stilted pathos to strained and verbal wit (often mere punning); and when a reformer like T.W. Robertson tried to come a little nearer to the truth of life, he was apt to fall into babyish simplicity or flat commonness.

Criticism has not given sufficient weight to the fact that English dramatic writing laboured for centuries--and still labours to some degree--under a historic misfortune. It has never wholly recovered from the euphuism--to use the word in its widest sense--of the late sixteenth century. The influence of John Lyly and his tribe is still traceable, despite a hundred metamorphoses, in some of the plays of to-day and in many of the plays of yesterday. From the very beginnings of English comedy, it was accepted as almost self-evident that "wit"--a factitious, supererogatory sparkle--was indispensable to all dialogue of a non-tragic order. Language was a newly discovered and irresistibly fascinating playground for the fancy. Conversation must be thick-strewn with verbal quibbles, similes, figures, and flourishes of every description, else it was unworthy to be spoken on the stage. We all know how freely Shakespeare yielded to this convention, and so helped to establish it. Sometimes, not always, his genius enabled him to render it delightful; but in most of the Elizabethans--though it be heresy to say so--it is an extremely tedious mannerism. After the Restoration, when modern light talk came into being in the coffee-houses, the fashion of the day, no doubt, favoured a straining after wit; so that the playwrights were in some measure following nature--that very small corner of nature which they called "the town"--in accepting and making a law of the Elizabethan convention. The leading characters of Restoration comedy, from Etherege to Vanbrugh, are consciously and almost professionally wits. Simile and repartee are as indispensable a part of a gentleman's social outfit as his wig or his rapier. In Congreve the word "wit" is almost as common as the thing. When Farquhar made some movement towards a return to nature, he was rewarded with Pope's line, which clings like a burr to his memory--

"What pert, low dialogue has Farquhar writ."

If eighteenth-century comedy, as a whole, is not brilliantly written, it is for lack of talent in the playwrights, not for lack of desire or intention. Goldsmith, like Farquhar and Steele, vaguely realized the superiority of humour to wit; but he died too early to exercise much influence on his successors. In Sheridan the convention of wit reasserted itself triumphantly, and the scene in which Lady Teazle, Mrs. Candour, and the rest of the scandalous college sit in a semicircle and cap malicious similes, came to be regarded as an unapproachable model of comedy dialogue. The convention maintained itself firmly down to the days of ***Money*** and ***London Assurance***, the dullness of the intervening period being due, not to any change of theory, but to sheer impotence of practice. T.W. Robertson, as above mentioned, attempted a return to nature, with occasional and very partial success; but wit, with a dash of fanciful sentiment, reasserted itself in James Albery; while in H.J. Byron it degenerated into mere punning and verbal horse-play. I should not be surprised if the historian of the future were to find in the plays of Mr. Henry Arthur Jones the first marked symptoms of a reaction--of a tendency to reject extrinsic and fanciful ornament in dialogue, and to rely for its effect upon its vivid appropriateness to character and situation. In the early plays of Sir Arthur Pinero there is a great deal of extrinsic ornament; especially of that metaphor-hunting which was one of the characteristic forms of euphuism. Take this, for example, from ***The Profligate***. Dunstan Renshaw has expressed to Hugh Murray the opinion that "marriages of contentment are the reward of husbands who have taken the precaution to sow their wild oats rather thickly"; whereupon the Scotch solicitor replies--

HUGH MURRAY: Contentment! Renshaw, do you imagine that there is no autumn in the life of a profligate? Do you think there is no moment when the accursed crop begins to rear its millions of heads above ground; when the rich man would give his wealth to be able to tread them back into the earth which rejects the foul load? To-day you have robbed some honest man of a sweet companion!

DUNSTAN RENSHAW: Look here, Mr. Murray--!

HUGH MURRAY: To-morrow, next week, next month, you may be happy--but
what of the time when those wild oats thrust their ears through the very seams of the floor trodden by the wife whose respect you will have learned to covet! You may drag her into the crowded streets--there is the same vile growth springing up from the chinks of the pavement! In your house or in the open, the scent of the mildewed grain always in your nostrils, and in your ears no music but the wind's rustle amongst the fat sheaves! And, worst of all, your wife's heart a granary bursting with the load of shame your profligacy has stored there! I warn you--Mr. Lawrence Kenward!

If we compare this passage with any page taken at random from *Mid-Channel*, we might think that a century of evolution lay between them, instead of barely twenty years.

The convention of wit-at-any-price is, indeed, moribund; but it is perhaps not quite superfluous, even now, to emphasize the difference between what the French call the "mot d'auteur" and the "mot de situation." The terms practically explain themselves; but a third class ought to be added--the "mot de caractere." The "mot d'auteur" is the distinguishing mark of the Congreve-Sheridan convention. It survives in full vigour--or, shall one say, it sings its swan-song?--in the works of Oscar Wilde. For instance, the scene of the five men in the third act of **Lady Windermere's Fan** is a veritable running-fire of epigrams wholly unconnected with the situation, and very slightly related, if at all, to the characters of the speakers. The mark of the "mot d'auteur" is that it can with perfect ease be detached from its context. I could fill this page with sayings from the scene in question, all perfectly comprehensible without any account of the situation. Among them would be one of those; profound sayings which Wilde now and then threw off in his lightest moods, like opals among soap-bubbles. "In the world," says Dumby, "there are two tragedies. One is not getting what one wants, and the other is getting it." This may rank with Lord Illingworth's speech in ***A Woman of No Importance***: "All thought is immoral. Its very essence is destruction. If you think of anything you kill it. Nothing survives being thought of." When we hear such sayings as these--or the immortal "Vulgarity is the behaviour of other people"--we do not enquire too curiously into their appropriateness to character or situation; but none the less do they belong to an antiquated conception of drama.

It is useless to begin to give specimens of the "mot de caractere" and "mot de situation." All really dramatic dialogue falls under one head or the other. One could easily pick out a few brilliantly effective examples of each class: but as their characteristic is to fade when uprooted from the soil in which they grow, they would take up space to very little purpose.

But there is another historic influence, besides that of euphuism, which has been hurtful, though in a minor degree, to the development of a sound style in dialogue. Some of the later Elizabethans, and notably Webster and Ford, cultivated a fashion of abrupt utterance, whereby an immensity of spiritual significance--generally tragic--was supposed to be concentrated into a few brief words. The classic example is Ferdinand's "Cover her face. Mine eyes dazzle. She died young," in ***The Duchess of Malfy***. Charles Lamb celebrated the virtues of this pregnant, staccato style with somewhat immoderate admiration, and thus helped to set a fashion of spasmodic pithiness in dialogue, which too often resulted in dense obscurity. Not many plays composed under this influence have reached the stage; not one has held it. But we find in some recent writing a qualified recrudescence of the spasmodic manner, with a touch of euphuism thrown in. This is mainly due, I think, to the influence of George Meredith, who accepted the convention of wit as the informing spirit of comedy dialogue, and whose abnormally rapid faculty of association led him to delight in a sort of intellectual shorthand which the normal mind finds very difficult to decipher. Meredith was a man of brilliant genius, which lent a fascination to his very mannerisms; but when these mannerisms are transferred by lesser men to a medium much less suited to them--that of the stage--the result is apt to be disastrous. I need not go into particulars; for no play of which the dialogue places a constant strain on the intellectual muscles of the audience ever has held, or ever will hold, a place in living dramatic literature. I will merely note the curious fact that English--my own language--is the only language out of the three or four known to me in which I have ever come across an entirely incomprehensible play. I could name English plays, both pre-Meredithian and post-Meredithian, which might almost as well be written in Chinese for all that I can make of them.

Obscurity and precocity are generally symptoms of an exaggerated dread of the commonplace. The writer of dramatic prose has, indeed, a very difficult task if he is to achieve style without deserting nature. Perhaps it would be more accurate to say that the difficulty lies in getting criticism to give him credit for the possession of style, without incurring the reproach of mannerism. How is one to give concentration and distinction to ordinary talk, while making it still seem ordinary? Either the distinction will strike the critics, and they will call it pompous and unreal, or the ordinariness will come home to them, and they will deny the distinction. This is the dramatist's constant dilemma. One can only comfort him with the assurance that if he has given his dialogue the necessary concentration, and has yet kept it plausibly near to the language of life, he has achieved style, and may snap his fingers at the critics. Style, in prose drama, is the sifting of common speech.

It is true, however, that, with equal concentration and equal naturalness, one man may give his work a beauty of cadence and phrasing which another man may entirely miss. Two recent writers of English dramatic prose have stood out from their fellows in respect of the sheer beauty of their style--I need scarcely name Oscar Wilde and J.M. Synge. But Wilde's dialogue can by no means be called free from mannerism,[1] while Synge wrote in a language which had a music of its own, even before his genius took hold of it.

It does not seem very profitable to try to concentrate into a definition the distinctive qualities of dramatic dialogue. The late Mrs. Craigie ("John Oliver Hobbes") attempted to do so in the preface to a charming play, *The Ambassador*; and the result at any rate the sequel--was that her next play, *The Wisdom of the Wise*, was singularly self-conscious and artificial. She found in "emotion" the test of dramatic quality in any given utterance. "Stage dialogue," she says, "may or may not have many qualities, but it must be emotional." Here we have a statement which is true in a vague and general sense, untrue in the definite and particular sense in which alone it could afford any practical guidance. "My lord, the carriage waits," may be, in its right place, a highly dramatic speech, even though it be uttered with no emotion, and arouse no emotion in the person addressed. What Mrs. Craigie meant, I take it, was that, to be really dramatic, every speech must have some bearing, direct or indirect, prospective, present, or retrospective, upon individual human destinies. The dull play, the dull scene, the dull speech, is that in which we do not perceive this connection; but when once we are interested in the individuals concerned, we are so quick to perceive the connection, even though it be exceedingly distant and indirect, that the dramatist who should always hold the fear of Mrs. Craigie's aphorism consciously before his eyes would unnecessarily fetter and restrict himself. Even the driest scientific proposition may, under special circumstances, become electrical with drama. The statement that the earth moves round the sun does not, in itself, stir our pulses; yet what playwright has ever invented a more dramatic utterance than that which some one invented for Galileo: "E pur si muove!"? In all this, to be sure, I am illustrating, not confuting, Mrs. Craigie's maxim. I have no wish to confute it, for, in the largest interpretation, it is true; but I suggest that it is true only when attenuated almost beyond recognition, and quite beyond the point at which it can be of any practical help to the practical dramatist. He must rely on his instinct, not numb and bewilder it by constantly subjecting it to the dictates of hard-and-fast aesthetic theory.

We shall scarcely come much nearer to helpful truth than the point we have already reached, in the principle that all dialogue, except the merely mechanical parts--the connective tissue of the play--should consist either of "mots de caractere" or of "mots de situation." But if we go to French critics for this principle, do not let us go to French dramatists for models of practice. It is part of the abiding insularity of our criticism that the same writers who cannot forgive an English dramatist what they conceive to be a stilted turn of phrase, will pass without remark, if not with positive admiration, the outrageously rhetorical style which is still prevalent in French drama. Here, for instance, is a quite typical passage from *Le Duel*, by M. Henri Lavedan, an author of no small repute; and it would be easy to find even more magniloquent tirades in the works of almost any of his contemporaries. I translate from the concluding scene between the Abbe and the Duchess:

> THE ABBE: "In our strange life, there are sometimes unexpected and decisive moments, sovereign, though we know not why. We feel it, that is all!--fulgurant moments, which throw, as it were, a flash of lightning upon our destinies, like those meteors which shine forth from time to time in the heavens, and of which none can say what their purple signifies, whether it be a cataclysm or an apotheosis. Well, it appears to me that we, you and I, are now face to face with one of these moments!"
>
> THE DUCHESS: "So I, too, believe."
>
> THE ABBE: "We must take care, then, that it be an apotheosis. That is why I want--Mon Dieu, madame! how shall I say it to you? Where shall I go to find the chosen words, the words of pure gold, of diamonds, the immaculate words that are worthy of us? All that you are, all that you are worth, I know, and I alone know. You have opened, that I might read it, the book of hours that is your mind. I am in no wise disquieted about you or your future; yet, that I may be fully reassured before we part, I wish, I wish you to tell me, to declare to me, that you are at this very moment in absolute repose, calm as a lake."

And so Monsieur l'Abbe goes on for another page. If it be said that this ornate eloquence is merely professional, I reply that his brother, the atheist doctor, and the Duchess herself, are quite as copious in their rhetoric, and scarcely less ornate.

It is a mistake to suppose that "literary merit" can be imparted to drama by such flagrant departures from nature; though some critics have not yet outgrown that superstition. Let the playwright take to heart an anecdote told by Professor Matthews in his ***Inquiries and Opinions***--an anecdote of a New England farmer, who, being asked who was the architect of his house, replied: "Oh, I built that house myself;

but there's a man coming down from Boston next week to put on the architecture." Better no style at all than style thus plastered on.

* * * * *

What is to be said of the possibilities of blank verse as a dramatic medium? This is a thorny question, to be handled with caution. One can say with perfect assurance, however, that its possibilities are problematical, its difficulties and dangers certain.

To discuss the question whether drama in verse is in its very nature nobler than drama in prose would lead us away from craftsmanship into the realm of pure aesthetics. For my own part, I doubt it. I suspect that the drama, like all literature, took its rise in verse, for the simple reason that verse is easier to make--and to memorize--than prose. Primitive peoples felt with Goethe--though not quite in the same sense--that "art is art because it is not nature." Not merely for emotional, but for all sorts of literary, expression, they demanded a medium clearly marked off from the speech of everyday life. The drama "lisped in numbers, for the numbers came." Even of so modern a writer (comparatively) as Shakespeare, it would scarcely be true to say that he "chose" verse as his medium, in the same sense in which Ibsen chose prose. He accepted it just as he accepted the other traditions and methods of the theatre of his time. In familiar passages he broke away from it; but on the whole it provided (among other advantages) a convenient and even necessary means of differentiation between the mimic personage and the audience, from whom he was not marked off by the proscenium arch and the artificial lights which make a world apart of the modern stage.

And Shakespeare so glorified this metrical medium as to give it an overwhelming prestige. It was extremely easy to write blank verse after a fashion; and playwrights who found it flow almost spontaneously from their pens were only too ready to overlook the world-wide difference between their verse and that of the really great Elizabethans. Just after the Restoration, there was an attempt to introduce the rhymed couplet as the medium for heroic plays; but that, on the other hand, was too difficult to establish itself in general use. Tragedy soon fell back upon the fatally facile unrhymed iambic, and a reign of stilted, stodgy mediocrity set in. There is nothing drearier in literature than the century-and-a-half of English tragedy, from Otway to Sheridan Knowles. One is lost in wonder at the genius of the actors who could infuse life and passion into those masterpieces of turgid conventionality. The worship of the minor Elizabethans, which began with Lamb and culminated in Swinburne, brought into fashion (as we have seen) a spasmodic rather than a smoothly rhetorical way of writing, but did not really put new life into the outworn form. It may almost be called an appalling fact that for at least two centuries--from 1700 to 1900--not a single blank-verse play was produced which lives, or deserves to live,[2] on the stage of to-day.

I have thus glanced at the history of the blank-verse play because I believe that it can never revive until we clearly realize and admit that it is, and has been for a century, thoroughly dead, while, for a century before that again, it was only galvanized into a semblance of life by a great school of rhetorical acting. The playwright who sets forth with the idea that, in writing a poetical drama, he is going to continue the great Elizabethan tradition, is starting on a wild-goose chase. The great Elizabethan tradition is an incubus to be exorcised. It was because Mr. Stephen Phillips was not Elizabethanizing, but clothing a vital and personal conception of drama in verse of very appealing lyrical quality, that some of us thought we saw in **Paolo and Francesca** the dawn of a new art. Apparently it was a false dawn; but I still believe that our orientation was right when we looked for the daybreak in the lyric quarter of the heavens. The very summits of Shakespeare's achievement are his glorious lyrical passages. Think of the exquisite elegiacs of Macbeth! Think of the immortal death-song of Cleopatra! If verse has any function on the stage, it is that of imparting lyric beauty to passionate speech. For the mere rhetorical "elevation" of blank verse we have no use whatever. It consists in saying simple things with verbose pomposity. But should there arise a man who combines highly-developed dramatic faculty with great lyric genius, it is quite possible that he may give us the new poetic drama for which our idealists are sighing. He will choose his themes, I take it, from legend, or from the domain of pure fantasy--themes which can be steeped from first to last in an atmosphere of poetry, as **Tristan und Isolde** is steeped in an atmosphere of music. Of historic themes, I would counsel this hypothetical genius to beware. If there are any which can fittingly be steeped in a lyric atmosphere, they are to be sought on the outskirts of history, or in the debatable land between history and legend. The formula of Schiller can no more be revived than the formula of Chapman or of Rowe. That a new historic drama awaits us in the future, I have little doubt; but it will be written in prose. The idea that the poetry of drama is to be sought specifically in verse has long ago been exploded by Ibsen and Maeterlinck and D'Annunzio and Synge. But there are, no doubt, themes which peculiarly lend themselves to lyrico-dramatic treatment, and we shall all welcome the poet who discovers and develops them.

One warning let me add, in no uncertain voice. If you choose to write a blank-verse play, write it in blank verse, and not in some nondescript rhythm which is one long series of jolts and pitfalls to the sensitive ear. Many playwrights have thought by this means to escape from the monotony of blank verse; not one (that I ever heard of) has achieved even temporary success. If you cannot save your blank verse from monotony without breaking it on the wheel, that merely means that you cannot write blank verse, and had better let it alone. Again, in spite of Elizabethan precedent, there is nothing more irritating on the modern stage than a play which keeps on changing from verse to prose and back again. It gives the verse-passages an air of pompous self-consciousness. We seem to hear the author saying, as he shifts his gear, "Look you now! I am going to be eloquent and impressive!" The most destructive fault a dramatist can commit, in my judgment, is to pass, in the same work of art, from one plane of convention to another.[3]

* * * * *

We must now consider for a moment the question--if question it can be called--of the soliloquy and the aside. The example of Ibsen has gone far towards expelling these slovenlinesses from the work of all self-respecting playwrights. But theorists spring up every now and then to defend them. "The stage is the realm of convention," they argue. "If you accept a room with its fourth wall removed, which nothing short of an earthquake could render possible in real life, why should you jib at the idea--in which, after all, there is nothing absolutely impossible--that a man should utter aloud the thoughts that are passing through his mind?"

It is all a question, once more, of planes of convention. No doubt there is an irreducible minimum of convention in all drama; but how strange is the logic which leaps from that postulate to the assertion that, if we admit a minimum, we cannot, or ought not to, exclude a maximum! There are plays which do not, and there are plays which do, set forth to give as nearly as possible an exact reproduction of the visual and auditory realities of life. In the Elizabethan theatre, with its platform stage under the open sky, any pictorial exactness of reproduction was clearly impossible. Its fundamental conditions necessitated very nearly[4] a maximum of convention; therefore such conventions as blank verse and the soliloquy were simply of a piece with all the rest. In the theatre of the eighteenth century and early nineteenth, the proscenium arch--the frame of the picture--made pictorial realism theoretically possible. But no one recognized the possibility; and indeed, on a candle-lit stage, it would have been extremely difficult. As a matter of fact, the Elizabethan platform survived in the shape of a long "apron," projecting in front of the proscenium, on which the most important parts of the action took place. The characters, that is to say, were constantly stepping out of the frame of the picture; and while this visual convention maintained itself, there was nothing inconsistent or jarring in the auditory convention of the soliloquy. Only in the last quarter of the nineteenth century did new methods of lighting, combined with new literary and artistic influences, complete the evolutionary process, and lead to the withdrawal of the whole stage--the whole dramatic domain--within the frame of the picture. It was thus possible to reduce visual convention to a minimum so trifling that in a well-set "interior" it needs a distinct effort of attention to be conscious of it at all. In fact, if we come to think of it, the removal of the fourth wall is scarcely to be classed as a convention; for in real life, as we do not happen to have eyes in the back of our heads, we are never visually conscious of all four walls of a room at once. If, then, in a room that is absolutely real, we see a man who (in all other respects) strives to be equally real, suddenly begin to expound himself aloud, in good, set terms, his own emotions, motives, or purposes, we instantly plump down from one plane of convention to another, and receive a disagreeable jar to our sense of reality. Up to that moment, all the efforts of author, producer, and actor have centred in begetting in us a particular order of illusion; and lo! the effort is suddenly abandoned, and the illusion shattered by a crying unreality. In modern serious drama, therefore, the soliloquy can only be regarded as a disturbing anachronism.[5]

The physical conditions which tended to banish it from the stage were reinforced by the growing perception of its artistic slovenliness. It was found that the most delicate analyses could be achieved without its aid; and it became a point of honour with the self-respecting artist to accept a condition which rendered his material somewhat harder of manipulation, indeed, but all the more tempting to wrestle with and overcome. A drama with soliloquies and asides is like a picture with inscribed labels issuing from the mouths of the figures. In that way, any bungler can reveal what is passing in the minds of his personages. But the glorious problem of the modern playwright is to make his characters reveal the inmost workings of their souls without saying or doing anything that they would not say or do in the real world.[6]

There are degrees, however, even in the makeshift and the slovenly; and not all lapses into anachronism are equally to be condemned. One thing is so patent as to call for no demonstration: to wit, that the aside is ten times worse than the soliloquy. It is always possible that a man might speak his thought, but it is glaringly impossible that he should speak it so as to be heard by the audience and not heard by others on the stage. In French light comedy and farce of the mid-nineteenth century, the aside is abused beyond even the license of fantasy. A man will speak an aside of several lines over the shoulder of another person whom he is embracing. Not infrequently in a conversation between two characters, each will comment aside on every utterance of the other, before replying to it. The convenience of this method of proceeding is manifest. It is as though the author stood by and delivered a running commentary on the secret motives and designs of his characters. But it is such a crying confession of unreality that, on the English-speaking stage, at any rate, it would scarcely be tolerated to-day, even in farce. In serious modern drama the aside is now practically unknown. It is so obsolete, indeed, that actors are puzzled how to handle it, and audiences what to make of it. In an ambitious play produced at a leading London theatre about ten years ago, a lady, on leaving the stage, announced, in an aside, her intention of drowning herself, and several critics, the next day, not understanding that she was speaking aside, severely blamed the gentleman who was on the stage with her for not frustrating her intention. About the same time, there occurred one of the most glaring instances within my recollection of inept conventionalism. The hero of the play was Eugene Aram. Alone in his room at dead of night, Aram heard Houseman breaking open the outside shutters of the window. Designing to entrap the robber, what did he do? He went up to the window and drew back the curtains, with a noise loud enough to be heard in the next parish. It was inaudible, however, to Houseman on the other side of the shutters. He proceeded with his work, opened the window, and slipped in, Aram hiding in the shadow. Then, while Houseman peered about him with his lantern, not six feet from Aram, and actually between him and the audience, Aram indulged in a long and loud monologue as to whether he should shoot Houseman or not, ending with a prayer to heaven to save him from more blood-guiltiness! Such are the childish excesses to which a playwright will presently descend when once he begins to dally with facile convention.

An aside is intolerable because it is **not** heard by the other person on the stage: it outrages physical possibility. An overheard soliloquy, on the other hand, is intolerable because it **is** heard. It keeps within the bounds of physical possibility, but it stultifies the only logical excuse for the soliloquy, namely, that it is an externalization of thought which would in reality remain unuttered. This point is so clear that I need not insist upon it.

Are there, in modern drama, any admissible soliloquies? A few brief ejaculations of joy, or despair, are, of course, natural enough, and no one will cavil at them. The approach of mental disease is often marked by a tendency to unrestrained loquacity, which goes on even while the sufferer is alone; and this distressing symptom may, on rare occasions, be put to artistic use. Short of actual derangement, however, there are certain states of nervous surexcitation which cause even healthy people to talk to themselves; and if an author has the skill to make us realize that his character is passing through such a crisis, he may risk a soliloquy, not only without reproach, but with conspicuous psychological justification. In the third act of Clyde Fitch's play, ***The Girl with the Green Eyes***, there is a daring attempt at such a soliloquy, where Jinny says: "Good Heavens! why am I maudling on like this to myself out loud? It's really nothing--Jack will explain once more that he can't explain"--and so on. Whether the attempt justified itself or not would depend largely on the acting. In any case, it is clear that the author, though as a rule somewhat lax in his craftsmanship, was here aiming at psychological truth.

A word must be said as to a special case of the soliloquy--the letter which a person speaks aloud as he writes it, or reads over to himself aloud. This is a convention to be employed as sparingly as possible; but it is not exactly on a level with the ordinary soliloquy. A letter has an actual objective existence. The words are formulated in the character's mind and are supposed to be externalized, even though the actor may not really write them on the paper. Thus the letter has, so to speak, the same right to come to the knowledge of the audience as any other utterance. It is, in fact, part of the dialogue of the play, only that it happens to be inaudible. A soliloquy, on the other hand, has no real existence. It is a purely artificial unravelling of motive or emotion, which, nine times out of ten, would not become articulate at all, even in the speaker's brain or heart. Thus it is by many degrees a greater infraction of the surface texture of life than the spoken letter, which we may call inadvisable rather than inadmissible.

Some theorists carry their solicitude for surface reality to such an extreme as to object to any communication between two characters which is not audible to every one on the stage. This is a very idle pedantry. The difference between a conversation in undertones and a soliloquy or aside is abundantly plain: the one occurs every hour of the day, the other never occurs at all. When two people, or a group, are talking among themselves, unheard by the others on the stage, it requires a special effort to remember that, as a matter of fact, the others probably do hear them. Even if the scene be unskilfully arranged, it is not the audibility of one group, but the inaudibility of the others, that is apt to strike us as unreal.

* * * * *

This is not the only form of technical pedantry that one occasionally encounters. Some years ago, a little band of playwrights and would-be playwrights, in fanatical reaction against the Sardou technique, tried to lay down a rule that no room on the stage must ever have more than one door, and that no letter must ever enter into the mechanism of a play. I do not know which contention was the more ridiculous.

Nothing is commoner in modern house-planning than rooms which have at least two doors and a French window. We constantly see rooms or halls which, if transported to the stage, would provide three or four entrances and exits; and this is even more true of the "central heated" houses of America than of English houses. The technical purists used especially to despise the French window--a harmless, agreeable and very common device. Why the playwright should make "one room one door" an inexorable canon of art is more than human reason can divine. There are cases, no doubt, in which probability demands that the dramatist should be content with one practicable opening to his scene, and should plan his entrances and exits accordingly. This is no such great feat as might be imagined. Indeed a playwright will sometimes deliberately place a particular act in a room with one door, because it happens to facilitate the movement he desires. It is absurd to lay down any rule in the matter, other than that the scene should provide a probable locality for whatever action is to take place in it. I am the last to defend the old French farce with its ten or a dozen doors through which the characters kept scuttling in and out like rabbits in a warren. But the fact that we are tired of conventional laxity is no good reason for rushing to the other extreme of conventional and hampering austerity.

Similarly, because the forged will and the lost "marriage lines" have been rightly relegated to melodrama, is there any reason why we should banish from the stage every form of written document? Mr. Bernard Shaw, in an article celebrating the advent of the new technique, once wrote, "Nowadays an actor cannot open a letter or toss off somebody else's glass of poison without having to face a brutal outburst of jeering." What an extravagance to bracket as equally exploded absurdities the opening of a letter and the tossing off of the wrong glass of poison! Letters--more's the pity--play a gigantic part in the economy of modern life. The General Post Office is a vast mechanism for the distribution of tragedy, comedy, melodrama, and farce throughout the country and throughout the world. To whose door has not Destiny come in the disguise of a postman, and slipped its decree, with a double rat-tat, into the letter-box? Whose heart has not sickened as he heard the postman's footstep pass his door without pausing? Whose hand has not trembled as he opened a letter? Whose face has not blanched as he took in its import, almost without reading the words? Why, I would fain know, should our stage-picture of life be falsified by the banishment of the postman? Even the revelation brought about by the discovery of a forgotten letter or bundle of letters is not an infrequent incident of daily life. Why should it be tabu on the stage? Because the French dramatist, forty years ago, would sometimes construct a Chinese-puzzle play around some stolen letter or hidden document, are we to suffer no "scrap of paper" to play any part whatever in English drama? Even the Hebrew sense of justice would recoil from such a conclusion. It would be a case of "The fathers have eaten sour grapes, and other people's children must pay the penalty." Against such whimsies of reactionary purism, the playwright's sole and sufficient safeguard is a moderate exercise of common sense.

* * * * *

Notes:
[1: So, too, with the style of Congreve. It is much, and justly, admired; but who does not feel more than a touch of mannerism in such a passage as this?--

MILLAMANT: "... Let us never visit together, nor go to a play together; but let us be very strange and well-bred: let us be as strange as if we had been married a great while; and as well-bred as if we were not married at all."

MIRABELL: "Have you any more conditions to offer? Hitherto your demands are pretty reasonable."

MILLAMANT: "Trifles!--as liberty to pay and receive visits to and from whom I please; to write and receive letters, without interrogatories or wry faces on your part; to wear what I please; and choose conversation with regard only to my own taste; to have no obligation upon me to converse with wits that I don't like because they are your acquaintances; or to be intimate with fools because they may be your relatives.... These articles subscribed, if I continue to endure you a little longer, I may by degrees dwindle into a wife."

This is very pretty prose, granted; but it is the prose of literature, not of life.]

[2: From the fact that I do not make an exception in favour of *The Blot in the Scutcheon* or *Stratford*, I must leave the reader to draw what inference he pleases. On the other hand, I believe that a reconstruction of Tennyson's *Queen Mary*, with a few connecting links written in, might take a permanent place in the theatre.]

[3: Mr. Israel Zangwill, in his symbolic play, *The War-God*, has put blank verse to what I believe to be a new use, with noteworthy success. He writes in very strict measure, but without the least inversion or inflation, without a touch of Elizabethan, or conventionally poetic, diction. He is thus enabled to use the most modern expressions, and even slang, without incongruity; while at the same time he can give rhetorical movement to the speeches of his symbolic personages, and, in passages of argument, can achieve that clash of measured phrase against measured phrase which the Greeks called "stichomythy," and which the French dramatist sometimes produces in rapid rapier play with the Alexandrine. Mr. Zangwill's practice is in absolute contradiction of the principle above suggested that blank verse, to be justified in drama, ought to be lyrical. His verse is a product of pure intellect and wit, without a single lyric accent. It is measured prose; if it ever tries to be more, it fails. I think, then, that he has shown a new use for blank verse, in rhetorico-symbolic drama. But it is no small literary feat to handle the measure as he does.]

[4: Not quite. The drama of some Oriental peoples recognizes conventions which the Elizabethans did not admit.]

[5: A conversation on the telephone often provides a convenient and up-to-date substitute for a soliloquy; but that is an expedient which ought not to be abused.]

[6: The soliloquy is often not only slovenly, but a gratuitous and unnecessary slovenliness. In *Les Corbeaux*, by Henry Becque, produced in 1889, there occur two soliloquies--one by Teissier (Act ii, Scene 3), the other by Madame de Saint-Genis (Act in, Scene 10)--either or both of which could be omitted without leaving any sensible gap. The latter is wholly superfluous, the former conveys some information which might have been taken for granted, and could, in any case, have been conveyed without difficulty in some other way. Yet Becque was, in his day, regarded as a quite advanced technician.]

www.bookjungle.com email: sales@bookjungle.com fax: 630-214-0564 mail: Book Jungle PO Box 2226 Champaign, IL 61825

The Codes Of Hammurabi And Moses
W. W. Davies

The discovery of the Hammurabi Code is one of the greatest achievements of archaeology, and is of paramount interest, not only to the student of the Bible, but also to all those interested in ancient history...

Religion   ISBN: *1-59462-338-4*   Pages: 132   MSRP *$12.95*   QTY

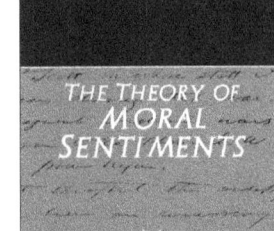

The Theory of Moral Sentiments
Adam Smith

This work from 1749. contains original theories of conscience amd moral judgment and it is the foundation for systemof morals.

Philosophy   ISBN: *1-59462-777-0*   Pages: 536   MSRP *$19.95*   QTY

Jessica's First Prayer
Hesba Stretton

In a screened and secluded corner of one of the many railway-bridges which span the streets of London there could be seen a few years ago, from five o'clock every morning until half past eight, a tidily set-out coffee-stall, consisting of a trestle and board, upon which stood two large tin cans, with a small fire of charcoal burning under each so as to keep the coffee boiling during the early hours of the morning when the work-people were thronging into the city on their way to their daily toil...

Childrens   ISBN: *1-59462-373-2*   Pages: 84   MSRP *$9.95*   QTY

My Life and Work
Henry Ford

Henry Ford revolutionized the world with his implementation of mass production for the Model T automobile. Gain valuable business insight into his life and work with his own auto-biography... "We have only started on our development of our country we have not as yet, with all our talk of wonderful progress, done more than scratch the surface. The progress has been wonderful enough but..."

Biographies/   ISBN: *1-59462-198-5*   Pages: 300   MSRP *$21.95*   QTY

www.bookjungle.com email: sales@bookjungle.com fax: 630-214-0564 mail: Book Jungle PO Box 2226 Champaign, IL 61825

The Art of Cross-Examination
Francis Wellman

QTY

I presume it is the experience of every author, after his first book is published upon an important subject, to be almost overwhelmed with a wealth of ideas and illustrations which could readily have been included in his book, and which to his own mind, at least, seem to make a second edition inevitable. Such certainly was the case with me; and when the first edition had reached its sixth impression in five months, I rejoiced to learn that it seemed to my publishers that the book had met with a sufficiently favorable reception to justify a second and considerably enlarged edition. ..

Reference   ISBN: *1-59462-647-2*   Pages:412   MSRP *$19.95*

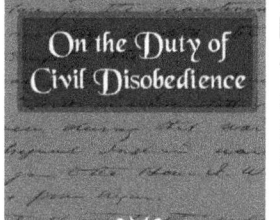

On the Duty of Civil Disobedience
Henry David Thoreau

QTY

Thoreau wrote his famous essay, On the Duty of Civil Disobedience, as a protest against an unjust but popular war and the immoral but popular institution of slave-owning. He did more than write—he declined to pay his taxes, and was hauled off to gaol in consequence. Who can say how much this refusal of his hastened the end of the war and of slavery ?

Law   ISBN: *1-59462-747-9*   Pages:48   MSRP *$7.45*

Dream Psychology Psychoanalysis for Beginners
Sigmund Freud

QTY

Sigmund Freud, born Sigismund Schlomo Freud (May 6, 1856 - September 23, 1939), was a Jewish-Austrian neurologist and psychiatrist who co-founded the psychoanalytic school of psychology. Freud is best known for his theories of the unconscious mind, especially involving the mechanism of repression; his redefinition of sexual desire as mobile and directed towards a wide variety of objects; and his therapeutic techniques, especially his understanding of transference in the therapeutic relationship and the presumed value of dreams as sources of insight into unconscious desires.

Psychology   ISBN: *1-59462-905-6*   Pages:196   MSRP *$15.45*

The Miracle of Right Thought
Orison Swett Marden

QTY

Believe with all of your heart that you will do what you were made to do. When the mind has once formed the habit of holding cheerful, happy, prosperous pictures, it will not be easy to form the opposite habit. It does not matter how improbable or how far away this realization may see, or how dark the prospects may be, if we visualize them as best we can, as vividly as possible, hold tenaciously to them and vigorously struggle to attain them, they will gradually become actualized, realized in the life. But a desire, a longing without endeavor, a yearning abandoned or held indifferently will vanish without realization.

Self Help   ISBN: *1-59462-644-8*   Pages:360   MSRP *$25.45*

www.bookjungle.com *email: sales@bookjungle.com fax: 630-214-0564 mail: Book Jungle PO Box 2226 Champaign, IL 61825*

QTY

	Title	ISBN	Price
☐	**The Rosicrucian Cosmo-Conception Mystic Christianity** by *Max Heindel*	ISBN: 1-59462-188-8	$38.95
	The Rosicrucian Cosmo-conception is not dogmatic, neither does it appeal to any other authority than the reason of the student. It is: not controversial, but is: sent forth in the, hope that it may help to clear...		New Age/Religion Pages 646
☐	**Abandonment To Divine Providence** by *Jean-Pierre de Caussade*	ISBN: 1-59462-228-0	$25.95
	"The Rev. Jean Pierre de Caussade was one of the most remarkable spiritual writers of the Society of Jesus in France in the 18th Century. His death took place at Toulouse in 1751. His works have gone through many editions and have been republished...		Inspirational/Religion Pages 400
☐	**Mental Chemistry** by *Charles Haanel*	ISBN: 1-59462-192-6	$23.95
	Mental Chemistry allows the change of material conditions by combining and appropriately utilizing the power of the mind. Much like applied chemistry creates something new and unique out of careful combinations of chemicals the mastery of mental chemistry...		New Age Pages 354
☐	**The Letters of Robert Browning and Elizabeth Barret Barrett 1845-1846 vol II** by *Robert Browning* and *Elizabeth Barrett*	ISBN: 1-59462-193-4	$35.95
			Biographies Pages 596
☐	**Gleanings In Genesis (volume I)** by *Arthur W. Pink*	ISBN: 1-59462-130-6	$27.45
	Appropriately has Genesis been termed "the seed plot of the Bible" for in it we have, in germ form, almost all of the great doctrines which are afterwards fully developed in the books of Scripture which follow...		Religion/Inspirational Pages 420
☐	**The Master Key** by *L. W. de Laurence*	ISBN: 1-59462-001-6	$30.95
	In no branch of human knowledge has there been a more lively increase of the spirit of research during the past few years than in the study of Psychology, Concentration and Mental Discipline. The requests for authentic lessons in Thought Control, Mental Discipline and...		New Age/Business Pages 422
☐	**The Lesser Key Of Solomon Goetia** by *L. W. de Laurence*	ISBN: 1-59462-092-X	$9.95
	This translation of the first book of the "Lemegton" which is now for the first time made accessible to students of Talismanic Magic was done, after careful collation and edition, from numerous Ancient Manuscripts in Hebrew, Latin, and French...		New Age/Occult Pages 92
☐	**Rubaiyat Of Omar Khayyam** by *Edward Fitzgerald*	ISBN:1-59462-332-5	$13.95
	Edward Fitzgerald, whom the world has already learned, in spite of his own efforts to remain within the shadow of anonymity, to look upon as one of the rarest poets of the century, was born at Bredfield, in Suffolk, on the 31st of March, 1809. He was the third son of John Purcell...		Music Pages 172
☐	**Ancient Law** by *Henry Maine*	ISBN: 1-59462-128-4	$29.95
	The chief object of the following pages is to indicate some of the earliest ideas of mankind, as they are reflected in Ancient Law, and to point out the relation of those ideas to modern thought.		Religion/History Pages 452
☐	**Far-Away Stories** by *William J. Locke*	ISBN: 1-59462-129-2	$19.45
	"Good wine needs no bush, but a collection of mixed vintages does. And this book is just such a collection. Some of the stories I do not want to remain buried for ever in the museum files of dead magazine-numbers an author's not unpardonable vanity..."		Fiction Pages 272
☐	**Life of David Crockett** by *David Crockett*	ISBN: 1-59462-250-7	$27.45
	"Colonel David Crockett was one of the most remarkable men of the times in which he lived. Born in humble life, but gifted with a strong will, an indomitable courage, and unremitting perseverance...		Biographies/New Age Pages 424
☐	**Lip-Reading** by *Edward Nitchie*	ISBN: 1-59462-206-X	$25.95
	Edward B. Nitchie, founder of the New York School for the Hard of Hearing, now the Nitchie School of Lip-Reading, Inc, wrote "LIP-READING Principles and Practice". The development and perfecting of this meritorious work on lip-reading was an undertaking...		How-to Pages 400
☐	**A Handbook of Suggestive Therapeutics, Applied Hypnotism, Psychic Science** by *Henry Munro*	ISBN: 1-59462-214-0	$24.95
			Health/New Age/Health/Self-help Pages 376
☐	**A Doll's House: and Two Other Plays** by *Henrik Ibsen*	ISBN: 1-59462-112-8	$19.95
	Henrik Ibsen created this classic when in revolutionary 1848 Rome. Introducing some striking concepts in playwriting for the realist genre, this play has been studied the world over.		Fiction/Classics/Plays 308
☐	**The Light of Asia** by *sir Edwin Arnold*	ISBN: 1-59462-204-3	$13.95
	In this poetic masterpiece, Edwin Arnold describes the life and teachings of Buddha. The man who was to become known as Buddha to the world was born as Prince Gautama of India but he rejected the worldly riches and abandoned the reigns of power when...		Religion/History/Biographies Pages 170
☐	**The Complete Works of Guy de Maupassant** by *Guy de Maupassant*	ISBN: 1-59462-157-8	$16.95
	"For days and days, nights and nights, I had dreamed of that first kiss which was to consecrate our engagement, and I knew not on what spot I should put my lips..."		Fiction/Classics Pages 240
☐	**The Art of Cross-Examination** by *Francis L. Wellman*	ISBN: 1-59462-309-0	$26.95
	Written by a renowned trial lawyer, Wellman imparts his experience and uses case studies to explain how to use psychology to extract desired information through questioning.		How-to/Science/Reference Pages 408
☐	**Answered or Unanswered?** by *Louisa Vaughan* Miracles of Faith in China	ISBN: 1-59462-248-5	$10.95
			Religion Pages 112
☐	**The Edinburgh Lectures on Mental Science (1909)** by *Thomas*	ISBN: 1-59462-008-3	$11.95
	This book contains the substance of a course of lectures recently given by the writer in the Queen Street Hall, Edinburgh. Its purpose is to indicate the Natural Principles governing the relation between Mental Action and Material Conditions...		New Age/Psychology Pages 148
☐	**Ayesha** by *H. Rider Haggard*	ISBN: 1-59462-301-5	$24.95
	Verily and indeed it is the unexpected that happens! Probably if there was one person upon the earth from whom the Editor of this, and of a certain previous history, did not expect to hear again...		Classics Pages 380
☐	**Ayala's Angel** by *Anthony Trollope*	ISBN: 1-59462-352-X	$29.95
	The two girls were both pretty, but Lucy who was twenty-one who supposed to be simple and comparatively unattractive, whereas Ayala was credited, as her Bombwhat romantic name might show, with poetic charm and a taste for romance. Ayala when her father died was nineteen...		Fiction Pages 484
☐	**The American Commonwealth** by *James Bryce*	ISBN: 1-59462-286-8	$34.45
	An interpretation of American democratic political theory. It examines political mechanics and society from the perspective of Scotsman James Bryce		Politics Pages 572
☐	**Stories of the Pilgrims** by *Margaret P. Pumphrey*	ISBN: 1-59462-116-0	$17.95
	This book explores pilgrims religious oppression in England as well as their escape to Holland and eventual crossing to America on the Mayflower, and their early days in New England...		History Pages 268

www.bookjungle.com *email: sales@bookjungle.com fax: 630-214-0564 mail: Book Jungle PO Box 2226 Champaign, IL 61825*

QTY

The Fasting Cure *by Sinclair Upton* ISBN: *1-59462-222-1* **$13.95**
In the Cosmopolitan Magazine for May, 1910, and in the Contemporary Review (London) for April, 1910, I published an article dealing with my experiences in fasting. I have written a great many magazine articles, but never one which attracted so much attention... New Age/Self Help/Health Pages 164

Hebrew Astrology *by Sepharial* ISBN: *1-59462-308-2* **$13.45**
In these days of advanced thinking it is a matter of common observation that we have left many of the old landmarks behind and that we are now pressing forward to greater heights and to a wider horizon than that which represented the mind-content of our progenitors... Astrology Pages 144

Thought Vibration or The Law of Attraction in the Thought World ISBN: *1-59462-127-6* **$12.95**
by William Walker Atkinson
Psychology/Religion Pages 144

Optimism *by Helen Keller* ISBN: *1-59462-108-X* **$15.95**
Helen Keller was blind, deaf, and mute since 19 months old, yet famously learned how to overcome these handicaps, communicate with the world, and spread her lectures promoting optimism. An inspiring read for everyone... Biographies/Inspirational Pages 84

Sara Crewe *by Frances Burnett* ISBN: *1-59462-360-0* **$9.45**
In the first place, Miss Minchin lived in London. Her home was a large, dull, tall one, in a large, dull square, where all the houses were alike, and all the sparrows were alike, and where all the door-knockers made the same heavy sound... Childrens/Classic Pages 88

The Autobiography of Benjamin Franklin *by Benjamin Franklin* ISBN: *1-59462-135-7* **$24.95**
The Autobiography of Benjamin Franklin has probably been more extensively read than any other American historical work, and no other book of its kind has had such ups and downs of fortune. Franklin lived for many years in England, where he was agent... Biographies/History Pages 332

Name	
Email	
Telephone	
Address	
City, State ZIP	

☐ Credit Card   ☐ Check / Money Order

Credit Card Number	
Expiration Date	
Signature	

Please Mail to: Book Jungle
PO Box 2226
Champaign, IL 61825
or Fax to: 630-214-0564

ORDERING INFORMATION

web: *www.bookjungle.com*
email: *sales@bookjungle.com*
fax: *630-214-0564*
mail: *Book Jungle PO Box 2226 Champaign, IL 61825*
or PayPal *to sales@bookjungle.com*

Please contact us for bulk discounts

DIRECT-ORDER TERMS

**20% Discount if You Order
Two or More Books**
Free Domestic Shipping!
Accepted: Master Card, Visa,
Discover, American Express

www.ingramcontent.com/pod-product-compliance
Lightning Source LLC
Chambersburg PA
CBHW080241170426

43192CB00014BA/2523